AF352744

ENGINEERING GLOBAL SOCIALISM

FRAMING THE GLOBAL

Hilary Kahn and Deborah Piston-Hatlen, series editors

ENGINEERING GLOBAL SOCIALISM

Ownership, Non-Alignment, and Corporate Culture in a Bosnian Company

Anna Calori

INDIANA UNIVERSITY PRESS

This book is a publication of

Indiana University Press
Herman B Wells Library
1320 East 10th Street
Bloomington, Indiana 47405 USA

iupress.org

First printing 2026

Cataloging information is available from the Library of Congress.

ISBN 978-0-253-07508-6 (hdbk.)
ISBN 978-0-253-07509-3 (pbk.)
ISBN 978-0-253-07511-6 (ebook)

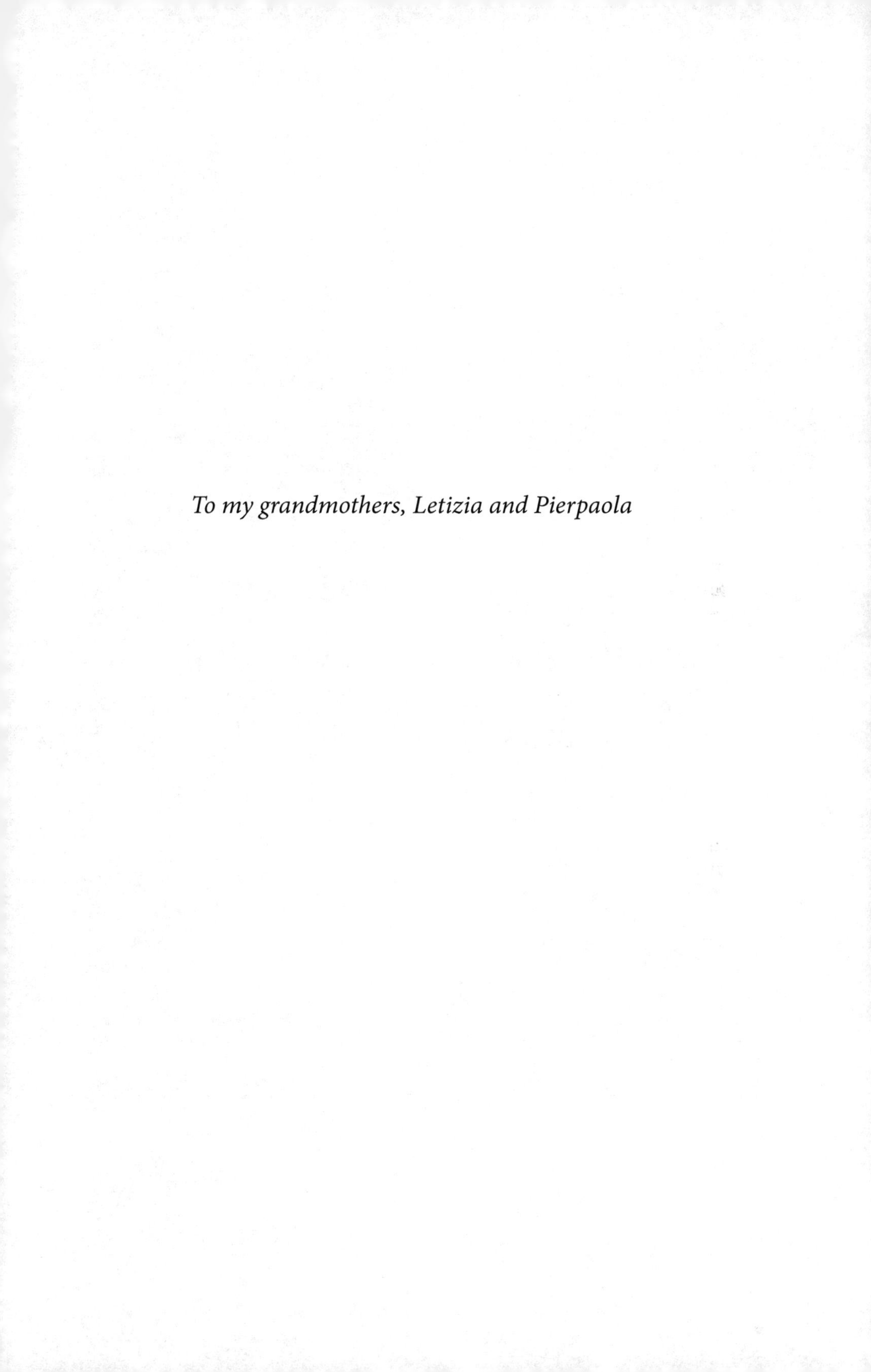

To my grandmothers, Letizia and Pierpaola

CONTENTS

ACKNOWLEDGMENTS

OVER THE YEARS IT HAS TAKEN ME TO write this book, I have come to realize that the most intriguing research—for me—happens completely by chance. And it is indeed by sheer chance that I found myself couch surfing in Sandra, Elena, and Dejan's apartment in Tuzla. I had never met people more enthusiastically committed to their country's history or more passionate about its food. It was through their familial love, friendship, and encouragement that I took my first steps as a young historian in the field—and that I got hooked on ajvar for life. Through our conversations, one thing became apparent to me: the world of work, its contentions, and its memory were what had glued a community together. I wanted to know much more about that world, the sentiments it sparked, and the memories it obfuscated.

I am forever indebted to all the people—in Energoinvest and beyond—who agreed to speak to me about their lives and memories, for all that they shared with me. It takes courage to sit with a stranger and share one's experiences, ideas, traumas, values, and desires. I will always treasure their words, their time, and their delightful hospitality. Although a fraction of what they shared ended up written on these pages, their words and expressions constitute the foundation and tapestry of this book.

I am also grateful to all the friends, scholars, and interlocutors who shared their contacts and helped me get in touch with people to talk to. Research often works like a snowball, but it is only through the support and contribution of a whole network that the snowball can start moving. A special thanks to Kathrin Jurkat, Saša Vejzagić, Alfredo Sasso, Chiara Milan, and Daniela Lai for sharing their early insights as young researchers in the field; crossing paths with them at the beginning of this research was foundational for what would come of it. I wish to thank Sladjana Ilić, Danka Belošević, Nevena Skrbić, Nevena Brajović, Katerina Ivanović, and Spomenka Brasić for all they taught me, for the countless times they hosted me, helped me with translations, showed me the ins and outs of their cities, corrected my *padeži*, and shared anecdotes and contacts with me. I owe a lot to all these incredibly strong women, and I have only admiration for who they are. I also wish to thank Milomir Kovačević, who kindly shared his powerful photographs with me.

I wish to thank all the staff at Energoinvest who made this research possible and, in particular, Lejla Logo and Bisera Hadžialjević. I would like to express my gratitude to all the archivists and staff I had the pleasure to work with—at the Archive of Yugoslavia; the State and the Federal Archive of Bosnia and Herzegovina; the Sarajevo, Tuzla, and Banja Luka city archives; and the National Library in Belgrade. A special word of gratitude to Vladan Vukliš and Tamara Ivanović, whose knowledge of the Bosnian and Yugoslav archive world is unmatched. I would also like to thank the economics professors at the economic faculties of Sarajevo, Belgrade, Zagreb, and Ljubljana for the time, views, opinions, and materials they so kindly shared with me. They offered precious guidance that helped me understand important aspects of economic transformation.

I would not have been able to turn this precious material into first a thesis and then a book without the expert guidance of my supervisors, Professor James Mark and Dr. Klejda Mulaj, who supported me every step of the way. I wish to thank James Mark from the bottom of my heart for giving me the opportunity to join his research team at the University of Exeter. He has supported and guided me long after I completed my PhD, and I owe him much gratitude for that. Beyond supervision, James offered mentorship: our discussions were as encouraging as they were motivating; his suggestions thoughtful and kind. If I have learned how to think like a historian, it is thanks to his inspiring and encouraging guidance.

As part of the project "1989 after 1989: Rethinking the Fall of State Socialism in Global Perspective," I had the pleasure of working alongside colleagues whose work I have ever since found awe inspiring. Drs. Ljubica Spaskovska, Ned Richardson-Little, Nelly Bekus, and Raluca Grosescu were fantastic companions in my PhD journey. Receiving their precious advice about research, career, and life after the PhD was heartwarming and reassuring. Together with Dora Vargha and Tobias Rupprecht, this group inspired me to delve deeper into the global history of socialism. Witnessing the development of these colleagues' amazing research was an extraordinary opportunity, one that filled me with curiosity and motivation to go forward, and I wish to thank them for that. I am grateful to Professor Florian Bieber for his precious insights on the earliest version of this manuscript.

Colleagues at the Imre Kertész Kolleg in Jena, and in particular Professors Michal Kopeček, Ondřej Vojtěchovský, and Máté Rigó, were brilliant in helping me work around some of the key questions of this book. Their expertise in entrepreneurship and business in the socialist world was only matched by their insatiable passion for hiking, and I am grateful they shared both with me.

My deepest gratitude to Professors Philipp Ther and Jannis Panagiotidis for welcoming me at the University of Vienna and giving me the intellectual space and strength to develop this book in its final stages. I wish to thank my friends and colleagues at the University of Vienna, whose support and friendship have accompanied me throughout the many iterations of this book, and their precious suggestions have undoubtedly made it better. I found in Goran Musić, Rory Archer, and Jelena Djureinović the sincerest, most generous, and most thoughtful companions one could hope for. Their passion and acumen in discussing anything from labor history to archival politics have always been a point of reference on how to take research seriously and life lightly. At times, I won't deny it, this journey hasn't been easy. Motivation fluctuates, and self-doubt creeps in. I was incredibly lucky to cross paths with Rosamund Johnston, Agata Zysiak, and Thục Linh Nguyễn Vũ: their bright views and sharp observations always brought a change of perspective when needed, one that recharged my enthusiasm and motivation to go forward. In them I found generous, compassionate, and insightful allies, and I am forever thankful for their friendship. I am particularly grateful to Rosamund Johnston for taking the time to read earlier versions of this work in full.

I would like to express my gratitude to the anonymous reviewers for the time and effort they devoted to reading and evaluating my manuscript. Their detailed feedback prompted me to critically reassess the book and refine both its arguments and its structure. I have greatly enjoyed revisiting and revising the draft with their insights in mind. I truly appreciate their thorough engagement with the work and am thankful for their kind and encouraging comments. I would also like to thank the editors at IUP, Bethany Mowry and Sophia Hebert, for the time and dedication they granted me. I have truly appreciated their patience and commitment throughout this journey, and I have valued and cherished their suggestions.

Finally, I wish to thank my family and friends for lending me their ears and for not taking me too seriously. My partner, Farhad, comes at the end here, but he's been there from the start: a home in all the places life led us to. His curiosity, his journalistic eye, and above all, his sense of humor have brought depth and lightness at every turn. His caring words have glued me back together after many crashes. He's coated our lives with the right dose of magic realism, and I am grateful that he did so.

ENGINEERING GLOBAL SOCIALISM

INTRODUCTION

The Bosnian Uprising of 2014

In February 2014, Bosnia and Herzegovina made it to the limelight of international news. One image caught the eye of media platforms around the world: it depicted protesters wearing Guy Fawkes masks in front of a burning government building, formerly the site of a large enterprise. Protesters were enraged by decades of corruption and privatization reforms that had brought the Bosnian economic system to collapse.[1] Popular unrest showed with the force of hundreds of Molotov cocktails the contested nature of "transition" in Southeastern Europe, where expectations and realities of transformation seemed unreconcilable. That year saw the most significant popular uprising in postsocialist Bosnia and Herzegovina. No picture could better represent the point of departure for this book.

Workers of formerly privatized firms were protagonists of these contestations. They witnessed not only the collapse of their workplaces but also the shift toward new property regimes and away from prospects of global integration. Transition had meant a double marginalization: away from the centrality of work within society and away from the centrality of their companies as global players. For them, transition was an unfinished business. Not only had it not delivered on its promises of prosperity, it had also relegated the enterprises at which they worked for their entire lives to being small, regional players: a major step down from the past grandeur of global relevance they could once claim.

This book follows the journey of the Yugoslav company Energoinvest and its workers as it navigated different promises of global integration—from socialist to market led—as well as the dissolution of a country, the destruction of war, and the complex reconstruction that ensued.

Energoinvest was one of the largest companies in Yugoslavia and was key to the country's economic development. Its experience provides an alternative success story of socialist globalization in the Yugoslav context, one that helps us reconstruct the understudied impact of (socialist) globalization in the socialist and postsocialist world. Zooming in on a single company provides a unique vantage point from which to understand the real and long-term implications of socialism's global promise for the history of Yugoslavia and its people. First, global socialism offered self-managed enterprises a global field of engagement with partners in the non-aligned world, through technical and economic exchanges. Second, it shaped workplaces by crafting a specific socialist corporate culture ingrained in a narrative of geopolitical relevance and capitalist competitiveness. Third, it delineated the structure of expectation for a generation of people who sought to reform—rather than do away with—state socialism.

To fully grasp the experience of late socialism and its transformation, this book argues, it is important to consider the different and at times conflicting promises of global embeddedness that shaped it. To do so, I employ the trope of "promise" as both an analytical and a historical category—as a tool to understand transformations, navigate the rationale of its protagonists, and unpack the disconnection between the experience and expectation of transformation within the microcosm of one workplace. Enterprises, as this book will show, were spaces where different, competing promises of progress through global integration coexisted: first, the promise of globality crafted under socialism; second, the promise of neoliberal global integration, to be achieved through privatization, liberalization, and the dismantling of socialism's clunky institutional structures.

The history of this one company mirrors in small the major transformations that a nation underwent as late-socialist regimes crumbled and war ensued. Energoinvest remained active throughout the Bosnian War, and so did its company journal, which continued to be published even in the dire circumstances of the siege of Sarajevo. This provides an invaluable and unique insight into a company at war. This micro perspective reveals at close range what kinds of expectations and debates emerged in the face of multiple transformations and a violent dissolution and how these went on to mold postsocialist workplaces. The choice of Bosnia, a country where the intervention of international economic institutions was perhaps more evident than elsewhere in the region, allows us to examine how neoliberal recipes were negotiated at the local level. Yet Bosnia is far from the only case where workers' identity and expectations were essential in shaping (transition) reforms in industrial areas across the world. In contexts as different as China and Venezuela, privatization and market reforms have been shaped by different class identities, ownership categories, and expectations of reform.[2]

Framing the Global Promise of Socialism

To understand the socialist global promise, its demise, and its lingering appeal in the postsocialist context, this book suggests it is important to look at the nexus between top-down, officially sanctioned visions of globality and bottom-up, day-to-day experiences of it. The Yugoslav League of Communists envisioned for its citizens a path to socialism paved through self-management and non-alignment, toward a future portrayed as bright and promising.[3] The promise of integration into the gears of a new economic world order, as well as that of a "socialist good life" of economic stability and prosperity, shaped the socialist world of work at various levels.[4] Beyond the mere posturing of relevance on the geopolitical or diplomatic arena, it entered people's daily lives through the worlds of work, production, and consumption.[5] In this double process—of shaping the world without while crafting the world within—state actors and diplomatic exchanges were only one element. Material culture, exhibitions, and monuments referring to the Non-Aligned Movement were designed as part of the state's project of nation building.[6]

In daily life, this promise materialized through several mediums, from consumer goods to news reports celebrating Yugoslavia's centrality on the world stage. While non-alignment touched most citizens through a TV screen, a newspaper page, or a national parade, for workers in globally export-oriented companies it had a direct implication for their lives. In places like Energoinvest, the pomp of a foreign delegation visiting a factory had more immediate bearings: it meant stability, new partnerships, new sales, new contracts. This book contends that it was this very global exposure, reinforced by Yugoslavia's political strategy of openness toward its non-aligned partners, that shaped workers' experiences and expectations of global (economic) change. This aspect offers a further point of entry into the uncharted field of labor and economic history of global socialist enterprises—as chapter 1 illustrates.

Companies were not just transmission belts of ideological and political control decided elsewhere; they displayed a high degree of agency in setting the direction of planning, international engagement, and reform—as chapter 2 highlights. They were central to the mutually constitutive processes of global-local negotiations that made the promise of Yugoslavia's path to global integration. Teodora Dragostinova has stressed the importance of understanding global processes from a pericentric approach, considering the role that local transformations and particularities played in shaping a plurality of socialist world making(s).[7] Indeed, "the global" is always a negotiation, a process that is created from the mutually constitutive relationship of the global-particular dynamic, as Hilary Kahn has shown.[8] Global processes and transnational interconnections must be understood as anchored in local practices, peoples, and perceptions. These processes are not "homogenizing and placeless" but producing different particulars.[9] The socialist global promise was equally important as a process that carved socialism's place in the world, as well as the world's place within socialism; in doing so, it crafted local understandings of the global.

Far from being isolated behind the Iron Curtain, the socialist world was embedded in transnational and global ties coconstitutive of the global economic order since the end of the Second World War, as James Mark and Oscar Sanchez-Sibony, among others, have shown.[10] Engaging in "socialist proto-globalization"—that is, the extensive industrial cooperation that resulted from integration between Eastern and Western European companies in the 1970s—was key to the effort to achieve the socialist promise. As Besnik Pula illustrates, socialist economies did, at least for some time, profit from this turn and did indeed improve their citizens' standards of living as a result.[11] As the Cold War effectively became a global phenomenon, with the two blocs increasingly competing to establish political and economic hegemony in the developing world, the socialist promise became effectively a global one. The nature of this desired hegemony was geopolitical as much as cultural and economic. Indeed, the Soviet Union and Council for Mutual Economic Assistance (COMECON) countries were adamant about establishing their own strategy for development and aid in the developing world, and they pursued it through military, economic, diplomatic, and scientific support.[12] From large infrastructural projects to student exchanges, the "Second" and "Third" Worlds became entangled in a web of economic and cultural transfers that gave rise to what scholars have termed an "alternative" globalization.[13]

The Non-Aligned Movement advocated for a specific model of global development based on an equitable international division of labor and trade and for the fostering of collective self-reliance and multilateralism through economic and technical cooperation. The initial exchange between a social-ist Eastern European country (Yugoslavia) and two developing countries (India and Egypt) with different socialist inclinations was crucial for the foundation of new avenues for "Third World" exchange and cooperation.[14] Although historiography on Second and Third World encounters has also referred to the Non-Aligned Movement as an important site of exchange, Yugoslavia features less prominently than other socialist Eastern European countries in the studies on East-South connections, particularly those of an economic nature. Conversely, scholarship on the Non-Aligned Movement interprets it as a diplomatic multilateral alliance concerned primarily with political and military transnational solidarity, where economic coopera-tion, though also present, was somewhat thwarted by the complications of achieving economic independence.[15] Formalizing and consolidating eco-nomic decolonization was possibly the most ambitious aspect of what Paul Stubbs defines as the non-aligned attempt at establishing a "globalization otherwise."[16] While caution is required not to err in "Yugo-centrism" and overstate Yugoslavia's centrality in the Non-Aligned Movement, it is equally important to foreground the role of a small, arguably peripheral country, as part of a broader process of crafting alternative socialist world makings.

Here, the very word *alternative* deserves further unpacking. Whether socialist globalization was an alternative to an already established capitalist one is a point of debate within scholarship and has important theoretical and methodological implications. Indeed, understanding global capitalism as the point of departure, to which socialism presented a counterbalance, risks reducing our understanding of globalization to mere economic terms and overstating the very global nature of capitalism. From the First Inter-national in 1864 to the declaration of a new international economic order (NIEO), socialist ideas, practices, and models were not only an alternative to an existing global order: they constructed it as well.

Johanna Bockman has suggested that the convergence toward neolib-eral capitalism can be seen as a forceful reaction to the worldwide appeal of noncapitalist forms of radical democratic governance, spread also thanks to socialist models.[17] On the other hand, Béla Tomka has questioned the extent to which socialist globalization was willingly conceived as an "alter-native" and the degree to which East-South connections could really com-pensate for limited links with the West. Socialist global engagement was, in this view, selective and uneven, characterized by only specific elements of global flows and interdependence in both geographical and temporal ways.[18] However, the characteristics of fragmentation, selectiveness, and unevenness can be applied to any form of globalization, not just the flows of interconnection between the socialist and developing worlds. Speaking of "alternatives" can help us pluralize the trajectories of globalization and understand them as characterized by flows of uneven intensity.

Furthermore, the voices and experiences collected in this book highlight the significance of "alternatives" not only as an analytical or historiographical category but also as a discursive trope used by the protagonists of this story: a conscious remark signifying divergence, difference, criticism. As chapter 7 illustrates, identifying with an alternative project was a source of commonality and a point of reference for many of those directly or indirectly involved with the socialist global project. This does not mean that instances of economic exchange were driven by aspirations completely different from those occurring elsewhere; often, profit making more than solidarity was a key driver of these interactions, though solidarity functioned as a privileged vehicle for their attainment.

Investigating "Socialist Corporate Cultures"

This book observes the inner workings of a socialist enterprise, its business ethos, its narratives, and its national significance through the lens of what I view as "socialist corporate culture." This was a set of values strongly tied to a sense of international relevance and supranational unity, as well as to the socialist ideology of workers' self-management and equality in work promoted by the party-state. To readers less familiar with the economic and business history of central and Eastern Europe, it may appear a paradox to talk of corporate cultures in the socialist world. After all, these were planned economies that allowed private enterprises to operate in very limited circumstances, if at all. Yet historiography on the region has shown the multifaceted and intricate ways in which a technocratic, managerial, or even entrepreneurial class existed and operated within socialist contexts.[19] In an effort to move away from a tradition that has been "taking the U.S. (or the West) as normal and normative," business historians have called for a transnationalization of their subject and argued for rebalancing and pluralizing business history by virtue of integrating perspectives from the socialist world.[20]

Since the mid-1980s, scholars in management studies and business history have been interested in dissecting "corporate" or "organization" cultures as complex systems of beliefs, symbols, and values shared by members; methods of decision-making or ways of thinking; and behavior patterns that bring organizations together by creating complex structures of meaning.[21]

This understanding has inspired scholars to approach corporate culture as primarily a cultural phenomenon, a process of mythmaking, and the creation of ritualistic narratives and objects. This approach has been mostly applied to deconstructing corporate narratives of large capitalist enterprises. In many instances, history itself has been used by different companies and corporations to establish their invented traditions, revitalize corporate brands, or even depoliticize or muffle problematic colonial pasts. At the same time, scholars have noted the significance of material objects—publications, posters, logos, lapel pins, coffee cups—as powerful signifiers of the ubiquitous nature of corporate cultures.[22] As Kenneth Lipartito has argued, by combining a focus on the materialities and mentalities of corporate cultures, business history can reveal, in new and important ways, how economic practices operate on people and how, in turn, different actors have agency in shaping corporate spaces, narratives, and objects.[23] In this respect, Yugoslavia, and Bosnia in particular, offers a fertile ground for decentering studies of corporate cultures by integrating perspectives other than Western capitalist ones. Thus, it is possible to examine the different ways in which corporate cultures functioned as transmission belts for the values and practices that underpinned socialist and ethnonationalist nation building.

Following the early insights of historian Charles Dellheim, this book approaches the study of socialist corporate culture by looking at the way it was founded, transmitted, perceived, and transformed through interactions within the company, as well as those between the company and the broader processes of transformation that interested the socialist world throughout the end of the twentieth century.[24] Without dismissing the fundamental differences that existed between socialist companies and their capitalist counterparts, it must be noted that some traits of the industrialist way of life were not so distant, particularly when one considers the "golden decades" of post–World War II industrialization. From Ivrea (Italy) to Detroit (US) and Sarajevo (Bosnia and Herzegovina), large industrial companies established themselves not just as centers of work but as benevolent providers of services, housing, and communities: as developers of industrial utopias, where narratives of corporate solidarity, unity, and progress ran strong. Energoinvest's corporate culture further cemented the overlap between company and society, as it embodied and enacted the rationalized myths of the socialist society through the workplace.[25] In their engagement with the developing world, companies and their employees found themselves at the forefront of Yugoslavia's construction of its own political promise—one of global integration through solidarity and cooperation and of simultaneous international and local growth and development. While building this outward-looking myth, enterprises also contributed to consolidating Yugoslavia's mythmaking for its own citizens: a mighty geopolitical power able to guarantee economic prosperity through international engagement. Not only were these companies pillars of economic development and national (re)construction after the end of the Second World War but they also mirrored within them the very principles and shared ideologies of the (socialist) nation in the making and functioned as sites of the diffusion and consolidation of the Yugoslav socialist project. Here, perhaps even more so than in the capitalist world, the constitutive ideologies of the company and the new socialist nation in the making showed the most overlap.[26]

Global socialism was a way for companies and management to legitimize their own narratives of corporate culture and relevance, as chapter 1 shows. Indeed, Yugoslav enterprises thrived on business partnerships with the socialist and developing world and crafted a corporate culture based on this geopolitical relevance. Although Yugoslavia's largest trade partners remained in Western and Eastern Europe, part of its industrial development—particularly for comparative latecomers like Bosnia and Herzegovina—was also anchored to the developing world. Though criticisms have been raised that the real magnitude of Second and Third World trade had a small bearing on the overall world trade, this does not diminish its importance.[27] Limiting our investigation to the trade relations that had the greatest impact on aggregate global trade statistics would be dismissive of the importance that other trade networks had in specific sectors or for specific commodities. Just as an example, the share of exports to developing countries to total exports was 19.7 percent in 1977, up from 7 percent in 1972.[28] Moreover, Yugoslav exporters were tied to developing countries in specific strategic sectors. In 1980, 65 percent of all its exports were highly processed manufactures, and Yugoslavia exported metal products to the developing world in the same share as it did to the Organisation for Economic Co-operation and Development (OECD) countries. By the 1980s, Yugoslavia's engineering, construction, and energy companies had become well-established competitors, particularly in the Global South.

Historicizing Competing Promises of Transformation

At the turn of the last decade of the twentieth century, both the promises of socialist and capitalist modernity, of Fordist and planned industrialization, appeared underwhelming and unsatisfying to larger groups of the population in both the East and the West. Though creating competing visions of the future, socialist and capitalist modernizations had promised equality in prosperity through industrialization, which came with specific ideas about the world of work and its position in society. At the time, a postindustrial future seemed to dawn on the world of work, marking the end of manufacturing and of the great "utopias of labor."[29] In the socialist world, this shift was accompanied by a series of reforms that entailed a radical transformation away from economic planning. Yet the promises of socialist reformism—much like those of the "socialist good life"—carried within themselves the "current of dissatisfaction with those very promises."[30]

This book follows Energoinvest through the nonlinear trajectory of reform attempts, along what can be defined as the long 1990s: from the first major market reforms of 1988 to the neoliberal privatization of 2002 and their aftermath. As chapters 3 and 5 show, competing visions of market integration and privatization were part of an ongoing struggle over the meaning of work, identity, ownership, and deservingness. What emerged are complex articulations of progress, which demanded a certain reorientation of selfhood, of the values and mentalities dictating the new social order one must live by; nevertheless, these also strengthened the role of a common past as a stabilizing force across changes, fluctuations, and transformations by reframing categories related to the world of work. The loss of this common past—first through the fallout of war and then through mass privatization policies—was a massive (and overlooked at the time) contributor to the instability that followed, as chapter 4 highlights. By foregrounding the experiences of those who are the apparent "losers" of transition, this book will show that, on the contrary, working-class identity was important in the way economic reforms took shape across the 1980s and 1990s, and global and market orientations, and the values attached to them, constituted a central element in legitimizing or resisting reforms. The industrial working class was not a passive receiver of institutional change; rather, it was an active subject of transformation.[31] As Stef Jansen suggests, viewing postsocialist reforms as "a textbook case of neo-liberalizing transition" that marginalizes anticapitalist workers would be an oversimplification, as it does not properly address people's complex views about economic reform.[32]

In contextualizing this shift, it is important to clarify the use of certain terms, the first being transition. Scholars have challenged a view of transition as a teleological trajectory and have warned against overemphasizing 1989's "rupture" effects, by highlighting the continuities that existed between the socialist and postsocialist times.[33] Many prefer to talk of transformation, a process *in fieri* that does not make a clear-cut distinction between the socialist and postsocialist condition or attribute normative connotations to the socialist, Eastern European, Balkan, backward "other" that needs to transition to a progressive, modern, Western European mode of living.[34] Indeed, to understand the nature of these processes, it is necessary to employ a *longue durée* approach and understand the history of transition as characterized by the long-term legacy of institutional structures, modes of living, and cyclical waves of reform. Throughout the book, the use of the prefix *post* (*post*socialist, *post*war) should be understood as just a way to loosely frame a chronological framework (after 1991 and after 1995, respectively), rather than defining a clear-cut break with the past. The use of *transformation* will refer to the period of economic and political changes that characterized socialist Europe between the late 1980s and the early 2000s. The term *transition* will remain if used by actors or in documents and reports.

Much like *transition, neoliberalism* is a highly contested term: it has come to encompass a set of ideas, a form of government(ality), a social construct, a historical process. Its use in the context of postsocialist "transformation" is as ubiquitous as it is ambiguous.[35] Marketization, liberalization, and privatization constituted the core of a neoliberal reform package in the region.[36] More than just a blueprint for reforms, the neoliberal turn was a developmental promise, one that entailed a new vision of progress through the withdrawal of the state, global integration into a unipolar and postindustrial world order, and a redirection toward individualized understandings of efficiency, productivity, and ownership, as chapter 6 shows. It also meant adapting workers and citizens to new reform principles, in Eastern Europe as much as in Latin America, Western Europe, and beyond.[37]

Rather than sanctioning a convergence of the transforming "East" toward an already neoliberal "West," the 1990s entailed a radical socioeconomic transformation of Europe in a postindustrial, post-Fordist key. As Philipp Ther has argued, Central and Eastern European socialism and its collapse were actually co-constitutive of a broader global shift away from Keynesianism, welfare policies, and a Fordist-industrial mode of production, thereby initiating a process of cotransformation that interested the whole European continent and beyond.[38] This global shift came with the deepening of huge inequalities, which create parallel visions of success and failure depending on which social group one observes.[39]

Identities at Work

Non-alignment played a key role in the world of Yugoslav work. The Yugoslav global project constituted an avenue for workers to create subjectivities and a sense of place within their society, through globally engaged enterprises.[40] It left an imprint on the lives of those who were not necessarily benefiting firsthand from what global socialism had to offer in terms of mobility or exposure; it is this imprint that this book focuses on. This has remained understudied, as scholars of Yugoslav labor history have primarily paid attention to the world of self-management or that of work migration (especially the experience of *gastarbeiters* in Western Europe).[41] In these accounts, workers appear untouched by one of the constitutive elements of socialist Yugoslavia, despite the country's eminent role as protagonist and cocreator of "socialist globalization." This is much more a disciplinary oversight than a historical reality: as this book shows, the Yugoslav project in its global formulation shaped the world of work and the lives of those who experienced it. Indeed, non-alignment was not just a project of a small number of very transnational actors, nor was it only experienced firsthand through mobility and migration across the socialist world. It was a much broader phenomenon that permeated different levels of society: it sifted through and trickled down indirectly even within otherwise very much local factories and industries. Scholars have noted the extent to which the experience of "the global" for people in the socialist sphere was not direct as much as it was mediated.[42] This, in my view, does not diminish the importance of these experiences or disqualify them from being part of "globalization"; after all, for most people the experience of globalization is indeed mediated and often indirect.

When Yugoslavia embarked in its first market reforms at the end of the 1980s, a new discourse of reformism, which set out to revise and improve the foundations of the Yugoslav project, emerged. Debates around economic reforms were not about the legitimacy of market reforms—most people were on board with that. The real friction emerged over the question of how much power could be handed over to the global free market without compromising the basic tenets of Yugoslav social ownership: workers' self-identification as owners of their factories and workplaces, as chapter 3 shows. The transformation of the work-ownership-identity nexus featured at the core of the privatization reforms of late-socialist governments, as well as postsocialist ones. It was necessary to cultivate mentalities, expectations, and values compatible with the economic vision laid out in the reforms. Socialist ownership had created a particular form of personhood—that of the worker-owner—which privatization set out to profoundly change.[43] Indeed, the neoliberal transformation was meant to accelerate the globalization of socialist societies and to mark a shift in subjectivities, from the socialist worker to the entrepreneurial individual.[44] This shift underpinned the fragmentation of the traditional working class, weakened by the simultaneous diffusion of globalized and precarious forms of labor—a transformation that has characterized traditionally industrial societies and even more so the postsocialist context.[45]

Yet workers' identities as owners of their factories emerged seemingly unscathed from the ashes of the socialist collapse. Why do people still identify as owners of their factories, even though these bear little resemblance to the once celebrated grandiosity of their socialist days? To understand this, it is key to observe workplaces as sites of multiple, at times competing, processes of identity transformation. In the case of postwar Bosnia, as this book will show, economic reconstruction and nation building sutured together the process of privatization with that of ethnicization. Energoinvest was at the center of a model of ethnic privatization that completely fragmented the former global giant along ethnic lines, as shown in chapters 5 and 6. The market-oriented entrepreneurial self, oriented to individualized private property relations, remained a mirage or a cautionary tale. Rather, new ethnonationalist forms of economic collectivism partly supplanted old socialist ones, through the complex interplay of citizenship and ownership as mechanisms of reward. Ethnic homogenization occurred parallel to, and because of, a process of privatization grounded on a narrative of compensation and deservingness, the same one that was at the root of socialism's own understanding of ownership. As this book shows, privatization and marketization created and reinforced new modes of economic living based on the juncture of worker, owner, and ethnic citizen. By showcasing people's attitudes toward these reforms—as mechanisms of reward and also sources of discontent—chapter 7 offers further nuance on the nexus of work, ownership, and (non)ethnic identity in a society undergoing transformation.

Bosnia is not the only postconflict society where ethnicity constitutes a prominent feature of privatization. In countries like Sri Lanka, Zimbabwe, El Salvador, and Sierra Leone, a reconfiguration of ownership rights intersected with processes of ethnicization and identity making.[46] Evidence from the case of Rwanda—where, similar to Bosnia, a structural adjustment and privatization program was introduced after the conflict—suggests that interethnic tensions were actually deepened by these reforms.[47] The case of a Bosnian company undergoing "ethnic" privatization is compelling for many scholars of these areas, as it gives a new perspective on what postconflict privatization means in terms of the reshaping of societies, as well as class and ethnic identities. This form of privatization puts this case study at the intersection of labor and identity studies, as it brings to the fore the ambivalence of workers' groups toward ethnicity in the workplace.

Introducing "Structures of Expectation" and the Hierarchies of Memory

An entire generation of workers started their professional lives at the heyday of industrialization and socialist internationalism, experienced the promises and letdowns of reforms, fought in the war, and adjusted to new postsocialist societies. Recording their life stories is crucial not only to preserve the memory of socialism, internationalism, and deindustrialization but also to help us understand how people process change. Through a collection of oral histories, displayed throughout the book, I sought to uncover and analyze memories, not just as a source but as narrators' interpretations of their experiences and past attitudes.[48]

Throughout my analysis, and particularly in the final chapter, I employ the concept of *structures of expectations* as characteristic of industrial modernization and of its transformation. *Structures of expectations* define something that is more than a feeling, more than habits of thought or industrial cultural forms: the set of expectations grounded on the values, practices, and narratives around which one's work life is structured—in our case, the promises of industrial prosperity, internationalization, and ownership. For this, I build on the concept of "residual structure of feeling" employed by scholars of deindustrialization to describe the sentiments that inform and construct the "ways of life (and) understandings of possibilities" that link people in postindustrial communities, permeating them with a collective sense of belonging that, though rooted in the past, is maintained in the present.[49] As Chiara Bonfiglioli suggested for the case of women in the (post)Yugoslav textile industries, a persisting industrial structure of feeling—rooted at the intersection of ideology, socioeconomic rights, and everyday practices—is evident in the sense of loss toward labor and welfare rights that emerges because of postsocialist deindustrialization.[50] While cognizant of the analytical importance of "structures of feeling" in the study of work in the post-Yugoslav sphere, I believe this concept only partly captures its complex nuances. It can risk essentializing the industrial and socialist experience of work into something eminently static and bound to a specific historical and ideological moment. More than feelings, what ties people to the memory of the industrial past is the persistent attachment to the promises and expectations it conveyed.

To illustrate the complex and dynamic relation between experience and expectation, I draw on Reinhardt Koselleck's formulation of "spaces of experience" and "horizons of expectation." These, Koselleck argues, are formal categories that constitute history and its cognition and produce relations between past, present, and future.[51] It is indeed the tension between experience and expectation that generates the historical passing of time and propels change and transformation forward. But what and how does this tension come about, how do people mediate it, and what can this mediation tell us about their strategies of coming to terms with historical change? It is with this theoretical framework in mind that I shall approach what my interlocutors had to say about their experience, not just through the lens of a romanticized past but through the complex interrelation of expectation and experience, which is historically contingent, ever changing, and not demarcated as "before" and "after." Reflecting on the complex temporality of "endings that are not over," Tanja Petrović suggests thinking in terms of affective afterlives. In the context of the memories of military service in the Yugoslav Army—the subject of Petrović's investigation—the feelings and affect mobilized by this experience are not simply evocative of nostalgia for a collective experience cemented in the past; rather, they are indicative of enduring future-oriented imaginaries and foreground the persistence of affective communities in the aftermath of state socialism.[52]

The question of affect toward past values and identity is a topical one in the study of industrial decline. Postindustrial communities are characterized, for Sherry Lee Linkon, by a "half-life of deindustrialization," whereby the "struggle with loss and change is central for working class people [who] still value industrial identity."[53] Much as in North America, in the former socialist countries people's responses to emerging conditions are still shaped by expectations and ideas from the industrial and socialist era. In this context, scholars of deindustrialization and postsocialism, among others, have extensively reasoned on the question of nostalgia. In the (post)socialist context, expressions of nostalgia for past socialist lives have been a crucial topic of investigation—through the lens of material culture, urban and everyday life, cultural production, memory and intergenerational dynamics, and affect; nostalgia has also been examined as a political phenomenon, a tool for critiquing the postsocialist transformation.[54] Crucially, this scholarship shows the importance of understanding nostalgia as an expression of people's disappointment in the unmet expectations of the future while maintaining a reflective and critical distance from the socialist past. Indeed, the socialist past becomes invested "with meanings that reflect present conditions, needs, and concerns."[55] For my interlocutors, too, the memory of socialist industrial work functioned as a process of interpretation of past and present, a crucial means to forge identities and reclaim representation. Their recollections were at times tinged with nostalgic undertones, though they were rarely of a "restorative" nature—that is, in Svetlana Boym's terms, an attempt or willingness to recreate a foregone past, a desired return to the lost home or a resurrection of the past. Rather, following Boym's distinction, these accounts displayed a reflective nature: they showed a readiness to call into doubt past truths and reflect on the complex ambivalences of longing for an irretrievable past that, perhaps, ought not to be restored.[56]

The process of remembering brought about a relational dialogue between past and present, shaped around the need to establish structure between sometimes conflicting memories. In fact, the suturing of state socialism's collapse, war, and deindustrialization in a matter of just a few years created distinctive and often conflicting sets of expectations. Restoring the values and practices of the old socialist corporate culture clashed with the need for recognition of workers' contributions during the war. Overlapping experiences of loss—of one's loved ones, workplace, and country—created ambivalence toward a shared past; further, it created conflicting expectations of a future that many could not see as a shared one. Making sense of a common experience in a divided workplace required ordering and structuring on the part of my interlocutors. I view this process as one of *hierarchical memory making.* What emerged from their accounts, in fact, is an awareness that contradicting, conflicting, or selective memories exist but that certain aspects of the past are more salient than others and ought to occupy a place of higher importance in the hierarchy of memory, first, because they are related to a set of values in which workers were socialized and which they were unwilling to let go and, second, because these memories are connected to specific structures of expectations. Through this selective process of hierarchical ordering of past experiences, people reflect critically on which aspects of their memories they wish to influence their present and future.

Sources and Methodology

For this book, I have relied on a combination of written and oral sources, which allows me to do three things: first, analyze internal dynamics of globally oriented enterprises; second, access structures of expectations that persist in workers' communities; and, third, provide new insights into the conceptualization, implementation, and challenges of reforms.

To examine how workers made sense of Energoinvest's trajectory, I collected thirty semistructured oral history interviews with former and current employees of Energoinvest. These employees ranged from highly skilled cadres and engineers to miners and factory workers who had started their work experience in the 1970s and 1980s. Although it would have been impossible to find workers from each of the hundreds of daughter companies of Energoinvest, I have tried to draw from a pool as geographically varied as possible. This snowballing technique led me to only a few female interviewees, as indeed the company employed a predominantly male workforce.[57] The situation was slightly more balanced concerning the management and highly skilled workforce of Energoinvest.

Besides employees, I was able to interview all the top managers of Energoinvest for the period I wanted to cover (1989–2008). Many of these directors have moved to the private sector or have bought their own companies.

Semistructured interviews allowed me to understand managers' lifeworlds and the ways they made sense of their jobs and environment. This kind of business oral history is particularly valuable in the study of corporate cultures, as indeed it helps in pluralizing company narratives and embedding them in society.[58] Christina Lubinski and colleagues have recently foregrounded the significance of entrepreneurial actions and the lived experiences of managers at the micro level as important explanatory factors in the history of transformations.[59]

Company newspapers offered one of the most fruitful insights into the life of the company, in its local and global dimensions. They provided useful evidence of debates occurring within workplaces about how market reforms were discussed and introduced in the late-socialist workplace.[60] Beyond providing detailed information on the state of the company (its global partnerships, revenue, projects, and development), these journals are also an important source to understand how management and workforce sought to represent themselves and perceived their positions within the company.

To understand how postsocialist transformation was envisioned and experienced, I relied on publications, magazines, and journals that collected debates on economic reforms.[61] I combined these with interviews and discussions with the local economists who had been active in drafting economic reforms and consulting local governments. In addition to interviewing economic experts, I recorded thirteen interviews with international advisers involved in the market and privatization reforms after 1995.

Chapter Outline

This book develops through seven thematic chapters. It starts with a bird's-eye view of the intellectual, social, and political history of the Yugoslav promise as an articulation of globally oriented visions of integration mediated through enterprises. The following chapter traces the effects of the crisis of global socialism on globally embedded enterprises. Chapter 3 delves into the crisis of the Yugoslav model and the promises of ownership reform under the last Yugoslav government. This is followed by a focus on the war in Bosnia as experienced within workplaces—through the eyes of worker-soldiers and the words of the company's journal. The war ushered in new promises of deservingness and reward, which, as chapter 5 shows, fractured workplaces by championing an ethnonationalization of the world of work.

This transformation then clashed with visions of the economic integration of former socialist corporations like Energoinvest, whose fate as globally embedded exporters was put into question, as documented in chapter 6. Although divided across ethnic and geographical lines, workers' communities were unwilling to let go of their expectations and visions of global integration. The seventh and final chapter reflects on this, by examining how hierarchical forms of memory emerge as global promises fade away.

1

SHAPING THE GLOBAL PROMISE

Entangled Globalizations, Non-Alignment, and Socialist Corporate Culture

In November 1966, Yugoslavia's president, Josip Broz Tito, paid a visit to the headquarters of Energoinvest, one of the largest and most profitable companies in the country. To welcome him in Sarajevo were the company's workers and its general director and founder, Emerik Blum, a former partisan and a Jewish concentration camp survivor. Congratulating the management and employees for the company's rapid growth in revenues and partnerships in the developing world, Tito remarked, "It is necessary that our Yugoslav industries work like Energoinvest so that we can remain competitors in the international arena and further our country's modernization."[1] What Tito endorsed in this visit was a key tenet of Yugoslavia's industrial policy at the time: domestic modernization and international market engagement went hand in hand. Referring specifically to Energoinvest—a company that had grown to be a respected competitor to Western firms in Africa and the Middle East—reveals the significance of developing countries for Yugoslavia's own economic strategy.

This kind of reasoning from a socialist leader should not come as a surprise. At the height of the global Cold War, socialist countries were very much committed to expanding their sphere of influence in the developing world. Establishing alliances—of an economic, diplomatic, and military nature—with the newly decolonized countries of the Global South had a symbolic as much as a strategic value for many socialist countries across Eastern Europe. Ideologically, the socialist promise was not just one of freedom and prosperity, of a better future, of growth and modernization. It was also one of global relevance. State-socialist regimes crafted and promoted an understanding of their countries as embedded in a large project of world making. This project had at its core a need to transcend the limitations and constraints of nation-states, the aspiration to create internationalist solidarity against imperial and fascist subjugation, and took further momentum with the wave of decolonization that swept across Asia and Africa in the aftermath of the Second World War.

Developing countries, and particularly those with socialist governments, had an interest in pursuing new alliances that would allow them to stand strong on their paths to economic and political independence.[2] From the Afro-Asian solidarity cemented in Bandung in 1956 to the first Non-Aligned Summit of 1961 and the Tricontinental Conference of 1966, the postcolonial world mobilized to find new avenues of exchange and cooperation that would eschew the Cold War's East-West divide. In doing so, they effectively constituted new paths toward what Adom Getachew has termed "anti-systemic world-making project."[3] As historians of development have shown, decolonized countries contributed to a redefinition of the existing relations and hierarchies of the global economic order.[4]

Yugoslavia viewed technical cooperation with emerging economies as the path to its own domestic industrialization and modernization while simultaneously providing *"trade, not aid"* for developing countries.[5] This global engagement, I argue, was not just a matter of foreign policy; it went on to shape the kinds of promises that socialist regimes made to their own constituents: there could be no internal development or modernization without international integration. Out of the Council for Mutual Economic Assistance (COMECON) since 1948, Yugoslavia had marked its distance from the Soviet orthodoxy by introducing a model of self-managed socialism and confederal federalism, espousing an increasingly market- and export-oriented path for its enterprises, and pursuing a strong foreign policy of non-alignment. After the initial postwar phase of reconstruction and domestic industrialization in the early 1950s, Yugoslavia's ambition as a political and economic player on the global chessboard grew stronger. Yugoslavia channeled its diplomatic efforts toward bringing together newly independent postcolonial developing countries under the aegis of the Non-Aligned Movement. Self-defined as an alliance against the bipolar Cold War framework, and yet arguably a product of this logic, the Non-Aligned Movement brought together a constellation of developing and postcolonial countries adhering to common principles of international solidarity, anti-imperialism and antihegemonism, peaceful coexistence, and multilateral cooperation. In pursuing a role of leadership in the Non-Aligned Movement, Yugoslavia aspired to hold a significant position as a diplomatic and economic power, by acting as an advocate of a more equitable political and economic world order that would not squeeze smaller countries in between opposing imperialisms.

Yugoslavia quickly positioned itself within the network of non-aligned countries as an ally, peer, and mentor. Official documents from the Federal Executive Council (the country's main executive body) show that, when reasoning about the question of uneven development between North and South, Yugoslavia defined itself as a formerly "half-colonial" (*polukolonija-lan*) country in reference to its history of low economic development under the thumb of Western political powers before the Second World War—a history similar to that of the newly freed postcolonial countries.[6] This self-understanding as a successfully developing country that had carved out its own space in global politics and markets allowed Yugoslavia to establish legitimacy, authenticity, and authority within the non-aligned bloc. It used this position as a springboard for championing its approach to local and international development, arguing that the two could, and should, go hand in hand. Indeed, a 1968 government report on Yugoslavia's technical cooperation makes this understanding abundantly clear: "Yugoslavia is an underdeveloped country, but it also actively participates in the development of technical cooperation with developing countries as it gives technical support and aid through expert and student exchanges and enterprises."[7] Against this background, Yugoslavia's aspiration was to simultaneously achieve national development through industrialization and secure a similar path for its developing partners. In its pledge to aid the developing world, it could not realistically draw from the same pool of resources that allowed the United States and the Soviet Union to be champions of aid in the early Cold War years.

Enterprise-Led Development: Crafting the Global Promise

Export-oriented self-managed enterprises constituted the backbone of Yugoslavs' approach to industrialization and economic development, both domestically and at the international level. Enterprises like Energoinvest would focus on foreign exports and expand international cooperation and outreach through joint ventures and partnerships. This would not only ensure domestic economic growth and modernization but also allow Yugoslavia to support developing countries in their quest for economic development. As pillars of economic development and industrialization, these enterprises were encouraged to develop a multinational nature and began to see themselves as cocreators of an "alternative," non-aligned, global order. Already in the early stages of the Yugoslav road to socialism, "the world market decisively shaped the re-ordering of economic, social and political life," and the country's industrial development was tied to foreign capital and socialist industrialization.[8] This tendency continued into the 1960s, when economic reforms were proposed to remedy Yugoslavia's economic woes as the country grappled with inflation and foreign trade deficit. The main goal was to reconcile further global market integration with the socialist-Yugoslavist principle of self-management—a strategy that would also be the centerpiece of the late-1980s economic reforms. The reforms removed some of the red tape around foreign trade and simultaneously granted workers more decision-making powers regarding investment and wages.

These first market reforms entailed a strengthening of Yugoslavia's market orientation, which allowed enterprises to engage in foreign trade. The introduction of market principles was also expected to create incentives for workers to feel more invested in their work and in the decision-making processes available to them. Thus, after these early market reforms, the Yugoslav economic model came to be structured around a combination of market competition (within the Yugoslav market and internationally) and self-managed enterprises (based on the social ownership of assets and profits).[9]

Yugoslavia's approach to enterprise-led technical cooperation picked up pace in the decade after the foundation of the Non-Aligned Movement as international cooperation among members clustered around demands for a reorganization of trade and development more favorable for developing countries. Yugoslavia, together with Hungary and Mexico, was a strong advocate of a programmatic set of recommendations proposing to rethink growth, industrialization, and development from the perspective of the existing structural disparities between North and South. Negotiating such imbalances was a cornerstone of the Non-Aligned Movement's multilateral strategy and culminated with the UN Declaration for the Establishment of a New Internearional Economic Order. This was a set of rival world ideas put forward in the mid-1970s by a joint effort of developing countries in multiple multilateral forums (the Group of 77 [G77], the Non-Aligned Movement, and the UN Conference on Trade and Development [UNCTAD]) to challenge the existing orthodoxy of unbalanced trade, promoting self-reliance and South-South cooperation.[10]

Propelling this exchange was a fundamental question that lay at the core of the non-aligned economic strategy: how to build a national path to economic decolonization and self-reliance without compromising aspirations to global integration. Indeed, the question of building and strengthening collective self-reliance was a topical one within the Non-Aligned Movement. Between the Third and Sixth Non-Aligned Summits (in Lusaka in 1970 and Havana in 1979, respectively), collective self-reliance became the core principle of the non-aligned rationale for development. In his opening speech at Lusaka, Zambia's president, Kenneth Kaunda, defined economic self-reliance supported by the acquisition of sufficient technical know-how as a "condition *sine-qua-non* for a successful national development effort"; further, he argued that it was "essential for nonaligned and developing countries to seek an effective strategy for their own development" and reduce dependence on developed nations.[11]

The Non-Aligned Movement was not the only forum where collective self-reliance was discussed. As the Second UN Development Decade opened with a reinforced commitment to support development and nascent South-South cooperation, several multilateral organizations became forums of discussion about "alternative forms of development."[12] As the Sri Lankan director of UNCTAD Gamani Corea wrote, collective self-reliance was a tool both to increase leverage for developing countries in the global economic arena and to intensify trade among themselves. According to him, it received a major impetus through the General Assembly's proclamation of a new international economic order (NIEO).[13] The political significance of collective self-reliance was such that the pressure to make it work within the developing world (and especially within the Non-Aligned Movement, which was one of its major promoters) was enormous. In fact, several declarations such as those signed in Colombo 1976 and Havana 1979 strengthened the commitment to reinforcing collective self-reliance, through a series of policy guidelines and recommendations.

The NIEO put forward in the mid-1970s as a joint effort of developing and socialist countries was configured as a set of rival world ideas that challenged the existing orthodoxy of the North-South divide in trade and development, promoting self-reliance and South-South cooperation. Rather than radically rejecting the principles and processes of transnational capitalism, the NIEO was aimed at redefining the existing economic relations of dependency between North and South, creating a space for smaller, post-colonial, developing countries to partake in the international division of labor as equal partners. In Yugoslavia—a major advocate of collective self-reliance in view of a readjusted international economic equilibrium—the NIEO was incorporated within state policy.[14] Thus, throughout the 1970s and 1980s, Yugoslav companies acted as agents of development, embedded in non-aligned economic networks between the East, the West, and the Global South. They sought to operationalize an NIEO even after this alternative was partly abandoned at the international level.[15] Large engineering, construction, pharmaceutical, and car-manufacturing companies established strong partnerships with non-aligned partners, from Cuba to Zambia and from India to Ethiopia. Most projects would be carried out under the aegis of the Federal Bureau for International Technical Cooperation with Developing Countries, which coordinated relations among the Yugoslav government, its enterprises, and their foreign counterparts. The system of market socialism in place since the 1960s meant that banks, rather than the state, would allocate finances and investments to enterprises.[16] The Yugoslav Bank for International Economic Cooperation (JUBMES) was a financial institution specialized in refinancing export credits granted by Yugoslav commercial banks and the Yugoslav national bank, to promote long-term industrial and financial cooperation between Yugoslav export companies and their foreign partners. It would grant loans to large Yugoslav companies like Energoprojekt, Rade Končar, and Energoinvest to establish their operations and trade partnerships with non-aligned developing countries, such as Libya, Zambia, Egypt, or India. Like JUBMES, banks such as Jugobanka (the Yugoslav Bank for Foreign Trade) and several Republic Banks (such as Zagrebačka Banka) financed commercial and trade partnerships between Yugoslav companies and the Global South. These banks, in turn, would often rely on foreign deposits and foreign borrowing.[17]

Through these loans, Yugoslavia would provide technical expertise and would complete infrastructural projects while training local experts. In return, it would obtain hard currency, oil, and other key import materials, like textiles, coffee, and sugar. In this context, Yugoslavia's geopolitical position as a leader of the Non-Aligned Movement was instrumental in its companies' global development.[18] Thus, Yugoslavia approached its path to industrial development and modernization by relying on its advantageous position within the global network of developing non-aligned countries. The company Energoinvest was a prime example of this strategy.

By recognizing non-alignment as an official state policy and an integral part to its identity, Yugoslavia crafted its own socialist promise as an eminently global one: the construction of an egalitarian workers' society would thrive on economic development and industrialization grounded on an organic integration into the global order. The Yugoslav model of "third way" socialism could serve as an inspiration for smaller developing countries in the Non-Aligned Movement that were, or had been, in the process of forging their own path to socialism (such as Egypt, Libya, Tanzania, and Zambia). While these countries developed their own national configurations of a socialist society, Yugoslavia was often viewed as a point of reference in the Non-Aligned Movement, not just as an ally but as a potential model to follow.[19]

Thus, a global orientation was ingrained in the Yugoslav project from its inception: through non-alignment and its economic and political ramifications, the socialist promise of progress and prosperity was coupled with that of global integration as two mutually reinforcing phenomena. The global promise, in turn, shaped the way Yugoslav citizens understood their position in their workplaces and communities and would go on to inform their spaces of experience and horizons of expectation. As we shall see, companies were crucial sites where a narrative of global relevance was cultivated and fostered among the workforce.

Shaping a Socialist Corporate Culture

Energoinvest, Energoinvest, your name is known all around the world. . . .
Our bridges, with steel arms, have covered softly the whole globe. . . .
Sarajevo, Yugoslavia, Europe, the whole world! Energoinvest![20]

This beatific and overjoyed song, which readers will easily find on YouTube, was composed and performed by two stars of Sarajevo's music scene in the 1970s and 1980s: Alija Hafizović, a former member of the prog-rock band Indexi, and Kemal Monteno, a famous pop singer. The piece was commissioned by the Sarajevo-based company Energoinvest and, in 1982, distributed by Yugoton—the largest record label and chain record store in the former Yugoslavia.[21] Meant as a celebration of Energoinvest's international successes, the song paid an exceptional tribute to a flagship company representing the ideal of Yugoslav self-managed internationalism. It was quite uncommon for musicians as popular as Monteno and Hafizović to lend their talents in service of what can be described as a corporate jingle, but then again, Energoinvest was no ordinary company.

Since its foundation in Sarajevo in 1951 as Elektroprojekt (soon to be renamed Energoinvest), the engineering company specialized in the design and construction of industrial equipment, particularly elements for energy and power production and for processing (such as switchgears and electrification projects). It rapidly expanded its designing activities by incorporating several already existing small- and medium-scale semi-industrial enterprises, also in view of recruiting more personnel.[22] The 1950s saw the rapid growth of large state-owned enterprises (Energoprojekt, Ingra, Rade Končar, and Pelagonija, to name a few) across Yugoslavia, particularly in the construction and infrastructure sectors. Energoinvest quickly rose to be one of the most successful self-managed corporations in the whole of Yugoslavia and a respected competitor on the global market—particularly after the liberalization of foreign trade in 1961. Though several large export-oriented construction companies emerged in Yugoslavia, they did not compete against one another but developed through complementarity, by focusing on different aspects of construction and engineering, as well as by operating in different markets.[23] Energoinvest's production was highly diversified: the company encompassed a variety of industries, from the traditional industrial sector (raw materials, mining, foundries) to the more technologically advanced (engineering, software development, electronics). By the mid-1970s, it had eleven research institutes that would provide technological development for its leading sectors (armature, pipelines, the electrochemical industry, and informatics). Energoinvest funded academic and research scholarships for its employees and contributed to the foundation of engineering and technical faculties at the University of Sarajevo.[24] A core of large companies within Energoinvest (research and marketing divisions) would coordinate the production in smaller factories and then proceed with distribution to partners and buyers around the world. Other smaller factories were involved in the extraction of heavy materials and mining or the building and export of engineering equipment, concrete, and metal reinforcement armatures across the globe.[25]

With the aim of boosting production for the foreign market, factories and research centers developed in Bosnia under the trademark of Energoinvest. In the 1970s, the company progressively assumed a leading role with its flourishing web of economic contacts and exchanges between the Global South, Western Europe, and the Soviet bloc. In this period, Energoinvest consolidated its global presence, establishing joint ventures in Libya (ELPCO, RASCO), Mexico (EnergoMex), Pakistan (EnergoPak), Egypt

Table 1.1. A shortened chronology of Energoinvest's expansion in the Yugoslav territory between 1953 and 1982

1952	By decree of the president of Yugoslavia, Elektroprojekt is founded: ninety-three workers; two years later had grown to thirty-two hundred workers
Between 1960 and 1967	Establishment of Metal in Priština (Kosovo), IRCE, IRCT, IRCA (Sarajevo); Jambor in Črnuće; Metaloplastika in Makarska (Slovenia); Svjetlost in Doboj; Sigma in Subotica (Serbia)
1967	Energoinvest has existed seventeen years: six engineer-project offices, four research development centers, eighteen factories and plants, seven thousand workers
Between 1969 and 1970	Bauxite mines established in Jajce, Vlasenica, Mostar, Bosanska Krupa; lead and zinc mines in Srebrenica; combine for nonferrous metals established in Prokuplje (Serbia)
Between 1970 and 1971	Vaso Miskin-Crni in Sarajevo; Livnica Čelika in Tuzla; HENA (with an oil refinery in Modriča, petrol refinery in Bosanski Brod, Terpentin in Višegrad, and Hempro in Gradačac) merge with Jugopetrol to form Energopetrol
1971	Energoinvest has twenty years of work and existence: twenty-two thousand workers, thirty-six production factories, six mines, four factories in construction, four scientific research centers, several specialized engineering and projecting offices, thirty-one companies abroad, seventeen in the country.
Between 1972 and 1982	Bosnaplast in Bosanski Petrovac; packaging factory in Bihać; factory for metal construction in Čapljina are established.

Source: Energoinvest List, February 29, 1988

(EVACO), and the Soviet Union (ENHA).[26] It also had partnerships in France, Germany, and the United States. Besides engaging in joint ventures, Energoinvest operated as a government partner in several projects, such as the construction of cement factories in Iraq and dams in Mexico.[27] By 1987, Energoinvest had a revenue of USD 425 million from its exports.[28] These companies exported high-quality, technically intensive products such as individual parts for electrical, hydroelectrical, and nuclear power plants; oil refineries; the processing of chemical materials; the extraction of non-ferrous materials; and the food industry. By the early 1970s, at the beginning of its second phase of international expansion, Energoinvest counted twenty-two thousand workers at thirty-one companies or joint ventures in seventeen different countries. At this time, *Fortune* magazine and the *Financial Times* wrote articles praising Energoinvest for its ability to be competitive on the world market while maintaining internal socialist principles of self-management.[29] Through funding provided by JUBMES, Energoinvest grew its exports: by 1988, its yearly export peaked at over USD 440 million, and the company was fifty-five thousand workers strong (roughly forty thousand in Bosnia) with over ten thousand expert cadres.[30] Its yearly contribution to the federation's export was roughly 4 percent, making it the third-biggest company in Yugoslavia in terms of both overall revenue and the number of employees.[31] By then, it had become the first exporter in Yugoslavia, with an expanded presence in over thirty-two countries.

As one of Yugoslavia's biggest and most successful companies, Energoinvest embodied one of the defining principles of the socialist project: a self-managed internationalism that would pave a path to a new kind of prosperity—a prosperity that, at least in theory, would not come off the back of the tyrannical structures of work that had been observed in capitalist systems. Nor would it come off the back of the noncompetitive centralization of the economy as understood by the cautionary tales coming from the Communist bloc. Yugoslavia would create a third way, unleashing democratic forces within the workplace where workers would act not as mere laborers for hire but as experts, decision-makers, and owners, forming a corporate leviathan within the competitive international market.

Since the 1970s, Communist leaders in Bosnia had encouraged economic policies fostering the development of its large industrial conglomerates, which rapidly rose among the ten largest companies in Yugoslavia.[32] Later on, during the market reforms of 1989–1991, the government of the last Yugoslav president, Ante Marković, gave priority in economic policy to the large companies operating in the export sector. A Bosnian Croat and former partisan, Marković had worked for more than two decades as director of one of the biggest Yugoslav electrotechnical companies (Rade Končar) in Croatia. His managerial and economic expertise at the head of a large, globally oriented socialist enterprise with significant business contacts across the globe shaped his attitude toward market reforms.[33] He argued that the export sector was the most profitable and competitive part of the Yugoslav economy, one that could ensure the rapid growth of production and revenues.[34] The companies involved in the export sector were the ones that had the most contacts with partners in the world market, on both sides of the Iron Curtain and beyond. Economists and researchers concluded that this sector would be the one most likely to use new technologies and to become a push factor for economic growth and development.[35]

Bosnia's industrial milieu benefited from the growth of around ten to fifteen successful globally oriented self-managed enterprises—each comprising a research and engineering core, a branch for imports and exports, and several smaller factories that produced for both domestic and foreign markets.[36] These large industrial conglomerates accounted for up to 35 percent of Bosnia's overall gross domestic product (GDP) and boasted joint ventures with international companies such as Volkswagen, Daimler-Benz, and Olivetti, as well as a myriad of smaller ventures in developing countries. Bosnia's biggest trade partners were developing countries in North Africa and the Middle East, as well as the USSR. In developing countries, Bosnia exported construction engineering and key components for civil and hydro-engineering.[37] In 1989, 40 percent of the overall export earnings of Yugoslavia came from the four major industrial conglomerates in Bosnia (Energoinvest, UNIS, Šipad, and Hidrogradnja).[38]

For large export-oriented socialist companies like Energoinvest in the 1980s, the global market had become a synonym of progress and modernization, precisely because of the prestige acquired at the international level. In the eyes of its managers, this enterprise was expected to contribute to, shape, and take part in the global market economy.[39] Entrepreneurs, reformers, and even representatives of the League of Communists in Energoinvest sought to modify the decision-making process and the structure of the company to compete more easily in the rapidly changing global market. As the League of Communists representatives remarked, "The market orientation of the whole Yugoslav economy will allow Energoinvest to develop further and ensure a more successful appearance in the international and domestic market."[40] Energoinvest was significant as both an economic competitor and a symbol of non-alignment. On a visit to Energoinvest's Egyptian joint venture and production facility EVAKO, Prime Minister Branko Mikulić praised the company as "the best and most concrete manifestation of the idea and concept of non-alignment."[41]

An intricate web of foreign economic relations with other companies was considered at the time "fundamental for the company's export and stability."[42] Božidar Matić was the last general director of Energoinvest in Yugoslav times and was first employed in the company as an engineer in the 1960s and was raised to the rank of research director and then general director in the 1980s. Though a party member with a staunch antireligious and antinationalist position, he was less politically oriented and more business oriented than his predecessor Dragutin Kosovac, a lawyer, former partisan, and high-ranking member of the party's Central Committee. During our interview, he often expressed his considerations about Energoinvest in a pragmatic tone. He remarked that it was important for his company to find itself "in between" East and West:

> We found a niche in this position. . . . If the import of a special computer was forbidden in the USSR but not in Yugoslavia, we procured it, and then together with the Russians, we would experiment with certain things. That helped the improvement of our level of expertise very much, and secondly, they paid us for that.[43]

Džemajl Vlahovljak, director of the Research Development Centre for Electro-energetics (Istraživačko-razvojni centar za elektroenergetiku, or IRCE) in the 1980s and then general director of Energoinvest in the 2000s, also stressed the non-aligned position of Energoinvest in a rather shrewd way:

> At the time of the Iran-Iraq War, we sold equipment [for electroenergy infrastructure] to both. Of course, we did not tell them; we hid that. We were traders, and it did not matter on whose side the politics of Yugoslavia was. However, we used the fact that Yugoslavia was a leader of that non-aligned world, that it was in such good relations with those less developed countries.[44]

Džemajl's rather blasé consideration of their company's ability to exploit Yugoslavia's perceived neutrality abroad for business purposes, recognized in a rather matter-of-fact way by many of my interlocutors, highlights an important nuance of the Yugoslav non-aligned promise: its complex military relations with the postcolonial world. Although the Non-Aligned Movement, and Yugoslavia within it, had been advocates for disarmament, demilitarization, and détente during the Cold War, they also armed conflicts and rebel groups around the world, following principles of socialist solidarity and support for struggles for self-determination. Thanks to its strong military sector, Yugoslavia was a key supporter of anticolonial liberation movements, and indeed this was part of delivering its global promise: solidarity through collective self-reliance. Yet, much as with cooperation and development, here too economic priorities increasingly took over more political considerations. As Milorad Lazić argues, since the 1970s Yugoslavia's military involvement in the Global South had been increasingly driven by economic concerns.[45] It is thus not surprising that for most of my interlocutors, be they managers or workers, the business benefits of dealing with a wide array of partners would calm any concern they may have had with the nature of these partnerships. To an extent, the rather economistic understanding of global relevance and success through economic (and military) partnerships may have obfuscated the potential issues that could arise within a heavily militarized country.

While Energoinvest was mostly dealing with partners from the non-aligned world and the USSR, it strove to maintain business contacts and partnerships in the West (the US and France in particular). Through the engagement of the American management and consulting firm McKinsey (a symbol of Western managerial principles), Energoinvest sought to improve its growth model and production organization to become more competitive on the world market.[46] Commended domestically as the epitome of economic non-alignment and praised in Western media by the likes of *Fortune*, the *Financial Times*, and *Der Spiegel* as "a fierce capitalist competitor," Energoinvest was still a self-managed company, organized according to the key tenets of Yugoslav socialism.[47]

Since the late 1940s, self-management had become a tangible and inextricable feature of Yugoslavia's economic philosophy and political identity. Top party ideologues and close allies of Tito's such as Boris Kidrič and Edvard Kardelj had theorized and designed a system of workers' self-management through workers' councils that would differ from Soviet models of the centralized, state-planned economy.[48] In 1958, political and economic reformers attempted to put economic and industrial production in the hands of "associated direct producers"—in other words, workers—who would be in charge of income redistribution as well.[49] At the beginning of the 1960s, new reforms extended this self-management model to all spheres of economic, social, and political life (health care, education, sociocultural activities).[50] From the mid-1970s, decentralization reforms determined that companies—or "working organizations" (*Radne organizacije*)—would become the basic economic decision-making units. Each working organization was subdivided into smaller production units. These smaller structures organized production (acting as parts of a bigger industry), as well as management and decision-making functions, through workers' councils and the board of directors.[51]

Energoinvest shaped its approach to a "global" socialist corporate culture by developing a program of research partnerships with other companies across the non-aligned world. Like other countries of the Eastern bloc, Yugoslavia too supported technical cooperation with the developing world through the exchange of experts and students. Although these exchanges were regulated at the federal level through bilateral agreements between countries and coordinated by the Bureau for International Scientific-Technical Cooperation (*Zavod za međunarodnu znanstveno-tehničku suradnju,* or ZAMTES), companies were often sites where international secondments and training would occur.[52] Building networks with non-aligned countries did not only mean hosting students or trainees through exchange programs or building opportunities for technical cooperation. It also entailed preparing its own workforce and experts for the language and rules of the business world, one very much characterized by highly educated international elites. These exchanges were a matter of great prestige for managers and employees of the company. Jakob Finci, who worked in Energoinvest's legal and trade departments throughout the 1970s and 1980s before becoming a prominent Jewish community leader and civil rights campaigner, was sent to Ethiopia and Kenya to oversee the construction of overhead transmission lines between Addis Ababa and Fincha'a. He himself participated in many international training sessions, and he explained their rationale as such:

> Energoinvest was the first company starting to send medium management and general staff abroad to learn languages, and I know that the praxis was to go to Britain to learn English because English is the language of business . . . because in all these non-aligned countries, there are not stupid people. People who are in charge of the businesses in Benin, in Ghana, in Ethiopia, all of them were educated in Oxford, Cambridge, huge universities, so they are not those "stupid Africans"—because the first attitude in Yugoslavia was "those are stupid Africans"—but at the end of the day they were very well educated, maybe even better than former Yugoslavs. And it was really necessary to be very well equipped, very well prepared for negotiations, answering each and every question and solve the problem together.[53]

This excerpt exemplifies the kind of pragmatic business ethos that characterized this company, but it also raises an important critical reflection on the quasi-colonial, Eurocentric if not blatantly racist attitudes that emerged as a result of these encounters. As a leader of Bosnia's Jewish community and himself an activist against ethnic discrimination in his own country, Finci, with this remark, shows how acutely critical he is of the assumptions and prejudices that underpinned Yugoslavs' own attitudes in this context.[54] He recognizes that the Yugoslavs, too, went to Africa with many misconceptions about their business partners. As Peter Wright and Catherine Baker have highlighted, race did in part mediate the relations between Yugoslavia and the postcolonial world. Although introducing itself to partners as a "developing" and "half-colonial" country, Yugoslavs also identified as "Europeans" and "white" in these encounters.[55] Yet questions of race and cultural difference were approached with a high degree of reflexivity in Yugoslav society, which was adamant about distancing itself from western European imperialist traits.[56] Although assessing the degree to which the question of race did shape business relations within the Non-Aligned Movement would be beyond the scope of this book, it is, however, important to note that my interlocutors were not ignorant of these dynamics or of the contradictions of non-aligned solidarity. The assessment of partners in Africa, for example, as being "in need of development," which could be bestowed by a more "developed" European nation, betrays undoubtedly a rather Eurocentric and hierarchical vision of the world order. At the same time, the fact that creating joint ventures and supporting expert exchange and scientific cooperation had to be done following the principles of solidarity and equitable development was not lost on those who took part in these projects.[57] As Dubravka Sekulić has shown for the case of Energoprojekt's architects and engineers involved in construction projects in Nigeria, working abroad was in part a way to learn the inner workings of a "real" market-based business environment; in part, it was a way to demonstrate the virtues of socialist solidarity abroad, thus "pointing further to the inherent ambiguity of Yugoslav socialism and its dual commitment to social solidarity and market competition."[58]

Mediating Influence and the Corporate Value of Expertise

Although Yugoslavia had espoused a "third way," "market-socialist" economic system since the early 1960s, it was still operating as a socialist planned economy. Companies like Energoinvest had a circumscribed, though varying, degree of business autonomy: planning commissions at the federal and national level, sanctioned by the League of Communists, would give general economic planning directions, in dialogue with and in response to the board of directors and workers' councils. Within each enterprise, councils had the right to allocate wages and investments depending on the yearly net income, as well as to elect directors and, in theory, influence productivity targets. Companies and workers' councils were of course not isolated from party influence, and indeed the membrane between the internal organization and the party directives and influence was rather porous. Besides workers and trade unionists, party activists exercised a significant political presence within factories, as political functionaries would sit within workers' councils. Even though at least two-thirds of each workers' council were supposed to be composed of production workers, studies conducted in the 1970s noted that "those with technical and managerial positions and party membership wield the most decisive influence."[59]

As Goran Musić has illustrated in his detailed study of self-management within two Yugoslav factories, there was a complex and ever-changing alliance between self-management bodies, professional management, and trade unions. This alliance was at times in friction with the party-state and at times willingly broken by it, particularly when the party presented fears of an overbearing "managerial technocracy" as a threat to the very principle of self-management.[60] Indeed, through its actions and presence within companies, the party-state kept "technocratic management" in check and propagated an idea that managers deserved those positions because of expertise *and* party loyalty. Indeed, this was a common feature of state-socialist systems across central and eastern Europe: state socialism "endorsed political loyalties and expertise as its main principle of stratification."[61] At the same time, an unspoken but rather concrete social contract existed within companies: workers were willing to pass "the initiative and responsibility for decision-making to the professional management and the specialists, as long as they felt that their measures were contributing positively to the company's total income."[62] Thus, in Yugoslavia, socialist self-management had managed to form, at least in some regions and companies, a microcorporatist alliance between management and labor.[63] Yet the professionalization of the managerial class and the growing real wage differences across skills created friction between self-management bodies and increasingly larger technocratic groups.[64]

Within Energoinvest, the way to stabilize this microcorporatist alliance and partly placate the potential conflict between management and work was to establish a corporate culture of internal social mobility based on ideas of expertise, prestige, and global relevance. To do so, as well as to bridge its international aspirations and its need for local development, Energoinvest invested extensively in research training and advancement. Through its research centers, it trained its cadres, who received university scholarships from Energoinvest in exchange for a professional period in the company. In the period between 1976 and 1988, according to the company's data, the percentage of less skilled workers fell from 14.5 percent to 10 percent, while that of highly skilled workers grew from 7.3 percent to 9.9 percent.[65] This kind of organizational integration and scientific management created another layer of loyalty among Energoinvest workers and further cemented an element of prestige within the company's workplace culture. When asked to describe their working environment, employees across skill levels mentioned this kind of attention to research and expertise as a defining trait of their company and as a matter of pride. They felt the company invested in their growth, creating human capital rather than simply extracting value from their labor. To them, this sort of commitment suggested that they had long-term security in their positions.[66]

Expertise and knowledge were also constitutive of a feeling of trust that employees had for their management. Highly skilled and blue-collar workers alike often expressed faith in the entrepreneurial capacity of their management; this was usually juxtaposed with the lack of knowledge and skills they found in the post-socialist context. For Edin, an engineer who received a stipend from Energoinvest to complete his studies and who was employed in an armature factory since 1986, the expertise and entrepreneurial values within Energoinvest were the basis for an orderly structure of management. Thanks to this, Edin continued, "the hierarchy was respected. We knew who had which task; we knew who was responsible for what."[67] Blue-collar workers shared his view as well. Asim, an employee in the armature factory TDS in Sarajevo, noted:

> It was possible to negotiate on work and operations; before we used to ask [the experts]; for some work you need to do this, for some you need to do that, and we decided with those workers who were experts on the matter, who were qualified . . . but today it is not like that.[68]

As Till Hilmar discussed for the case of care workers in East Germany and the Czech Republic, in their accounts of "transformation" people remarked on the importance of skills to create a sense of continuity and consistency in their coping methods. In other words, skills are intertwined with a sense of recognition and belonging, which is often juxtaposed with the present condition.[69] Indeed, the narrative of a corporate culture that values expertise and, through that, flattens out issues of inequality is still present among Energoinvest workers. As Mirsad, a member of Energoinvest's union before and after the war, recalls:

> [Before the war] there used to be capable people. That's why there was no room for that story [of people complaining that engineers had higher salaries]. Let's say the development service, let's say for example, it made a lot of tools in machine production. That's why you could not, before the war, in that former

> system of the 1980s, you could not say anything to anyone because that man
> was working, because that man put on a coat, came to production, saw what
> the problem was, then solved it, since he is a mechanical engineer, so do it. Iris
> [one of Energoinvest's subcompanies] used to make computers, so we also had
> a couple of computers here, which was advanced for the time. So that these
> people were capable and so that no one could call him names, why does he
> have such a salary? Because that man was working. Now it is the case that they
> do nothing and receive double salary. We have a development service here for
> ten to fifteen years, they have not done anything.[70]

Hindsight colors these perspectives, of course. Mirsad's remark that "you could not say anything to anyone" has here a double interpretation: one wouldn't dare criticize colleagues with higher expertise and higher salaries because they had earned such positions through their expertise. At the same time, one could not criticize them for the same reasons, as these differences were products of a system that legitimized them through the discourse of shared productivity and benefits to be attained through the socialist collective effort. This kind of consideration of expertise as a core value of the company's corporate culture, one that is seen as missing in the postsocialist context, reveals the extent to which corporate values were formalized and internalized. The value of expertise and trust in the company's ability to select capable personnel became a naturalized aspect of Energoinvest's corporate culture. A result of this process, corporate scholars argue, is that "the corporation no longer is simply a model of efficiency or a means of production. It becomes a model for society. It comes loaded with values that often are *expressed* in what seem to be objective and formal structures of efficiency and rationality."[71] In many ways, throughout its history Energoinvest was held as a model for, and a mirror of, Bosnian society.

Crafting the Corporate Culture: Company Newspapers as Transmission Belt

Since the early 1960s, Yugoslav enterprises had published extensive daily, weekly, or monthly enterprise journals and company newspapers. These publications had the task of informing workers and their councils about issues related to the fulfillment or realization of their self-management rights.[72] According to the Communication Research Section of the Yugoslav Sociological Association, these journals were meant to provide a "decrystallization" of political communication, thus bridging the gap between the organized consciousness of the ruling class and the spontaneous consciousness of popular masses. Sociological studies carried out at the time showed that bulletins and papers issued by enterprises retained significant importance as sources of information for workers, second only to workers' assemblies.[73] These journals were, to a certain extent, the transmission belt for the party's or the management's rhetoric, but at the same time they reported quite closely on discussions between different groups in the company.

The "myth" of Energoinvest was an intentional endeavor on the part of the management. The aim of the company periodical and other cultural activities was to familiarize all employees with their global contacts and also to present its operations in a positive light and thus instill pride and create an attachment to the company and the workplace. Zdravko had worked for many years on the editorial board of the company's newspaper. When I interviewed him in his Sarajevo apartment in 2016, he shared many good memories of working in the editorial office, proud of his contribution to the workplace. He recalled:

> The propaganda created a "cult" of Energoinvest. Energoinvest took the liberty on its own, and through the paper, to consider itself "more Catholic than the pope," meaning that it would present itself as the best at this and that.[74]

Although mediated by the company's communication strategy, its periodical was still a space for debate and discussion among employees. Workers could contribute to it and use it to gain information about their company and colleagues. Voices of dissent from company policies, though often filtered by the editorial board, were still present on the periodical's pages. Letters, photographs, poems, and jokes submitted by workers also created a sense of bottom-up participation by the collective in its own internal news.

The company's successful mythmaking was cultivated on the pages of its company journal, *Energoinvest List*, as well as those of its numerous subsidiaries. In every issue, two to three pieces of different lengths reported on Energoinvest's new or ongoing international operations. These articles would also feature interviews with foreign partners or company directors, often stressing the kind of respect and significance that the brand Energoinvest represented around the world.[75] Further, Energoinvest developed its image of a socialist corporate culture around the slogan of "Brotherhood and Unity," espousing—at least in language—the principles of equality and coexistence of all the Yugoslav nations and national minorities, as well as the unique destiny carved out for them by the virtues of non-alignment and self-management.[76] Energoinvest was not simply in the business of

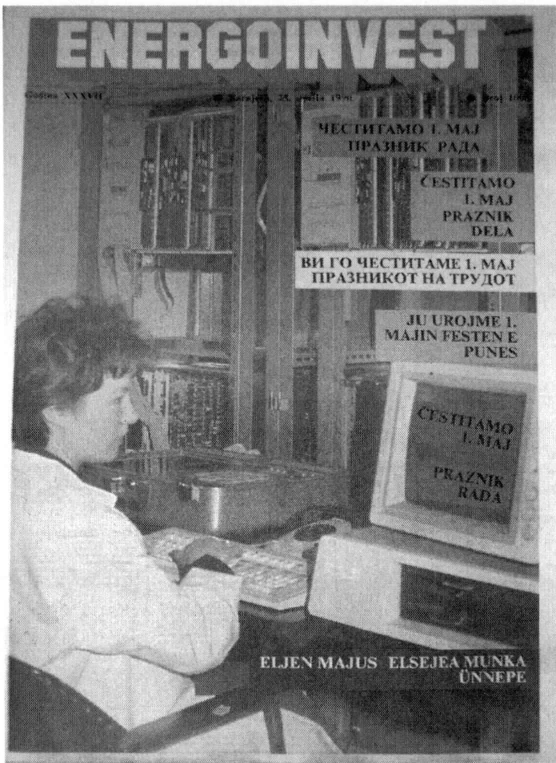

Figure 1.1. First page of Energoinvest's company journal,
April 25, 1990, wishing its workers a happy Labor Day
in all the official Yugoslav languages. Credit: Narodna
Biblioteka Srbije

antinationalism to pay lip service to an ideological tenet; supranationalism was a core principle of its business ethos. It was good for business to be able to present itself as ethnically, religiously, and nationally mixed and pluralistic so that potential partners in predominantly Muslim, Catholic, or Orthodox countries would not perceive any significant cultural barrier.

On the pages of the workplace newspaper, Energoinvest's management would repeatedly declare its commitment to the "civil religion" of "Brotherhood and Unity" and pan-Yugoslav solidarity, defining Energoinvest as a "truly Yugoslav economic firm."[77] This meant fostering an idea of a labor force united by self-organization and work, undivided by nationalism. Occasions were marked for celebrations to cement a spirit of inclusion and cross-national solidarity within the workforce. For example, employees would hold celebrations for Labor Day involving workers from different factories. Moreover, throughout the whole decade of the 1980s, the company periodical held special issues for the commemoration of Tito's death (May 4, 1980), republishing parts of his most famous speeches on Yugoslavia, socialism, and "Brotherhood and Unity." Referring to Tito's message, the paper remarked on the importance of rejecting the "theories of one single ruling nation [*nacija*]" in Yugoslavia.[78]

The company's corporate culture was also grounded in its self-representation as an institution that was committed to fostering cohesion among the different populations and nations that composed Yugoslavia. Take, for example, the case of Energoinvest factories in Kosovo. Here, the company had established a couple of factories producing electrical equipment. These were relatively successful and, as the workplace paper highlighted, contributed to the economic development of Kosovo, as well as to that of self-management and unity in the province.[79] At the time, Kosovo was the least developed of Yugoslavia's provinces, lagging behind in terms of GDP, production rates, and industrialization levels. This had become a serious point of contention between Yugoslav republics, particularly the richer Slovenia and Croatia, which questioned the mechanisms of resource redistribution within the Yugoslav federation. Energoinvest carved for itself the role of "developer and pacifier" in the country, especially after animosities started emerging between the Serbian and Albanian ethnic populations in the 1980s. Toward the end of the 1980s, workers' protests had become a pressing political issue for the federation and had started to preoccupy the company's management—especially since they began to lean increasingly toward nationalist and separatist claims. The director of Energomontimi, one of the factories in Kosovo's capital city, Priština, stated, "If Yugoslavia had behaved in Kosovo as Energoinvest has done, we would not have any problems. . . . Energoinvest has achieved much more than any other collective, or than Yugoslavia, when it comes to solid investment in Kosovo . . . it has built bridges of friendship and elevates the symbols of brotherhood and unity at a level that can serve as a model for the whole Yugoslavia."[80]

With this remark, Energoinvest sought to foster its corporate image as a company that "built bridges"—physically and metaphorically—and that was committed to advancing development, both domestically and internationally. One of the key economic foundations of the Yugoslav federation was a mechanism of the internal redistribution of resources, which entailed that poorer republics and autonomous regions would receive subsidies for development from richer ones. Kosovo, as the poorest region, was dependent on such subsidies. Indirectly, then, commending Energoinvest for behaving even better than Yugoslavia was a reference to its ability and willingness to redistribute subsidies to its lesser developed partners. This was indeed a thorny issue in late-socialist Yugoslavia, one that saw richer republics like Croatia and Slovenia pushing for further economic and political decentralization (to maintain further control of economic resources in a moment of increasing crisis) and poorer republics supporting a recentralization of economic and political mechanisms.[81]

This rather ideological, top-down declination of a socialist corporate culture coexisted with a company-specific narrative of global relevance, which marked Energoinvest's specificity and value in the eyes of its employees. This was grounded on frequent remarks on the company's strengths, which lay in its ability to compete on the global market, establish partnerships across the Iron Curtain, and rely on its highly qualified, but competitively priced, expert workforce.

Reporting on the company's international achievements was not just a prerogative of the company journal. *Oslobođenje*, the largest Bosnian daily newspaper, published regular features on the company's endeavors in Libya, Zaire, Thailand, Iraq, Algeria, and even China, where Energoinvest established the first Yugoslav-Chinese cooperation.[82] Indeed, the 1980s were a moment of great expansion and growth for these joint ventures, as Yugoslavia further opened its economy to transnational partnerships and foreign private capital. It was in this context of the expansion and proliferation of international deals that most of my interlocutors started their working lives in the company, participating in an environment that fostered expertise development and international training for many of them.

Working (in) the Miracle: Workers' Experiences of the Global Promise

Across Central Eastern and Southeastern Europe, a key tenet of socialism as an alternative modernization project was that of ensuring a satisfactory degree of employment, equality, access to leisure activities, and consumer goods. As Patrick Hyder Pattison illustrates, improving the standard of living for its citizens was part and parcel of the socialist state's social contract with its citizens, and indeed this was a process of mutual negotiation between the state and its citizen-worker-consumers and a source of legitimation for the socialist state.[83] In particular, workplaces were key spaces of such negotiation, melding the nexus between (promises of) production and consumption. Export-oriented enterprises like Energoinvest were vital in this nexus: not only could they ensure access to foreign markets and function as vital evidence and source of legitimization for the socialist "global" project but, crucially, they could offer employment, housing, services, and access to consumer goods to their employees.

The very urban development of a city like Sarajevo, where Energoinvest had its headquarters, is testament to this role. Bosnia's capital has a peculiar topography: it is oblong, with a great West–East extension compared to its relatively narrow North–South axis. Engulfed in a narrow valley, it develops alongside the river Miljacka. Parallel to it runs Sarajevo's busiest artery, Zmaja od Bosne. It connects the old town, surrounded by hills, with the newer part of the city. Packed trams transport passengers back and forth along this route, and several high-rise buildings punctuate its skyline. Right off this busy street is the building of Energoinvest. This is an important point of reference for many city dwellers, as it marks the crossroads connecting the two highly populated neighborhoods of Grbavica and Pofalići to the city's main artery.

Visible from many parts of the city, this building was pointed out to me as soon as I mentioned the topic of my research to anyone I met in Sarajevo, be they interviewees, friends, archivists, or taxi drivers. Referring to it affectionately as "our former giant" (*Naši bivši gigant*), most people mentioned the same two details that they considered illustrative of the company's (lost) grandeur: the number of its employees (fifty-five thousand) and its connections across the globe. These remarks would be followed either by various details describing the company's prosperity during socialism or by bitter consideration about its dilapidated status.[84] The reference to its global connections sparked my interest. I expected Bosnia—a former socialist country—to have its fair share of state-owned companies with large numbers of employees. However, I found their global connections had been neglected in mainstream discussions about the socialist workplace (which had become largely synonymous with *isolation* within popular post–Cold War narratives in the Western world).

Indeed, this was a very common first remark from most of my interlocutors. The workplace was a physical space where people were exposed to the Yugoslav "global promise" in immediate and tangible ways. Mladen's testimony exemplifies this convergence. He worked in the 1970s and 1980s as an engineer in IRIS, Energoinvest's leading software and research center:

> [Energoinvest] was the biggest exporter in former Yugoslavia, and they really exported products in Indonesia, Mexico, Africa, and Third World countries, where it used that position of former Yugoslavia in the non-aligned. . . . [W]e were really proud of working there. Salaries were not high, but that was the price of solidarity, of development, of finding new areas. When I started, you know, computers were only just at the beginning, so we got a huge project because Energoinvest responded to such a project. And that was Yugoslavia.[85]

Like Mladen, all the other employees of Energoinvest I interviewed had mnemonic associations that tied their work, their company, and their country into a singular experience. Energoinvest, Yugoslavia, and non-alignment overlapped in their narrations, as spaces where they experienced—directly or indirectly—the principles of internationalism and solidarity, manifested in the form of competitive global trade and non-alignment during the Cold War. Yugoslavia became a unique space—carving its own path in a bipolar world and fostering its own brand of national belonging—and its workplace became a microcosm of these broader tropes. In the experiential space of the workplace, workers became witnesses to and participants in the non-aligned, global aspirations of their company as an embodiment of those of the wider nation. To work for the export market, rather than domestic production, was far from an irrelevant aspect of workers' daily lives. In the space of the workplace, non-aligned solidarity, socialist modernization, and an industrial ethos all collapsed in the word *Svijet* (World), often uttered in the same sentence as Energoinvest. Mate, a blue-collar worker in Energoinvest's large aluminum complex in Mostar, recalls:

> In the production line where I was working, we were making parts for military industry, that means guaranteed money, everything was guaranteed because Yugoslavia was non-aligned, so we made planes for Libya, in cooperation with Romania. Actually, helicopters. So we worked, there were jobs. There was a salary. Now, it was never something that you could praise from today's perspective. But you had something. You did not have to pay the doctor, the school. You studied for free here. If you know, you sign up to the university, attend it, finish it, and you did not have to pay anything.[86]

Like Mladen's before him, Mate's experience of work, the sense of security he derived from it, is marked by the contours of Yugoslavia's engagement with non-alignment. In many of these factories, even blue-collar workers got a glimpse of the Yugoslav global project, one that shaped their working lives in tangible ways. Workers concretely experienced non-alignment and market engagement in their workplace on a daily basis. This is what shaped their occupational identity and their affect not only toward their workplace but toward the global project it represented.

When asked about his job, one of the first things that Branimir proudly remarked was that in his factory (RAOP, a daughter company of Energoinvest that produced high-voltage switchgears), "over 80 percent of our production was destined to Libya, Indonesia, Czechoslovakia."[87] For Branimir, the very act of producing for the foreign market—in a society that for many other purposes did not feel particularly "globalized" to him—had an important symbolic meaning. It was as if knowing that his work would have such a far-reaching impact, thousands of kilometers from his factory in Sarajevo, had broadened his space of experience: concrete pieces of himself—the components he produced—were shipped across the world, and he was, in his words, "proud of that."[88] Many of my interlocutors related to this feeling and to the sense of security that came from having significant, steady orders coming from abroad. This sense of pride was due to not only the international trade in the product of their labor but also the international recognition of the name of their company. Employees felt a sense of international engagement and relevance even without leaving their factories in Bosnia. They derived a sense of "geopolitical dignity" in being participants in a project that considerably shaped Yugoslavia's global outlook.[89]

At Energoinvest, the socialist corporate culture was not just a creation of party cadres and senior management, nor was it just imposed through propaganda. With workers actively participating in some of the internal decision-making processes, many came to see themselves as unofficial ambassadors of the enterprise. In the company paper, workers had room to debate current issues, comment on their work and lives, and organize different events. Workers coordinated many leisure and recreational activities within the company, in Bosnia and across Yugoslavia, and doing so nurtured a sense of collectivism and attachment. It was indeed commonplace for large socialist conglomerates to organize various leisure activities for their employees. Workers were able to have group or family vacations at the company's leisure facilities on the coast in the summer and at the skiing resorts near Sarajevo in the winter. This further contributed to employees' perception of their own status and privilege as part of Energoinvest.[90]

Across state's borders, different workers' groups organized sports activities and tournaments. Among the best known were the Trekking and Hiking Society (Planinarsko društvo Energoinvesta, which still exists today) and the sports event Energofis, a sort of Yugoslav-wide Olympic Games for employees of Energoinvest.[91] These kinds of bottom-up initiatives nurtured a sense of belonging among workers, who contributed to building the spirit and narrative of the company as a global giant. In 2017, during my field research, I spoke to Branimir in a café near his apartment. Branimir was a highly skilled worker in a switchgear factory in what would become "East" Sarajevo. During our conversation, he recalled with considerable fondness the leisure activities and fun he associated with working at Energoinvest. He remembered that sports and leisure activities provide be a moment of socialization beyond the workplace, one that for him symbolized the values of cohesion, collectiveness, and friendship (*drugarstvo*), which he wanted Energoinvest to embody:

> We had Energofis, the sports games of the workers of Energoinvest. We would also meet workers from those factories that were our competitors too. And we would go as the team representing Energoinvest. And after the end of the games, we would have a party, where we would dance and eat, there would be drinks and music. It was great. And that also created a spirit of Energoinvest. In some ways, to put it literally, *we were proud because we were workers of Energoinvest.*[92]

In addition to a sense of camaraderie, workers listed material benefits that both uplifted morale and boosted their loyalty toward the company. The founder and director Emerik Blum was the mayor of Sarajevo in the early 1980s, an important figure in the Bosnian minister of industry and mining, and a member of the Sarajevo Winter Olympics organizing committee. Not only did his name lend a lot of prestige to the company name but, thanks to his political weight and prestige, Energoinvest built large industrial complexes across the city and employed a significant proportion of its workforce. This led to fast industrial development in Bosnia, and especially in Sarajevo.[93] Neighborhoods such as Alipašino Polje, Dobrinja, and Novi Grad benefited from the development of social housing that Energoinvest initiated. The company owned many factories in the area and had built or acquired property for its workers there; it is estimated that over forty thousand citizens were living in this area.[94] Although the housing system was often slow and flawed since it tended to privilege managers, cadres, and clerks, it nevertheless created a sense of security among those workers who could benefit from it.[95] Energoinvest was thus strongly embedded in the cultural, social, and economic life of Bosnia and its capital.

Firms and factories in what Stephen Crowley and David Ost have defined as "workers' states" were characterized by specific organizational cultures based on the sense of identification and values that workers established with their workplaces.[96] Across socialist Eastern Europe, though arguably in Western Europe as well, people were employed their whole lives by a single enterprise, and this shaped not only their biographies but also their views and expectations.[97] Much as with other socialist countries, the Yugoslav industrial workplace was an important space of socialization for workers. Here, "the socialist discourse on the significance of factory labor and the working-class community reinforced and co-shaped the sense of belonging to the factory."[98] Self-management and market socialism had given many Yugoslav workers a sense of emotional attachment to their workplace—though of course sentiments varied across regions, sectors, gender, class, and skill levels. The workplace constituted a place where a specific labor and class identity was forged, one where workers came to socialize and share a feeling of belonging to a promising future.

2

THE CRACKS IN THE PROMISE
OF GLOBAL SOCIALISM

Debt and Restructuring in the Time of Reform

THE 1970S SAW A CONSIDERABLE EXPANSION OF AID and development efforts from the socialist world toward the Global South. Yet this was also a decade of significant amounts of borrowing as the "Third World" began accessing loans from both Western countries and socialist lenders, taking advantage of low and competitive rates. In addition, private commercial banks offered loans to developing countries, piling on even more debt. While the socialist world lent capital, machinery, and industrial equipment to the Global South, it also borrowed a great deal from the West.

Debt was a binding instrument in the relationship between the developing world and the socialist economies (and vice versa).[1] This degree of indebtedness in the Global South had a significant impact on the socialist economies of eastern Europe. Indeed, after providing generous loans to the Global South and relying on trade to balance the deficit with the West, the East had become "dependent on the South."[2] Although the developing world accounted for just 17 percent of Yugoslavia's overall import and export in 1980 (with the majority going to Organisation for Economic Cooperation and Development [OECD] countries), in certain sectors such as metal and nonmetal production (aluminum and bauxite), shipbuilding, and energy transformation (switchgears, power substations), Yugoslavia held trade relations with the Global South as sizable as those with OECD countries. Iraq was Yugoslavia's fourth-largest trading partner after Italy, West Germany, and the USSR, whereas more than 20 percent of Yugoslavia's imports came from Latin America, particularly in the form of agricultural products.[3]

In socialist countries like Zambia, Panama, and Cuba, not only were Yugoslav companies able to offer cheaper contracts than their Western counterparts for the relatively fast construction of energy infrastructure but they were also able to respond to these countries' requests to establish joint venture companies—with shared ownership, capital, and know-how—with a higher degree of flexibility than Western companies involved in the same areas could offer. As an example, in Panama, Yugoslav companies were engaged in supporting the country's ambition to untether itself from US dependency in the field of trade and energy. Companies like Energoinvest were approached to build oil refineries that would be cheaper than US ones. Moreover, Yugoslavia agreed to import large quantities of bananas from Panama at subsidized prices, slightly higher than what US banana cartels were offering. In Zambia, Yugoslav companies like Energoprojekt and Energoinvest established joint ventures in crucial sectors like transport and energy, while Italian companies like Fiat or Impregilo were less eager to respond to similar proposals from the Zambian side.[4] From the perspective of its developing partners, Yugoslavia appeared more accommodating to their constraints and wishes. Yugoslav economic experts viewed preferential relations built with the developing world as a competitive edge over Western firms.[5]

The Yugoslav promise was a complex balancing act between integration into the world market, on the one hand, and economic self-reliance, on the other. The two oil shocks of 1973 and 1979, as well as the debt crisis that shook most of the developing world in the early 1980s, brought to the fore the pitfalls of global interdependencies. Because of the debt crisis, borrowing countries in the developing world found themselves less and less able to service their debt, delaying payments of Yugoslav loans.[6] This was not the case only for the countries of the Global South but for socialist countries as well. Poland and Romania, for example, had also relied on borrowing from Western banks, as well as international financial institutions such as the World Bank and International Monetary Fund (IMF). These became key players in countries experiencing debt distress and were able to impose harsh conditionality measures to achieve fiscal stability. This renewed developing countries' economic dependency on the Global North. Faced with internal economic constraints, major players such as the Soviet Union and Yugoslavia partly retreated from their development commitments in the Global South, signaling the "unravelling of 'Third World' solidarity."[7]

For a country like Yugoslavia, which had relied on foreign credit and cheap oil imports from its non-aligned partners to finance its growing industrial sector, export-led growth amounted to what Susan Woodward has defined as a "Faustian bargain": in the name of a self-reliant path to economic development, based on an ambitious program of fast industrialization, Yugoslavia pursued a policy of global market integration that had exposed it to its fluctuations.[8] Yugoslavia's strategic position as a small socialist country with a comparatively open economy and a between-the-blocs position had further exposed its domestic economy to the vulnerabilities of external shocks.[9] As Woodward highlights, the Yugoslav League of Communists had created economic conditions that pushed unemployment upward, ultimately hollowing out the very foundations of their political consensus.[10] The gradual but steady dependence on foreign capital had two major consequences. First, because of a shift in the Western demand for exports, Yugoslavia prioritized investment in industries "that required far more governmental involvement in capital investment."[11] Second, this rendered the country particularly vulnerable to the swings of the world economy.

By the early 1980s, Yugoslavia had entered a phase of recessions and great economic instability. This was due to both the heavy reliance on foreign capital (in the form of loans and of remittances of Yugoslav workers abroad) and the alleged internal inefficiency of the production sector and organization of labor through self-management.[12] In addition, competition from the booming export sector of the East Asian Tigers also put a dent in Yugoslav enterprises' competitiveness on the global market and imperiled the country's strategy of export-led growth. Having to finance export growth by borrowing heavily from international financial markets and relying on hard currency imports led Yugoslavia into a "debt trap" with a downward spiral of trade deficit, increased inflation, and a staggering USD 20 billion foreign debt by 1980.[13] To an extent, Yugoslavia was not just exposed to a crisis beyond its control; it was a making of its own design as well.[14] Its internationalization was dictated by the ideological, political, and geostrategic need to maintain a position of relevance within the Non-Aligned Movement and by the recognition that such a position had enabled Yugoslav companies to compete with Western ones in the developing world.

The Promise of Reform in the Socialist East

The political and economic zeitgeist of the 1980s is often associated with the acronym TINA: "There is no alternative." This slogan, attributed to Margaret Thatcher, has often been used to signify economic policies championed by (neo)conservative forces on both sides of the Atlantic. After the oil shocks and the debt crisis, a new program of harsh monetarist anti-inflationary policies, deregulation, and market liberalization, promoted domestically within the US and UK, spread rapidly to the developing world as well as socialist countries in Eastern Europe. The advent of large-scale market-oriented reforms in Latin America and Central and Eastern Europe appeared to confirm this: there was, indeed, no alternative.

The liberal fever was contagious: a wave of economic and democratic reforms swept across socialist countries in Central and Eastern Europe, heralding different degrees of market liberalization and privatization. Yet a closer look shows that reforms in the former socialist bloc consisted of much more than a monochrome canvas of normative economic mores. In fact, there was a high degree of variation among postsocialist countries, shaped around local trajectories of reform.[15] The spectrum ranged widely between Berlin and Sofia, Belgrade and Warsaw. Far from giving in to the one-size-fits-all model of market transition promoted by Western advisers committed to the ideas of the Washington Consensus, the first market reforms across socialist Eastern Europe found their roots in endogenous economic thoughts and traditions.[16] In fact, market reforms in the socialist world were a long time coming, the result of a snowballing of reform that had been ongoing in Eastern Europe for several years.[17]

Scholars like Johanna Bockman, Gil Eyal, and Adam Fabry have questioned the extent to which the triumph of neoliberalism should be seen as the common denominator for the market reforms in late-socialist eastern Europe.[18] Many reformers intended to finally realize the models of democratic market socialism they had been advocating for since the 1960s. Local economic experts had been long familiar with market principles and the possibility of embedding them in a socialist system and had been engaged in transnational dialogues on alternative economic models across the Iron Curtain.[19] As Johanna Bockman has shown in her study on late-socialist reforms, the late 1980s in Yugoslavia and Hungary saw the revival of market socialist models as the preferred outcome of economic transformation; reformers were engaged in giving new impetus to the development of radical democratic institutions as the base underpinning market socialism. The late 1980s across the socialist world were thus a moment of real hope, one where the promise of a specific kind of reformed market socialism came tantalizingly close to being actualized. Economists who had been advocating for a system of democratic market socialism since the 1960s found themselves reinvigorated in the 1980s, and indeed for a while they were able to push for reforms that were in no way meant to do away with socialism but rather to democratize it. With the new political environment ushered in by the collapse of socialist and communist rule came a more "authoritarian" and neoliberal vision of economic policy, one characterized by competitive markets, hierarchical firms, and the narrowing of workplace democracy. Indeed, "the victory of neoliberalism was in spite of, not because of, those economists who developed models of democratic market socialism that they had hoped to implement after 1989."[20]

In Yugoslavia, too, the market reforms of the late 1980s had been a long time coming and in fact could be viewed as a countermovement away from the model of decentralized production that had been implemented since the mid-1970s. Responding to a resurgence of nationalisms and to the fear of a liberal counterrevolution, the constitutional reforms introduced in 1974 had significantly decentralized economic powers in favor of republics.[21] From then on, Republican governments carried out most of the decision-making concerning industrial and development policies, as well as the foreign trade sector after 1977.[22] In conjunction with this, a new Law on Associated Labor was introduced in 1976 that replaced the central decision-making organs of each company with a hierarchy of various decision-making units. Each large firm became a complex organization of associated labor (*Složena Organizacija Udruženog Rada*, or *SOUR*) composed of several working organizations (*Radna Organizacija*, or *RO*), in turn subdivided into single, smaller production units called basic organizations of associated labor (*Osnovna Organizacija Udruženog Rada*, or *OOUR*).[23] These smaller structures carried out production (as part of a larger industry), as well as management and decision-making. This decentralization was supposed to devolve power more directly to workers' councils within each OOUR, which would now have control over working conditions, the management of productive assets, and the redistribution of income.[24]

Despite these reforms—and according to some people, because of them—the 1970s coincided with a period of economic slowdown that intensified into a decline in the 1980s. The economy stagnated because of a combination of different factors—namely, the overlap of the debt crisis with a fall in productivity. The consensus among economists was that the decentralization and the overbureaucratization of decision-making within enterprises was an obstacle to technologic and research development, which in turn affected industrial productivity and efficiency.[25]

Those experts called on rethinking the Yugoslav economic system emerged from a neoclassical economics tradition critical of decentralization and supportive of market socialism, as Johanna Bockman has evidenced.[26] Though not adamant about eradicating self-management, they were committed to erasing what had been the most direct forms of workplace democracy, as a system that overbureaucratized decision-making, slowed down companies, and tied them closer to the state. Mihajlo Crnobrnja—a professor of political economy at Belgrade University, former director of the Serbian Council for SocioEconomic Planning (1986–1989), and Yugoslav ambassador to the European Economic Community (EEC) (1989–1992)—recalls how the proposals for reforms were intended to adapt socialism to a changing internal context:

> We economists always presented [reforms]as an internal need, as a consequence of the fact that we went way out in expanding the rights of the workers with . . . the Law on Associated Labor of '76. So our explanation and our justification for entering the global market was not that people expect that of us, that Americans, the European Union, and so on—it was quite the reverse! We made a move [the law of '76] which was—well, let's not call it silly—but which was economically unwise, and we needed to correct it now in order to be competitive.[27]

As experts further noted, instead of empowering workers, the decentralized system of Basic Organizations of Associated Labor had led to a poor use of resources and a high cost of labor, which threatened Yugoslav enterprises' competitiveness on the global market.[28]

Several Yugoslav presidents in the 1980s (Sergej Kraigher, Branko Mikulić, and Ante Marković) established Commissions for Reforms, where economic experts and policymakers were tasked with a major and substantial makeover of the Yugoslav economic system. Although most economists in advisory positions emerged from either Belgrade or Ljubljana, the key centers of reformist economic debates, Bosnian economists were not entirely at the periphery of the reform effort and were particularly observant of the economic transformations occurring across Central and Eastern Europe. Bosnian party officials and economic advisers welcomed Mikhail Gorbachev's reforms with a certain degree of optimism: Perestroika signaled that the USSR was moving away from planned orthodoxy and toward a reformed socialism inspired—scholars argued—by the Yugoslav model.[29] They viewed this as the ultimate evidence of "the end of a relatively unsuccessful phase of development of the Stalinist model of socialism, one that would open to a new phase of socialism's historical advantage."[30] Further, it was evidence that the Soviets had finally given in to the superiority of the Yugoslav model of market socialism. At a meeting of the Bosnian Council for International Relations, for example, experts remarked that Yugoslavia should "stop devaluing what, in our conceptions and ideas, are the experiences of our Non-Aligned Movement and our achievements, which has served as an inspiration to Gorbachev and his followers."[31] Perhaps even more so than their northern counterparts, Bosnian economists were adamant that reforms would not retreat into more parochial economic policies but that the transformations ongoing in other parts of the socialist world would galvanize further change.

After a few attempts to initiate change, the first major reforms were set in motion by the government of Branko Mikulić in 1988.[32] The federal government introduced the Law on Enterprises (Zakon o Preduzećima), which legalized the existence of multiple forms of enterprises (enterprises with private, public, or mixed ownership and corporations) and set the terms under which they were to be managed (through a shareholders board or an elected board of trustees, for example).[33] This was a significant move, as it paved the way for broader ownership rights and market reforms that had the potential to transform the enterprise sector. However, Mikulić did not enjoy widespread political support and was criticized for failing to control an inflation crisis. Although his program for reforms had initially enjoyed support and obtained some results, it was none other than a Bosnian company that fast-tracked his demise. The financial scandal that hit the Bosnian food production giant Agrokomerc shook the Yugoslav economic and political system to the core and dealt a final blow to Mikulić's leadership. The scandal—defined by some as the Yugoslav Watergate—revealed a system of financial improprieties committed by its general manager, Fikret Abdić, who had risen to a position of esteem and leadership within Bosnian politics because of the support he received from Hamdija Pozderac, one of the key figures in the Bosnian Communist Party from the 1970s onward. Agrokomerc's management was accused of issuing nearly USD 900 million in worthless unsecured promissory notes, which dealt a heavy blow to Yugoslavia's creditworthiness as it approached the IMF for debt restructuring. Moreover, this came as the country was facing a three-digit inflation rate, which, some argue, was made even worse by the scandal. Without full support from the party or the broader population, Mikulić was ousted in 1988 after a vote of no confidence and consequently resigned from his position.[34]

In December of the same year, Ante Marković became the new (and last) prime minister of federal Yugoslavia. His proposed concept of "New Socialism" was influenced by both his experience as a company director and the intellectual milieu and debates that had flourished in the second half of the 1980s within the economics profession in Yugoslavia. In line with his predecessor, Ante Marković relied on a team of economists as well as members of the entrepreneurial field to devise a new reformist strategy. Bosnian experts invited to advise the Commission for Reforms worked extensively on recommendations for economic transformation, including ways to improve self-managed decision-making processes within companies.[35] The issue that concerned them was whether Bosnian companies would be competitive enough to keep up with the Western countries' rush toward the newly opened markets in the now crumbling Soviet bloc.[36] This aspect was particularly pressing in the context of an emerging European common market of increasing geopolitical relevance. In a country like Bosnia, for example, which strongly depended on trade with the Soviet Union and non-aligned partners, economists discussed how "the dichotomy that forces us to choose between Non-Aligned markets and the EEC is false, and we should keep ties with both."[37] Bosnian foreign trade decision-makers viewed the non-aligned market as an integral part of the Yugoslav model of economic growth and development. The prospect of closer ties with the EEC was not supposed to obliterate Yugoslavia's peculiar geopolitical position or to submit its development strategy or multilateralism completely to the hegemonic powers of the IMF and the World Bank. Indeed, Yugoslav reformers were acutely aware that competing paths and models of global integration were at play. What they defined as the "mounting hegemony of the neoconservative strategy of economic growth . . . based on neoliberal premises" was itself a global tendency pushing paths of global integration in a completely different direction, one that would expand the gulf between an ever more powerful global capitalist class and the impoverished working class.[38] In Bosnia, the goal was to gradually reform its economic system to incentivize productivity and competitiveness in its enterprises, always with a large presence on the global market in mind: the "shock of the global" could only be absorbed through further global integration. Yet this could only be ensured if, in parallel, a recentralization of management and decision-making powers occurred within enterprises.

Weathering the Crisis: Energoinvest in the 1980s

As developing countries encountered difficulties in satisfying their balance of payments, export-oriented companies that depended on global exchanges experienced severe shortages. JUBMES, Yugoslavia's export finance bank, had until then supported the foreign business of Yugoslav enterprises. This specialized bank refinanced 65–70 percent of export credits by commercial banks, supporting companies' operations abroad.[39] With the debt crisis of the 1980s, however, JUBMES experienced a severe lack of resources, which in turn impaired companies like Energoinvest, which was now unable to count on its credit. Furthermore, the economic crisis affected many developing countries, particularly in Central and Latin America, making it even more difficult for Energoinvest to collect its payments from partners abroad. Moreover, the dependency on oil producers and foreign markets created issues for exporters like Energoinvest, which were reliant on trade with countries associated with the Organization of the Petroleum Exporting Countries (OPEC). The difficulty in importing oil, combined with the crisis of hyperinflation and foreign debt, created shortages that significantly affected the country's stability and its companies' revenues.[40] For example, by 1991, the growth in the prices of raw materials, services, and energy had diminished Energoinvest's export revenue by a staggering USD 134 million. For Yugoslav companies, this meant having to accept payments in crude oil rather than foreign currency, which further deepened their dependency on foreign lenders.[41]

Lack of financing on the Yugoslav side, compounded by debt insolvency on the side of non-aligned partners, cornered the Yugoslav economy into a serious crisis. Countries like Cuba, for example, had established trade agreements and economic cooperation with Yugoslav companies thanks to financing from Yugoslav creditors.[42] As the island entered a period of economic crisis due to the rapid deterioration of assistance from the Council for Mutual Economic Assistance and the Soviet Union, it found it increasingly difficult to settle its payments with Yugoslavia. This further destabilized enterprises like Energoinvest that had a significant share of the export of machinery to the Cuban sugar industry.[43] The workers directly involved in producing for the Cuban market noted with concern that production had slowed down because of the delay in payments.

Cuba was far from the only country with which Yugoslavia started having difficulties in terms of payments. The aggravation of the Iran-Iraq War in the second half of the 1980s put a significant dent in the economic prospects of enterprises dealing in the area, which had been crucial for the country's own export sector and import of crude oil. In the eye of the storm of the debt crisis, the Mexican operations of Energoinvest (such as its joint venture EnergoMex) were facing severe problems in deliveries and were under threat of closure multiple times.[44] Similarly, debt repayment started to be an issue for Energoinvest operations in Zambia. Among the many Yugoslav companies involved in Zambia, Energoinvest was particularly vocal in showing significant preoccupation with unpaid claims to Yugoslav enterprises for the services they had provided. In fact, many large enterprises involved in Zambia, like Energoinvest, the truck manufacturer Fabrika automobila Priboj (FAP), and the construction company Energoprojekt were owed, respectively, USD 16.8 million, 9.8 million, and 1.5 million. When the discussion came to Energoinvest, the company representatives said that having over 60 percent of unpaid claims made it impossible to continue working and asked that the debt be repaid immediately. During one of the regular meetings of the Yugoslav-Zambian Joint Committee for Economic Cooperation, held in Lusaka in 1983 and presided over by Zambia's president, Kenneth Kaunda, the atmosphere was palpably tense. The head of the Zambian delegation informed the Yugoslav counterpart that Zambia was going through a difficult time in terms of the economic sector, and because of this, it was finding it difficult to fulfill some of its international obligations, such as the payment of debts to its partner countries. Nevertheless, Zambia reassured the Yugoslav delegates that they were doing "everything they could to revive the economy," citing examples of the arrangement Zambia had concluded with the IMF for further loans.[45] Many of these repayments did not materialize and were in fact dragged into the complicated postwar, postsocialist situation, where it was even more difficult to assess whom to repay—whether the Bosnian state, as a potential successor of the Yugoslav state, or Energoinvest itself.

For Energoinvest and many companies alike, building their raison d'être and business strategy on tight economic partnerships with the non-aligned world revealed itself to be a double-edged sword. In October 1990 and then June 1991, hundreds of metalworkers from Sarajevo went on strike because they had not been paid for their work, because of delayed payments from their buyers in Iraq, which at the time was involved in the Gulf War.[46] It has to be said, however, that Energoinvest workers participated in strikes to a lesser extent than their colleagues in other Bosnian companies, or indeed in other conglomerates in Serbia, Montenegro, and Croatia.[47] They remarked that, in comparison with other factories and companies, their situation was not that bad, because they still had a lot of production requests to fulfill.[48] Indeed, at the beginning of 1990, Bosnia had established a record high for exports, above the Yugoslav average, and Energoinvest was mentioned as one of the key factors in this, thanks to its global connections and trade endeavors.[49] Although the strategy of relying extensively on non-aligned partners appeared less beneficial than before, it was evident to workers and reformers alike that autarchy or isolation was not a viable solution.

The exposure to and embeddedness in an increasingly global business world had led Energoinvest managers to adopt the kind of management jargon and practices that had been increasingly codified throughout the 1980s. They spoke about market reforms as a way to further internationalize production, a positive step to enhance a "technological and market profile and thus increase business performance."[50] Several interviews with the general directors of the Energoinvest group between 1987 and 1991, which were reported in the company paper, show a management increasingly concerned with the inability to attract foreign investment. On these pages, it was frequently remarked that a centralization of management abilities would allow the company to "be more efficient, not subjected to state intervention," and ultimately "be able to pursue normality in accordance with Western standards" and thus provide "more quality and cheaper services than those obtained with the previous system."[51]

An emphasis on efficiency and productivity soon became a thorny issue. In many companies of the Energoinvest group, workers mobilized the traditionally socialist principle of "distribution according to one's work" to argue against the kind of overbureaucratization of self-management and the lack of accountability they saw on the management side. "We hope that the number of executive personnel will diminish and that their work is valued by what they do" stated a workers' representative in Sarajevo's Livnica Armature.[52] In the oil refinery of Modriča (in the north of Bosnia), workers lamented issues of overemployment and mismanagement—particularly on the side of the administration responsible for drafting production and business plans. According to a worker interviewed in the company's paper, "We all want to work. The problem is that there is eighty of us in my department and we do not know what to do. The fact that workers do not have things to do is not our fault; we are happy when we have to work. Others are paid to prepare the program [of production]. If they do not know how to do that, they should be responsible."[53]

This remark, like many that appeared in company periodicals at the time, suggested that workers were not satisfied with the management's planning of production. It was also a time of severe production shortages and high indebtedness, which fueled dissatisfaction among workers—particularly those whose companies depended on trade and exports. Many workers of the most productive and richest companies were dissatisfied with having to share profits with less profitable ones—an issue that mirrored, at a smaller scale, the question of the uneven development of Yugoslav republics.[54] As a workers' representative remarked at the time, "We are in favor of lending to others [other companies of the group] but only until it has a purpose . . . if a factory is on its knees, we shouldn't prolong its agony."[55] The president of the workers' council of a refinery in the Energoinvest group—a sector that had been comparatively less affected by the crisis—suggested that "those who achieve and create profit should benefit from the result of their work."[56] Thus, the scarcity of resources created by the economic crisis in the developing world, as well as the mounting instability within Yugoslavia, exacerbated fractures within companies and their workforce—between those still able to attract foreign investment and those in need of financial support.[57]

Competing Expectations

The Law on Enterprises (*Zakon o Preduzećima*) introduced in 1988 allowed for the transformation of self-managed organizations of associated labor (*organizacije udruženog rada*, or *OUR*) into companies. Crucially, this legalized the existence of multiple forms of enterprises (enterprises with private, public, or mixed ownership; corporations; and so forth) and further regulated how they would be managed (through a management or shareholders board, by an elected board of trustees, etc.).[58] The Marković reforms introduced the possibility for the smaller units within each company, to "organize themselves as enterprises."[59] This formalized the kind of decision-making agility that the managements of large companies like Energoinvest had advocated for many years. In fact, to further pursue their market and globally oriented raison d'être, they had argued that a stronger "corporate" outlook was necessary to be more competitive and attract foreign investment. In this direction, Energoinvest pursued a transformation into a holding. According to a gazette issued to inform workers of the imminent changes, companies would be connected "through capital to Energoinvest holding by transferring in it the shares of a value of at least 51% of the total net value of each enterprise" without compensation or rights of management.[60] The general director of Energoinvest at the time, Božidar

Matić, declared that this "new organization (was) based on the most successful practice of corporate organization," in which efficiency would be ensured "by giving precedence to people's intelligence, creativity and entrepreneurship . . . which will not lead to the socialization of the effects of bad work, but to the development of ideas which will affirm self-management and leadership."[61]

These shifts were thus justified through the rhetoric of efficiency, centralization, and debureaucratization employed throughout the period of reforms, but they also drew on issues that had been raised within workers' councils. Only through a de facto recentralization of management would the company "be more efficient, not subjected to state intervention," and thus provide "better quality than what was obtained with the previous system."[62] Marking the distinction between "the state," which was responsible for mismanagement, lengthy bureaucratic processes, and lack of efficiency, and "the company," a guarantor of quality, productivity, and market success, was another way to mobilize Energoinvest's corporate culture to galvanize workers' consensus. Yet workers disputed whether limiting the scope of self-management would bring a guaranteed higher efficiency.[63] Again, the disagreement over what qualified as "efficiency" showed the cracks between management and workforce around the question of reforms.

Although the company's workers' council decided in favor of transforming Energoinvest into a holding—a company with most of the capital or shares of subsidiaries in a corporate group—this eventually created a schism between the mother company, which aimed to recentralize capital, and some smaller subsidiary (or daughter) companies, which were attempting to cash in on the reforms' concession of property rights to workers. Some foundries in Tuzla and Sarajevo, as well as the mines in Srebrenica and the aluminum factory in Mostar (all part of the Energoinvest group), opposed a merger with the central branch of Energoinvest. While factories experiencing some financial difficulties (due to the nature of their production, the scarcity of resources, or the outdated equipment) feared to be caught in situations where they would have to rescue other partners from bankruptcy, more successful ones like the aluminum complex in Mostar deemed it "unacceptable" to give 51 percent of their profits and assets to the central holding. This complex, which was worth USD 140 million and was thus the most profitable within Energoinvest, decided to distance itself from the main company and become a stand-alone holding.[64] Employees had in fact vocally opposed the merger with Energoinvest, and both management and workers made clear that they did not want "to be bothered about the problems of other parts of Energoinvest."[65] Hence, strong because of its cadres, knowledge, market contacts, and profit, this complex saw in the reforms the opportunity to break free from the centralized power of the company and attempt to pursue the business individually. As a result, the promise of global integration had become tantalizing for many within Energoinvest, a promise so significant to create internal fracturing and centripetal pressures for independence. Worker-shareholders were now more motivated to pursue economic activity independently—a consequence perhaps unforeseen by the reformist government.

In addition to the perceived improvement in the opportunities of a stand-alone enterprise, compared to those of a holding option, the question of redistribution was also an important one that shaped workers' sentiment toward this transformation. This kind of reasoning—not wanting to "be bothered about the problems of other parts"—echoed, in small part, several republics' issues with being part of a socialist federation. Indeed, richer countries like Slovenia and Croatia had grown increasingly irritated with the federal rules that imposed a mechanism of redistribution of wealth to poorer republics and autonomous regions, like Kosovo or Macedonia. One of the main points of contention that had accelerated the fracturing of the federation and of the party-state was precisely the question of the redistribution of resources. These questions and debates had shaped Yugoslavia's political landscape throughout the 1980s, particularly as the economic crisis intensified. Thus, workers and managers were familiar with the different arguments in favor of or against further economic decentralization. Wanting to put a halt to the mechanisms of solidarity through subsidies was not just a prerogative of national politicians; indeed, it characterized discussions within companies. For these reasons, several companies of Energoinvest opted out of the holding option; perhaps the largest defection was that of Aluminij Mostar, at the time justified as being driven by economic reasons as well as new ethnopolitical influences.

Not everyone had been ignorant of this potential outcome. Božidar Matić, a former director of Energoinvest at the height of the Marković reforms (between 1989 and 1993), had supported the transformation of the whole of Energoinvest into a holding and had pushed for the central branch to retain its control over the smaller ones. During our interview in his study at the Academy of Science in Sarajevo, he recalled a conversation he had had with former prime minister Marković in 2011, a few months before his death. Over lunch, Marković was reminded of what the president of Energoinvest already told him in 1990. Matic had warned the prime minister back then that the new Law on Enterprises allowing each subsidiary to decide whether to remain within larger companies would be destructive:

> I told [Marković] that all the small [companies] who feel that they can be independent, they will leave enterprises, and you will have holdings without property or production. That's it. However, he said, "This is democratic," this and that. "Well, here's your democracy," I said.[66]

What Matić had feared unfortunately materialized. Global aspirations within Energoinvest revealed themselves to be divisive as well. With the Law on Enterprises, the transformation into a holding entailed a fracturing between those companies that thought they could make it alone in the global market and those that preferred to stick to the central company. The global promise, once meant to unify companies and guarantee prosperity through global integration, now entailed competition and fracturing rather than solidarity. A socialist corporate culture started to crack under the pressures of reforms that, paradoxically, were meant to strengthen and enhance it.

3

DELIVERING CHANGE?

Remaking the World of Work in the Early Privatization Reforms (1988–1990)

I N HIS 2018 BIOGRAPHICAL DOCUMENTARY FILM ON THE last Soviet leader's legacy, the German director Werner Herzog asks Mikhail Gorbachev what he would like his epitaph to say. Gorbachev answers concisely: "We tried."[1] Gorbachev was perhaps the most famous reformer of his time whose ambitious reform programs have been met with both praise and criticism. In Europe and beyond, he popularized the words *glasnost* and *perestroika*—synonyms of a changing world—and inspired reformers in the socialist world to open up their economies to private capital.

The last Yugoslav president, Ante Marković, is at times compared to his counterpart in the Soviet Union for trying—and, according to some, failing—to introduce sweeping political and economic reforms before they were interrupted by the outbreak of war. His attempts at reform are thus written off as irrelevant against the greater historical events that subsequently absorbed Yugoslavia, but as I argue in this chapter, even "failed" reforms matter. Indeed, it is important to problematize evaluations of reforms in post-1989 Central and Eastern Europe (and any reform, for that matter) on a gradient from more to less successful.[2] This may have further reinforced a view of the postsocialist condition as a convergence toward a neoliberal model of development. A closer look shows that reforms in the former socialist bloc consisted of much more than a monochrome canvas of normative economic mores. In fact, localized neoliberal varieties emerged.[3] Neoliberalism was, of course, not a prerogative of Eastern Europe: Latin America constituted a significant testing ground for the emergence of locally embedded varieties of neoliberalism, often driven by the need to build stronger, rather than weaker, states. The spectrum of variation ranged widely between Berlin and Sofia, Belgrade and Warsaw, Moscow and Buenos Aires. Lagging behind or diverging from the neoliberal path, however, should not be seen as a failure to reform or a success in resisting it. Rather, it should be understood in its own right, as a result of complex top-down and bottom-up negotiations that determine the trajectory of transformation. These reforms were crucial in shaping the expectations around (and hence the experience of) the postsocialist transition. This chapter further unpacks the promises of reformism across the collapse of socialist Yugoslavia by focusing on changing ownership regimes throughout the 1980s and early 1990s.

The System Is Broken, but Can It Be Fixed?
Self-Management in Crisis

From the Soviet bloc to Cuba, from China to Yugoslavia, socialist regimes had spent decades "making"—unmaking and remaking—the "socialist man" in different ways. This meant creating a civic spirit that would facilitate the objectives of the new state: conforming to the ideals of the social revolutions and educating, socializing, and disciplining workers according to the Marxist political thought and tradition.[4] Socialist regimes were spaces of perpetual top-down and bottom-up transformations concerning subjects' socioeconomic lives. In turn, acts of adaptation and defiance emerged in response to what was prescribed ideologically.[5]

The political discourse of early Yugoslav socialism often mirrored the glorification of the "shock worker" (most dedicated worker) of the communist regimes.[6] However, as Yugoslavia progressively distanced itself from the influence of Soviet communist ideology, its party veered toward an understanding of work as the liberator of people from any form of labor alienation—even that imposed by the state. During the split with the Council for Mutual Economic Assistance (COMECON), which lasted until 1953, Boris Kidrić and Edvard Kardelj, the top party ideologues and close allies of President Josip Broz Tito, started to theorize a system of workers' self-management that would differ from the Soviet models of state-planned economy. In 1958, party cadres and prominent economists concurred that social production and income redistribution would be managed by "associated direct producers"—in other words, the workers.[7] Socialist employment was meant to break away from the need for self-managers to sell their own labor or depend on the top-down state-led redistribution of salaries and income. The notion that by doing so workers' management had returned to the workers the fruits of their labor became central to the making of the Yugoslav self-manager.[8] In combination with self-management, the Yugoslav system relied on a particular configuration of social, rather than state, ownership. Social ownership had been a fundamental tenet by which Yugoslav socialism further distanced itself from Soviet configurations of state ownership. The socialization of ownership in the industrial sector was generally understood to mean that "nobody [could] possess the means of production, but that everybody should have the right to use them."[9] According to Edvard Kardelj, working people would "work, create, think and build a society where the means of production [were] socially owned."[10]

This model was meant to give workers shared decision-making power over matters pertaining to their work, incentivizing hard work and better decisions about how their enterprise should be run, who should receive what share of the profits, and how resources should be allocated and invested. This was what we understand today as the democratization of the workplace. But it was also meant to instill a sense of personal responsibility, cultivating a rational "producer-consumer" in charge of decisions regarding production and the redistribution of income derived from it. Thus, since the early days of self-management, workers' motivation and self-realization were understood to be tied to their role as (self-)managers, producers, and owners.

Throughout the 1960s and 1970s, numerous sociological studies in Yugoslavia investigated workers' productivity and motivation in Yugoslav industries.[11] Sociologists showed that workers were primarily interested in and motivated by higher salaries, a good working environment, and meaningful work, rather than participation in collective decision-making.[12] Moreover, when it came to crucial issues related to their work (the distribution of wages, investment decisions, housing), a number of studies found that blue-collar workers did not enjoy the same decision-making power as their colleagues in the management cadres.[13] Scientific communities across the country had started criticizing socialist self-management and workers' councils, which they deemed incapable of guaranteeing a "free and harmonious development for the economy" or even solving "the problem of equitable distribution" of wages.[14] Against the backdrop of this economic malaise, debates on merit, compensation, "productive" and "nonproductive" labor flared up in the political and economic circles.[15] Many scholars argued that self-management had led to a "catastrophic demotivation of workers" by creating "a climate for shirking [*nerad*]."[16]

The criticism of self-management was expressed loud and clear in the workplaces too. Part of the workforce—especially white-collar workers—blamed self-management for its endemic inability to "filter good workers from bad ones."[17] For example, a representative of the workers' union in the Bosnian mining town of Srebrenica remarked, "It is necessary to clearly divide work from nonwork . . . and pay the production, creative and innovative work adequately."[18] Indeed, this language echoed what Marković himself had declared less than two years earlier in one of his addresses to the Federal Executive Council: Reforms would "induce socially owned enterprises to differentiate between good and bad workers and to form mechanisms of work and business motivation. It [would] also be necessary to enable competition between employed and unemployed workers, i.e. make it impossible to monopolise a job position."[19]

Workers across the Yugoslav federation used the term *shirking* or *nonwork* to define all those who enjoyed the benefits and status of being workers without actually producing—those who were physically present in the workplace but did not fully engage with the requirements of their task.[20] "Shirkers" (*neradnici*) or "unemployed employees" were considered to be workers who profited from the socialist system's lack of punishing mechanisms for those who did not fully respect employment agreements. Academic publications from the time seem to agree with this diagnosis.[21] However, as one would expect, nobody thought that they themselves were shirkers. According to blue-collar workers, it was the managers who did not engage in manual labor, while management and cadres said that it was the shop-floor workers who were idle and unproductive.[22]

This mounting discontent led to widespread worker mobilization across Yugoslavia. In Serbia, Montenegro, and to a lesser extent Croatia and Bosnia, workers protested decreasing wages, worsening living conditions, and a ballooning of the technocratic-managerial class. The case of Serbia and Croatia led to the antibureaucratic revolution of 1988–1989.[23] Workers' dissent was directed toward management structures, technocratic elites, and the party-state, as decentralization reforms had created smaller factories that were overstaffed with white-collar workers and often faced shortages of production workers. Protesters' demands were primarily directed toward a rediscussion of wage policies and the mechanisms of decision-making in self-managed enterprises.[24] As Susan Woodward illustrated, the system's inability and unwillingness to deal with the growing issues of unemployment ultimately corroded its authority and solidity.[25]

Much as in other republics, discontent was looming in Bosnia. Company journals were often an outlet and forum for workers to voice their concerns. Though these journals were not free of editorial bias—with cherry-picked voices lending legitimacy to the official party line—they nonetheless documented general trends in the debates within the workforce. The debates from the time reflect a combination of demands for equality based on the expectations and promises of Yugoslav socialism, with requests for efficiency based on new liberal narratives of market objectivity.[26] At Energoinvest, the company journal featured interviews with workers that discussed these issues; these articles included voices from all the workers' collectives across Bosnia and thus provided an extensive space for discussion beyond the central branch in Sarajevo. Many of those interviewed in the company journal at the time openly reproached their colleagues for idleness and blamed self-management for allowing such behavior to go unpunished. For example, Zijo, a machine worker, said on the company pages: "Everyone gets a wage in proportion to what he or she does, that we divide work from nonwork. We constantly say that, but we do not behave like that. If my colleague does not work, he gets 75% of the salary, but if I fulfill my work, I only get 25% more."[27] Sometimes, one would see a partial admission of personal shortcomings in the journal as well. A worker from a wagon factory expressed his view on unproductivity rather audaciously: "None of us works eight hours in their workplace; if we did, we would make wonders . . . we should say these things and openly discuss this; I am annoyed that in my sector we have half-workers [polu-radnici]; they're half in the factory, half working the land. But I live only off this work, and nothing else. And at the end of the month, we both get the same."[28]

Others believed that the spirit of collective ownership, and thus collective responsibility, needed to be revived in society in general. For example, in 1987 a machine worker and political activist in the automation factory Procesna Automatika in Sarajevo reminded his colleagues: "We must invest more effort in changing the understanding and relations toward social ownership. I am concerned that many think that social ownership is nobody's, but it is everybody's, and all together, equally, we need to take care of it. I think that with better behavior we would have better results."[29]

Many of the testimonies collected in the company journal reveal a working class much concerned with questions of access to work, equal salaries, ownership, and the necessity of reforms. They also highlight a rather fractured understanding of where responsibility for the economic distress lay—whether in the system and bureaucracy, company management, or other colleagues. Despite widespread mobilization, diverging tendencies characterized the Yugoslav labor movement in the 1980s. Regional differences, an unevenness in internal development, and the decentralization of political and economic decision-making produced a labor movement that did not have an en masse response to growing unemployment, though it was affected by it.

The economic turmoil of the 1980s plunged Yugoslavia into a crisis that shook its conceptual foundations. The late socialist reforms were not just a set of emergency measures set in motion to steer Yugoslavia out of the economic crisis. They also picked up on a widespread and long-term dissatisfaction with the system of self-management and social ownership—a dissatisfaction that intensified after the decentralization reforms of the mid-1970s. The solution was to reform the system, in continuity with the series of macro- and microeconomic reforms that had accompanied the evolution of the Yugoslav economic system since the 1950s. These entailed a rethinking of the sociopolitical role and status of the socialist worker, as much as they involved formulating new principles of economic development or regulating social and managerial relations within enterprises.

Inventing Owners: The Sentimental Residue of Social Ownership

A Yugoslav-wide survey carried out in 1990 revealed a country at a crossroads, unsure of its next move but eager to forge its own path. On the one hand, the data showed that 56 percent of the population surveyed believed that ownership reforms were a good solution to the economic crisis. This survey also showed that there was an almost unanimous agreement on a stricter work discipline in the workplace. On the other hand, policy proposals such as "to change attitude towards work, introduce a market economy, or seek expert advice or support the development of SMEs" all scored between 12 and 18 percent.[30] Furthermore, people disagreed over the measures needed to achieve economic stability. When asked if they would be willing to put up with lower employment rates and the dismissal of workers made redundant by new technology for the sake of economic stabilization, 44 percent answered yes, 40 percent said no, and 17 percent were undecided.[31] Although the ownership element of reforms enjoyed much popularity among Bosnian workers, the growth strategy was generally more divisive and contested. There was a majority consensus that markets had to be reconciled with labor protections. In the court of public opinion, these nuances generated a meaningful albeit unresolved tension: the need to "change everything so that everything could stay the same," to quote a famous line in the Italian novel *Il Gattopardo*.[32]

Redefining social ownership became another policy of New Socialism to revitalize motivation and incentives within workplaces. Many Yugoslav economists, sociologists, and lawyers were involved in redefining social ownership: to whom it belonged and whether it could be compatible with new market structures, individual ownership, and the fundamentals of socialism.[33] Branko Horvat in 1976 wrote that the "dogma of the identity between private ownership and capitalism, and between state ownership and socialism is false."[34] The concern with social ownership was not purely of an intellectual nature, nor was it simply relative to market reforms. The power of social ownership to create strong bonds between workers and their workplaces was not lost among reformists. Pioneering sociological and oral history studies conducted across Yugoslavia in the 1980s had already documented a strong feeling of ownership ties that bonded workers to their factories as co-owners (*suvlasnici*).[35] Workers interviewed for these studies mentioned the redistribution of profit through the deliberation of the workers' councils and the possibility for employees to reinvest additional profit within the technological and infrastructural development of each company as factors that supported that sense of co-ownership. Reformers recognized that this appreciation for the principles of social ownership was important to the workers. Instead of throwing the baby out with the bathwater, they had to redefine social ownership without any insult or injury to the sentimental value it carried for workers.

New Socialism was to act as a transformative and invigorating force here as well: social ownership could be transformed and improved into workers' shareholding. As Johanna Bockman has evidenced, employee ownership was indeed a preferred solution for many reformers across Central and Eastern Europe, as a result of reformers' neoclassical orientation toward decentralized workers' ownership and their exposure to transnational debates. Employee stock-ownership plans had been popularized across Europe and North America since the early 1980s, while countries like Chile and Peru had already been experimenting with socialist models of social ownership in the 1960s and 1970s.[36] In the US, by 1991 the number of companies with at least 20 percent employee ownership had grown tenfold in comparison with 1981.[37] On the pages of Yugoslav economic journals, local and international authors promoted the diffusion of workers' buyouts as a potential solution for the Yugoslav context, as they involved "a re-marriage of ownership and control" through market decentralization and self-management.[38] Yugoslav reformers did not just look to the US for inspiration: similar initiatives were widespread in the United Kingdom and West Germany, as well as Southern Europe and China. During a 1988 summit about the complex definition of ownership, Yugoslav economists praised a case from West Germany where an owner decided to bequeath his company "to the workers who had worked there" instead of following the usual custom of leaving it to his family.[39] The experience of other labor-managed corporations like the multisectoral Mondragòn Corporation in the Basque Country were often referred to as examples of successful, reformed self-management.[40] Furthermore, the case of China during the 1980s, where social ownership was converted into collective ownership in view of gradual privatization, was taken as another example of a reform of social ownership that did not mean to do away with the socialist experience. Drawing from this breadth of experiences and examples, Yugoslav reformers envisioned employees' shareholding as one of the most pragmatic solutions for the Yugoslav context.[41]

While a variety of models and approaches to privatization persisted across socialist eastern Europe, so did understandings of the very role of privatization within reforms. As Yugoslav deputy prime minister Živko Pregl put it at the time, "Ownership restructuring is not an end in itself; rather, it is a means of increasing economic prosperity."[42] This position is particularly interesting compared to what the Czech privatization minister Dušan Tříska declared around the same time: "Privatization is not just one of many items on the economic program. It is the transformation itself."[43] Similarly, in Hungary privatization was presented as the backbone of (neoliberal) reforms in the late 1980s.[44]

Though there was plenty of dissatisfaction with how social owner-ship had been implemented, reformers were aware that workers appre-ciated the social and ethical dimensions of collective ownership. Jože Mencinger, the Slovenian minister of economic affairs in the early 1990s and one of the main proponents of the shareholding model during the 1980s, recalls what influenced his position:

> I remember when I went to the countryside around 1990, and I thought, "OK, now we will privatize these factories." The answer of these people was "You are stupid, what are you talking about? These factories belong to us!" It was really a kind of a feeling of ownership, much more real than I thought it was . . . so I said, "OK, for now probably the best owners I can invent will be insiders, i.e. workers."[45]

Mencinger was one of the key architects of the Slovenian model of gradu-alist reforms. For him, this memory carries a poignancy about the nature of gradual reforms: they are an attempt to reconcile (or renegotiate) cer-tain established cultural values to align them with pragmatic concerns over the evolving demands of modernity, technology, and economic competition—for example, by achieving higher productivity while re-specting workers' attachment to their workplaces instead of threatening it. It is also likely that these comments were made to signify an ideologi-cal and almost moral distinction from his counterparts in other post-Yugoslav countries accused of disregarding workers' needs during the privatization process.

Ante Marković himself viewed the clumsy institutions of social owner-ship as the "original sin of self-management."[46] Picking up on workers' discon-tent, he proposed a "New Socialism" that, in his view, could finally actualize self-management's potential to put workers "at its center" while simultane-ously motivating them to contribute their fair share of productive labor.[47] In 1990, following the advice of the Commission for Reforms, Marković's presi-dency introduced the Law on Social Capital (*Zakon o Prometu i Raspolaganju Društvenim Kapitalom*).[48] This gave enterprises the power to issue shares and sell them internally to workers currently or previously employed, with a dis-count proportional to the years spent working in the company. These shares could subsequently be sold on an internal stock exchange; workers would thus participate as shareholders, "owners of the social capital."[49] This would formalize their status as social owners by giving them individual, rather than collective, rights of ownership. Decision-making powers over ownership would be limited to the board of shareholders, while executive decisions (over investments, new research, and new joint ventures) would now pertain to a management board, not to a workers' council.[50]

Members of the Marković Commission for Reforms believed that this kind of transformation would be an additional incentive to motivate workers and foster their sense of responsibility toward work.[51] The prosperity of the company—and thus the dividends afforded to shareholders—would become linked to the individual responsibility of the worker, bolstering motivation and morale in the workplace. Workers would have a vested interest in the financial stability and profitability of their company, as they would share the profits and risks associated with the quality of labor they were willing to provide.[52] Furthermore, this would potentially avoid alienating or antagonizing workers. The New Socialist person was now envisioned as a worker-shareholder, motivated by and efficient because of a tighter bond with the company.

This shift was accompanied by the transformation of enterprises into joint stock companies and was meant to attract capital and liquidity into enterprises while reducing inflation. This would not mean a "return to capitalism" but rather a reformulation of Yugoslavia's economic character—the combination of market socialism and self-management.[53] This clarification was important to maintain the political line of cautious reformism in front of the highest representatives of the Communist Party. The economist Živko Pregl, Marković's deputy, argued that it was necessary to improve competition and motivation in workplaces.[54] On the pages of *Komunist*, the official publication of the League of Communists of Yugoslavia, the Central Committee issued a declaration in support of the development of "democratic socialism" in Yugoslavia, envisioning that the introduction of different forms of ownership (private, collective, mixed) would offer new private incentives without compromising the promise of the collective.[55]

By the end of 1990, the federal government estimated that "in only six months, around 2 to 5 percent of social capital had been privatized."[56] A few months later, roughly one thousand enterprises had made internal share offers and initiated the procedure of gradual privatization through employees' buyouts. The percentage of shares on sale for internal ownership varied between enterprises: in the case of Energoinvest, for example, only 49 percent of the overall shares could be sold through this method. According to the management at the time, a higher percentage would be too similar to public ownership and thus would hinder the possibility of attracting foreign investment.[57]

Corporate Influence on Reform Policy

In the late 1980s, the general directors of several large self-managed enterprises started working in close collaboration with the Commissions for Reforms under the Branko Mikulić and Marković governments. It was not unusual for reformers at the time to seek feedback from large enterprises to verify whether reforms were proceeding on the right path. At the end of 1988, the vice president of the Federal Executive Council, Janež Zemljarič, visited Energoinvest and other large enterprises, where he met with the general managers and discussed plans for reform. As Zemljarič declared, such discussions between the federal government and managers of large enterprises would bring "an improvement regarding liquidity, motivation of workers, and accumulation, and this [would] lead to further stabilization."[58] Large exporting firms like Energoinvest, Energoprojekt, and Marković's own Rade Končar already enjoyed significant political influence due to their importance to Yugoslavia's global economic integration. Moreover, their company managers belonged to a traditionally influential social group and had shown strong reformist inclinations, in Slovenia as well as Bosnia and Croatia.[59]

Meetings between federal officials and company directors gave Marković's team the opportunity to test and discuss reform ideas with entrepreneurs to win the support of the business community.[60] For instance, in July 1990, after one of these meetings, the government issued a statement noting that Marković had the support of Yugoslavia's general directors. This was not false advertising; Marković enjoyed the support of industry heads, not least because of his professional experience as general director of one of Croatia's largest enterprises.[61] Consensus and support among company directors were instrumental to Marković's success and stability in government. As a former company director himself, he knew that. The industry took him as one of their own and trusted him to understand their needs when it came to reforms.

Bosnian enterprises played a special role in shaping and facilitating Marković's reforms. In comparison to its counterparts in the North (such as Croatia, Slovenia, and Serbia), Bosnia was a latecomer with respect to industrial development. However, it industrialized rapidly, developing large conglomerates, such as Energoinvest, UNIS, FAMOS, and Agrokomerc, that saw meteoric growth in a short period of time. The 1984 Winter Olympics held in Sarajevo were a recognition of Bosnia's development as a key player in the Yugoslav economy. Emerik Blum, the former founder of Energoinvest and mayor of Sarajevo, was a member of the Olympics Organizational Committee. Professor Žarko Papić, an economic adviser in the federal government during the second half of the 1980s, remarked:

> Energoinvest and other big companies had an impact, literally the most direct impact, not only on concrete issues but on economic policies. . . . The prime minister would receive a delegation of those large firms, who would tell him what was working, and what was not and so on.[62]

Indeed, in the 1980s a new technocratic wave had risen from Bosnia—one of powerful directors, well connected with both the higher echelons of the party and the increasingly global business environment. It carved its own political identity too. Where some republics, such as Slovenia, leaned on pro-market reforms, others, like Serbia, were opposed to them. Bosnia, however, became a hub of a business culture that aimed—at least in theory—at bridging both positions by finding suitable compromises between the needs of the markets and the workers. The managers of these companies became instrumental to Marković's New Socialism project because they were eminently and vocally pro-Yugoslav and espoused Marković's federalist vocation. Supporting a gradual transformation of enterprises, oriented toward employee and management buyouts, would have allowed them to maintain their positions of leadership within their companies. On the contrary, the advent of quick and radical privatization reforms, with a strong entrance of foreign capital, would have potentially marginalized them. In turn, to strengthen his leadership, Marković built on the consensus he found in Bosnia—among the party, the entrepreneurial circles, and the wider population. In fact, his proposal for economic change and political pluralization was initially applauded by Bosnian citizens.[63] At the beginning of 1990, Bosnian companies had already started showing signs of recovery, a success they attributed, in part, to the economic wisdom of the Marković reforms. By May 1990, the approval of his leadership was very high—over 72 percent in the whole Yugoslavia and 92 percent in Bosnia.[64]

Enterprises, too, developed their own discourse of gradual reformism, which would further open the Yugoslav economy to market principles. Several company managers participated in the Bosnian Republic Council for Economic Development and Economic Policy. Within this body, they discussed further marketization reforms and ways to incentivize productivity and efficiency.[65] Former managers interviewed for this book often described themselves as the last people who sought to reform socialism to salvage the best of it. This was also evident in their critical stance toward the more aggressive set of privatizations that came after the war and in their willingness to distance themselves from the postsocialist reforms that brought many companies to the brink of collapse, if not bankruptcy. Žarko Primorac was an economist and a manager at Energoinvest, and in 1989–1990 he was also a member of the federal commission tasked with reforming companies. During our interview in his Zagreb residency, he recalled:

> We thought that the companies must be more efficient [efikasnije]. You cannot regulate through a law that someone would be more efficient, and you cannot prescribe any regulation, the only thing that you can think of is some form of economic instrument, which will make me, or any other person, interested in being more efficient. And that is how we decided for internal shares.[66]

This excerpt reveals a fundamental turning point in the history of reforms, one that defined the promise of reformism: finding in ownership reform the solution to the question of workers' productivity and motivation in the workplace.

Not all managers were equally convinced of the reforms' unique and noncapitalist features. In the summer of 2016, I had the chance to meet Stevan Santo in the northern Serbian town of Subotica. Santo had been the minister of industry and energy under the government of Ante Marković, chosen because of his fame as a well-respected enterprise director in Vojvodina (Serbia). We spoke at length about his role in the government, his work as an entrepreneur before and after his government experience, and his friendship with Marković. They both shared roots in the world of enterprises, as well as a certain pragmatism in the approach to reforms. Santo's cultural and geographical proximity to Hungary (Subotica is located very close to the border) made him particularly attentive to the political and economic developments in the COMECON countries and to Yugoslavia's distinguishing features in this context. He recalled:

> When we formed the government, it was already 1989, neither Ante Marković nor we could say that we will abolish socialism. Here it was not the same thing as in other parts of eastern Europe. There, socialism was a synonym with Soviet occupation, so if you said there "Let's abandon socialism," you would win the elections and that's it. But here it was different; people did not want

to change socialism completely; they had it best and had the highest social security. I know that Marković was an intelligent man and understood that politically he simply could not present the reforms in such a radical manner [like other eastern European countries] . . . so he came up with the platitude of socialism with a human face.[67]

Although this slogan (Socialism with a human face) was coined in the context of reformist attempts during the Prague Spring of 1968, it is significant that Stevan Santo would refer to Marković in a similar fashion. This consideration suggests that, upon embarking on a major transformation of the Yugoslav economic system, some members of Marković's government were aware that they did not have much room to maneuver. What Santo describes is a partial disconnect between the expectations of reformers and those of their political constituents: he depicts Marković as dressing a liberal agenda in the language of gradualist reformism to make it acceptable to the party and the general population. Yet a liberal direction for economic transformation and a genuine commitment to reforming socialism were not necessarily antithetical. On the contrary, Marković and his government committed to integrating a liberal discourse into their program of reforms, without doing away with what they viewed as the positive legacies of socialism. Reforms were thus a partial reprogramming of society, an attempt at fulfilling the promise of socialism rather than doing away with it.

Reformers sought to remake property relations according to what they perceived as an emotionally charged characteristic of Yugoslav self-management: workers' attachment to their workplaces and their self-identification as owners of their factories. Marković's New Socialist approach drew from a long tradition of market-socialist reforms that held workers as central pillars of social and ownership transformation. Yet it did not just signal a move toward reforming and actualizing self-management. It also determined the culmination of socialism's attempt at "making" individuals, imbuing them with certain socioeconomic values and ethics, this time by marrying ownership with labor. Though the already influential circle of experts, managers, and company directors dominated the discussions of reforms, the seed of reformed socialism, the aspirations and values it espoused in the face of change, would prove to have an enduring hold over the broader membership of Yugoslav society. In addition, the legacy of these discussions would prove fateful for the trajectory of postsocialist reforms.

4

OUR WORLD CAME TUMBLING DOWN

The Workplace at War

In the summer of 1991, I invited a couple of paragliding pilots from Vienna to come to Sarajevo to make a presentation of that new sport, and they said they will come. And that was around May 1, and we were talking about next month, which means June or maybe July 1991, and then the bridges on the Sava River fell down [in September 1991, a bridge that connected Bosnia and Croatia across the Sava River was blown up as part of the initial Yugoslav army offensive], I mean the war started . . . and I was just thinking about my paragliding pilots from Vienna that won't be able to come to Sarajevo and that we would have to postpone their visit. And I was working here diligently engaging TV and the Olympic Center to make that presentation. That summer, that was our last summer on the coast, you know . . . funny atmosphere, some airplanes flying low above the sea, and we were swimming, and I did not worry much, no. Some games, it will end up very soon, you know . . . and I brought my paraglider, and I took off from the mountain above, and it was a sensation at the time, a paraglider over that part of the coast, and people there still remember crazy Mladen flying on the horizon in '91 . . . and after that September it was Dubrovnik [the Yugoslav Army's attack on the Croatian city that commenced in October 1991], and I mean for everybody . . . I mean I must have been crazy, I did not read these signs, I was not worried, and it appears now that most people knew that the war was getting closer. No, I, I did not. . . . Naive, stupid, optimist: I don't know how to describe myself.[1]

This picture of beachgoers and paragliders, aloof in the face of an impending war, describes the dissonance experienced by Mladen when his expectations—or perhaps, hopes—of peace were upended by the brutal conflict that followed. Mladen mentions the bridges on the Sava River. Although this is an ex post facto reflection on the war that shook the former Yugoslavia—and Mladen's life—to the core, it is an important starting point to reflect on the theme of expectations. Why was it important for Mladen to think back to his paragliding against the background of an impending war? Why did he choose to reflect on the stark contrast between his feelings at the time and the events that were about to unfold? Was it the absurdity of going on vacation on the eve of the war? The memories described by Mladen, and the feelings they represent for him, offer us a way into the categories of experience and expectation that are crucial to understanding how my interlocutors came to terms with major transformations in their lives. Mladen's visualization of the space around him (the seaside, the destroyed bridges, the airplanes) and the horizon of his expectation (his focus on the paragliders from Vienna, his regret for not picking up on serious signs of imminent conflict) mark the contours of his narrative and embody the relationship between past, present, and future in his account.

In this chapter, we zoom in on the workplace at war. We shall see that the workplace was at first a space of resistance to the impeding war polarization, and it morphed into a space of division mirroring broader social changes as the war proceeded to fracture geographical, ethnic, and social ties. As workers were recruited into opposing warring factions, workplaces became spaces where those divisions were reproduced and at times amplified. Unpacking the complex dynamics of the workplace at war shows workers' responses and engagement with the war not as monolithic but rather as scattered through time and space. More than a moment of rupture, the war entailed a forceful, though temporary, shrinkage of people's geographical and social horizons. To tell the story of a former socialist corporation across transformation, it is important to excavate how it weathered its darkest period.

Talking about the War

Speaking of war in the former Yugoslavia is never an easy matter, and as a foreign researcher, I was particularly aware of that. During my first fieldwork experience in Bosnia collecting oral history interviews on antinationalism, my interlocutors had lamented their discomfort with foreigners "coming to Bosnia just to ask us about the war." Many were annoyed at people not wanting to know anything else about the country, as if nothing else had existed before or after 1992–1995. For this reason, I was careful and deliberate in not prompting questions about the war, letting people raise the topic only if they wanted to. Though I had a good command of Serbo-Croatian at this point, I was aware of my own positionality as a foreign young woman, who did not share the same social, linguistic, geographical, or cultural background as the workers I spoke with and who was lucky not to have lived through the traumatic experiences they shared. While I kept this in mind throughout the course of each interview, when the conversation reached the topic of the war, I was particularly sensitive to these differences. The traumatic experience of war was something I could empathize with but not fully comprehend as those who had lived it firsthand; I could only sense the bewildering trauma it had left behind.

For the generation of workers I spoke with, most of whom were also war veterans, the memory of the war is still fresh and carries many difficult emotions. The loss of family, friends, and coworkers made the experience unspeakable to them. The conversation literally stopped when, overwhelmed with emotion, people could (or would) no longer verbalize their trauma. Memories pertaining to the collapse of their workplaces prompted similar reactions. Work and war, place and affect remain deeply entangled in people's narratives of loss. This was such a traumatic and transformative event that it would almost always come up in a conversation even if not directly probed. It cut deep, tearing apart the narrative stability of people's lives, enclosing time within the parentheses of "before" and "after."[2] This was one of the many ruptures they indicated, as they often went back and forth between the trauma of the war and that of losing their workplaces.

The space of the workplace remained a crucial point of reference for the people I spoke with. Through their continued experience of the physical space of work, as well as the connections with their coworkers, they sought to build continuities across the rupture of the war. With the dissolution of Yugoslavia, the value system in which its citizens were socialized had crumbled. This was a moment in which the Yugoslav promise of "Brotherhood and Unity," of a federation united in ethnic and national differences, came tumbling down, together with the pledge of prosperous self-management and full employment. Each in a different way, the people I interviewed sought to piece together fragments of their lives separated by the chasm of war, by anchoring their narratives to their place of work. Since the workplace had represented the fundamental building block on which the broader social order was constructed, preserving and rebuilding it after the war carried a significant meaning for many survivors. They were faced with not only the chaos of war but the might of an international order that would completely redesign the economy and the social model of work people had come to understood as uniquely their own.

Through the narration of those who lived through such events, I wanted to understand how the war had reshaped the world of work.

The topic of ethnicity, identity, and belonging featured prominently in these sections of the interviews. People described their workplaces during and after the war as crucial sites of complex changes in interrelational dynamics; issues of inclusion and exclusion, resistance, contested return, and the microethnicization of social categories were discussed at length. At the same time, identification with ethnonational groups was not mutually exclusive with other aspects of people's identity—such as belonging to the same social class or to a veteran group. Following the constructivist approach to ethnicity that views it as contingent, constructed, and historically reproduced, I approached people's understandings of their own or others' ethnonationalist identity not as static but as fluid constructs. Ethnonational identity was just one of multiple social identities my interlocutors referred to, as they themselves were hesitant to reify ethnonational groups as internally homogeneous entities with fixed behaviors and agency.[3] Narrating the workplace at war was crucial to understanding how the internal dynamics of the workplace were transformed in the postwar, postsocialist context.

Ethnicity in the Socialist Workplace

"Nobody cared what your surname was": many of the interviews I collected started in this way. I was struck by the recurrence of this remark, uttered in this exact form across multiple interviews. Rather than lamenting indifference in the workplace, this elocution expressed a common understanding about the importance of ethnicity in the workplace. In today's Bosnia, names and surnames are often the first identifier of someone belonging to a specific ethnic category. Pointing out the indifference to such distinctions was a way for workers to indicate that the atmosphere on the shop floor was rather different from what they experience today. In their testimonies, they often express regret at seeing such divisions in the new political landscape, where ethnic categorization constitutes the foundation of social organization.

This, after all, was a generation that had grown up in state-socialist times, where the party's rhetoric of "Brotherhood and Unity" had been widespread, also within workplaces. In the words of Fedja Burić, Bosnia was a "metonymy" for socialist Yugoslavia and as such carried the badge of the socialist dream of a multiethnic federation.[4] In the demographic censuses of 1981 and 1991, Bosnia fared higher than the national average in terms of people declaring their ethnicity as "Yugoslavs."[5] As Ljubica Spaskovska has noted in her study of youth culture and politics in late-socialist Yugoslavia, young people had internalized "the basic postulates of the Yugoslav polity—its parallel ethno-territorial and its supranational character," in the form of "layered Yugoslavism," where the national identity coexisted with the Yugoslav, supranational one.[6] Although my interlocutors were of a slightly different generation, their accounts also reveal the pervasiveness of Yugoslavism as something that existed with, rather than instead of, an ethnonational sense of belonging.

Many workers I talked to depict their prewar workplaces as spaces of diffused and nondivisive ethnic demarcation. Branimir, for example, was a technician in the Energoinvest Rasklopna Oprema (RAOP) factory in Lukavica (now East Sarajevo, Republika Srpska). He recalls how he would go to play handball with other workers of Energoinvest, to train for the pan-Yugoslav games, Energofis. He put it thus:

> I did not know their surnames. I knew that one was *Haso*, for example, but I did not know or did not care that *Haso* meant *Hasan* [a typically Bosnian Muslim name]. In our factory, for example, half of the workforce was Serb; the other half was Croat and Muslim. We all worked together. I do not remember there being frictions before the war.[7]

Branimir's remark exemplifies a shared attitude among workers I spoke with: ethnicity was present in the factory, since people were aware of their colleagues being Bosnian Serbs, Croats, or Muslims, but this was not a source of friction. The performance of everyday tasks, work interactions, and collective activities such as participation in workers' councils and sports initiatives all created among workers bonds that contributed to demystify "the other" and form long-term relations.[8]

Religion, too, was a matter discussed and experienced in workers' everyday lives. Much like ethnicity, this element is also thought to pertain only marginally to the life of the workplace. Dževad recalls that, as a Muslim, he left his faith outside the workplace because, as he points out, his company allowed him to practice his religion:

> I was a practicing Muslim then, in Tito's time, and still am. And I used to go to the mosque, and nobody had issues with that. There were around 1,100 employees in my factory [Livnica Armature, Sarajevo], and some of us would go to the mosque on Friday, and so would I. So from 12 to 1 p.m., I was absent from the workplace, but we had our internal regulations, so each employee

> had six hours a month for private things, if you had to run some errands or you had to go to the doctor and so on . . . so I was a Muslim, but outside the workplace.[9]

In their descriptions of the workplace, workers often mentioned the irrelevance of religious and ethnic backgrounds, (in)directly highlighting that the code of conduct at the time was to keep such personal details discreet.

This was spelled out even more explicitly by Božidar Matić, the last director of socialist Energoinvest:

> Energoinvest was completely anational. Its principles were Yugoslav. National sentiment and religion were for the home, for the afternoon, as we said. Afternoon activities. In the company we did not feel any nationalism until 1990. When the whole society around you got entangled in nationalism, logically that penetrated companies. But look at the first three presidents of Energoinvest; they weren't Muslims. First one was Emerik Blum, a Jew; second, Braco [Dragutin] Kosovac, a Serb; third, it was me, a Croat. But we did not look at that; that just happened on the basis of professional expertise. And the less religion mingles with secular societies, the more chances these have to be a healthy society. If a society were to be a body, then nationalism would be the disease that destroys it.[10]

As it emerged throughout our interview, Matić was a staunch believer in a strong separation of politics and religion, science and belief. For him, the only way for Bosnia to become a prosperous and democratic country was to be a secular one. Quoting Karl Marx, he referred to religion as the "opium of the masses."

At times, it seemed that ethnicity and religion were deliberately omitted or glossed over in the accounts of the socialist workplace. In a group interview at Energoinvest-TDS in Sarajevo, a factory worker hinted at divisions in the workplace before the war but was quickly silenced by his colleagues, who dismissed him as being "a drunk."[11] This incident was rather indicative of the complex and layered narratives and counternarratives that existed around the delicate intersection between work and ethnicity. This generation of Bosnian workers had, in many ways, espoused the secular and supranational foundations of Yugoslavism. At the same time, this generation also remembered the repression of nationalist movements across different points throughout Yugoslavia's socialist history and may have further wanted to remark, perhaps involuntarily, on the unspeakable nature of nationalist issues within the loci of socialist consensus. At the same time, one must also dissect the dissenting voice: Why was it important for this interviewee to indicate his dissent in front of his colleagues? Did he want to debunk the myth of a multiethnic harmony in socialist Yugoslavia? Or was this perhaps his personal way of reminding his colleagues that "something must have been wrong" for Yugoslavia to disintegrate the way it did? The silence and discomfort that followed this interaction made clear to me that the conversation, for that moment, had to end there, suspended between these two interpretations of the collapse.

The desire for a different present, one devoid of the ethnonationalist rhetoric that permeates the sociopolitical order of contemporary Bosnia, brings forth the memory of a different past. Speaking of very personal recollections of this shared past and, at times, omitting those aspects that would not fit this narrative was a way for my interlocutors to vouch for and reinforce the validity of prewar ethnic harmony against accusations of romanticizing the past.[12] In our interviews, only a few workers openly spoke about tensions in the workplace, usually in connection with the period right before the war. Munevera was a technician employed in Energoinvest's central branch in Sarajevo. She recalls:

> Right before the war, we saw that things started to be divided, that groups started to separate . . . I want to say, the orthodox. For example, there was a woman, a colleague of mine, I found her nice, and I made an effort so that she could get a job with us . . . she had two kids, so I thought, "Come on, let's help her out." Afterward, we were in the same hierarchical position, except I had been there for longer. One day she asked me quite abruptly, "Come on, do some photocopies." To me? I left it there, but that is how that group started to separate. A kind of impatience appeared, and we could feel that atmosphere . . . I do not want to speak in national terms, but . . . for example, my boss, who was a Muslim, was supposed to go on a business trip, but our new director, a Serb, sent his own cousin instead![13]

Besides this remark, Munevera, just like most of my other interviewees, stressed many times that she did not want to discuss workplace relations strictly in ethnic terms. The issue of preexisting ethnic frictions in the workplace was often downplayed as insignificant to the socialist workplace and limited to a few instances that became warning signs of a looming war. This generation of workers, after all, was socialized within the Yugoslavist value system—one where the party's ideological control was also expressed through discourses of interethnic solidarity among workers as a pillar of the new socialist society. The party's capillary presence (and membership) within enterprises consolidated a particular code of conduct whereby ethnicity had to be left outside the factory door. Bringing up workplace grievances was also a way for people like Munevera to partly demystify a vision of the socialist workplace as devoid of frictions. In our conversations, people often grappled with this ambivalence: making sense of the war meant coming to terms with early signs of ethnic frictions, even in the workplace. On the other hand, reinforcing the memory of interethnic solidarity is a way of critically distancing oneself from the pervasive ethno-nationalist discourse and fragmented social order of contemporary Bosnia, as well as a strategy to preserve the legacy of socialism and propose a counternarrative to its mainstream dismissal.[14]

This is not to say that workers are suppressing ethnic identity or that they are remembering their past "wrong." Rather, they are trying to make sense of the contradictions of a system that promoted supranational values but disintegrated across ethnonational ones. Indeed, when encouraged to speak about it, some prefer to recollect the interethnic harmony of the workplace, while others pause over uncomfortable signs that foretold the war. These differences reveal diverging attitudes toward ethnicity: as something that must be actively critiqued and removed from workplaces or something to be reckoned with to move forward. Deliberately downplaying the memories of prewar ethnic frictions was also a strategy for my interlocutors to position themselves within the new postsocialist context, as agents critical of a system that made them feel excluded or marginalized but within which they must operate. As Ognjen Kojanić argues, narratives of the past that may be tinged with nostalgia allow subjects to position themselves within the new postsocialist, neoliberal context and are, at times, techniques of the self to reshape their subjectivities within a profoundly transformed context.[15] With these remarks, my interlocutors showed that they preferred a system and structure that considered ethnicity secondary; even if they had been witnesses to, or agents of, ethnic friction in the prewar past, what mattered now was to indicate their distance from such attitudes by sharing a counternarrative of the past. One thing became apparent from this exchange: memories forge the past; they do not only reflect it.

These comments also showed the boundaries of my own position and chosen methods, and indeed highlighted, in a few moments, the interpretive challenges that inevitably arise when dealing with live testimonies. As the anthropologist Andrew Gilbert suggests, interviews are events of "self-making" that are "inter-subjective," whereby people reflect on their past in a certain way to actively shape the way interlocutors see them.[16] People may have wanted to present themselves under a particular light because of the way they saw me—a younger "Westerner"—in front of whom, perhaps, it was important to present prewar Bosnia as a country of multiethnic harmony; my "Westerness" may have also inspired a need to discuss how the omnipresence of nationalist discourses had been reinforced by the institutionalization of nationalism that came with the Dayton Peace Agreement, which ended the war in 1995. Analyzing interviews collected a generation after the war, at a time when antinationalist discourses had picked up pace, requires sensitivity to the interpretive challenges posed by these dynamics.

The Looming Threat of Nationalism

In an official, state-led Yugoslav-wide survey carried out at the beginning of 1990, Bosnian respondents described their Yugoslav identity as connected with loyalty to supranationalism. Most respondents characterized workplace relations between members of different national groups as being congenial.[17] In urban settings across Bosnia—where most of the industrial production took place—workers were the demographic group most likely to declare themselves as Yugoslavs in the national census; they did so almost three times more than other Bosnian citizens.[18] This kind of supranational identification was seen as particularly relevant, and indeed mobilized, as the political discourse in Yugoslavia assumed increasingly more nationalist tones. In company journals, workers' voices—possibly carefully selected—were published to demonstrate that the feeling of pan-Yugoslavism was an organic force that emanated from the workplace, an affective space where not only were livelihoods earned but differences diluted and communities forged. The workplace was where Yugoslavia could be constructed, where it could become a reality and prove its potential as a space simultaneously bound up in Cold War politics and offering an alternative to its status quo of bipolarity.[19] It was important for workers, and for the company, to discuss their distance from a radicalized discourse that many saw as dangerous. As a factory worker in the northeastern town of Gradačac wrote in 1990, "In our factory . . . there's a multinational composition of citizens. And because of this, in this environment, we never had national frictions. . . . It hurts my soul when I read that Tito and the League of Communists are blamed for this situation because it is not true."[20] This comment was made in direct opposition to the rhetoric of the new nationalist forces that fired up the political campaigns before the first multiparty elections of 1990—with a strong and open criticism of the shortcomings of the Yugoslav federation and the one-party system.

Similar criticisms of growing radicalization emerged in other companies at the time. Workers in Croatia and Serbia were adamant about vocalizing their strong antinationalist stance, as they perceived nationalism to be a problematic tool of distraction from what were essentially labor-related issues.[21] As Goran Musić and Jake Lowinger have shown, nationalist propaganda used workers' mobilization as a sign of ethnonationalist friction within a workplace; the apparent "ethnic radicalization" of workers was the result of management and political leadership co-opting workers' (class-based) demands into an ethnonationalist framework. There is evidence that workers of large conglomerates across Yugoslavia were also strongly against the mounting nationalist rhetoric that characterized Serbian politics in the early 1990s.[22] In his study of the Polish trade union Solidarnošć, David Ost also noted how the union organized labor anger "away from class cleavages and toward identity cleavages instead"—with problematic consequences for both the new democracy and the union itself.[23]

The antinationalist sentiment among industrial workers in Bosnia was similarly conveyed, and it remained strong even as the socialist federation was collapsing. A group of factory workers of Livnica Armature, an Energoinvest foundry in Sarajevo, expressed their strong rejection of the nationalist rhetoric that was becoming dominant. They wrote in their factory journal in 1990:

> We are against those who look for nationalism instead of class and people and in that way manipulate workers and their interests by sparking nationalist feelings. . . . We are promised national identity with which to express hatred against others, and [by doing so] we will split the country we built together. . . . We do not want to be put one against each other; we are workers facing the same problems.[24]

Workers responded with growing uneasiness to the nationalist rhetoric by now pervasive in the Yugoslav political environment. These comments were made as the country was bracing for the first multiparty elections, which featured political campaigns characterized by increasingly incendiary tones. Through speeches and demonstrations, workers of Energoinvest tried to maintain a supranational, interethnic solidarity, derived from what they had collectively understood as the spirit of Energoinvest and Yugoslav socialist self-management. This was not the only case of workers' antinationalism, as similar responses to growing radicalization emerged within other companies in the former Yugoslavia.[25]

After the elections and the clear victory of nationalist parties, national media started reporting ethnic-related incidents, with episodes of vandalism, such as the covering of monuments with ethnonationalist slogans. Similarly, news circulated about workers going on strike to protest ethnic-based nepotism, as was the case for the workers of Fočatrans, in the southeastern town of Foča (now Republika Srpska). According to the press at the time, Muslim employees abandoned the strike after rumors that their (Serb) colleagues were targeting the director because of his Muslim origin.[26]

In this context, some worrying signals emerged in Energoinvest factories too, particularly in ethnically mixed communities such as Mostar (35% Bosnian Muslim and 34% Bosnian Croat) or Zvornik (59% Bosnian Muslim and 38% Bosnian Serbs).[27] For example, in Zvornik, a city at the border with Serbia, Energoinvest had a range of extraction mines and factories. Here, the nationalist and military escalation of 1992 had created tension and fear among the population, and it had negative consequences for imports and exports between Bosnia and neighboring Serbia.[28] On the pages of the company's journal, employees often wrote about the difficulties they were experiencing in an increasingly fractured community. These letters and articles mostly appealed to their fellow workers and citizens to maintain the spirit of brotherly togetherness that had characterized their city.[29] In a climate of increased hostility and fear of an imminent attack, the company even organized an evening with music, food, and celebration, called *Hajde da se družimo* (Let's hang out), bringing together three hundred workers from all the factories of Zvornik and Mali Zvornik (on the other side of the river Drina, in Serb territory) to show that "the Drina does not divide people."[30] This initiative defied the increasingly toxic nationalist rhetoric that was affecting communities across Bosnia, and it provides evidence that the workplace was indeed a space where national tendencies and supranational identities were produced and contested.

The Descent into War

The political crisis that swept the country and plunged it into the spiral of war saw the preponderance of identity politics mobilized by rising ethnonationalist forces. At the same time, different sets of explanations have illustrated how ethnic and national identities came to be preponderant in the early 1990s—for example, a crisis of legitimacy of the socialist state in providing equality and recognition to its citizens; an economic crisis that lacerated the country's tenuous economic federation and further accentuated the divide between richer and poorer republics; the rural-urban divide that characterized Yugoslav society; civil society demobilization; or dilemmas over security.[31] Political and structural flaws also contributed to the fragmentation of the Yugoslav federation, as much as did identity politics in the hands of new nationalist elites.

Despite the promising initial results and the rather widespread support that the economic reforms enjoyed, the presidency of Ante Marković was short-lived. The severity of the economic crisis dovetailed with the mounting political frictions that emerged between nationalist movements and within the Yugoslav League of Communists. Single republics developed different visions of political and economic control and self-determination. Within Slovenia, the richest and most developed country of the federation, aspirations for more economic and political autonomy had grown stronger throughout the 1980s. Serbia strongly opposed this line: its leadership saw the loss of federal unity as a threat to the political and economic stability of the remaining countries. Under Slobodan Milošević, the Serbian Communist Party had taken an eminently nationalist stance, arguing for stronger powers for Serbia over the autonomous provinces of Kosovo and Vojvodina; in Kosovo, protests of the ethnic Albanian population had vocalized disagreement with the Serbian government's treatment of minorities and were met with radicalized nationalist responses from Belgrade.

Numerous sociopolitical movements had emerged, pushing for democratization, pluralism, and the enhancement of civil liberties throughout the Yugoslav federation, as well as much stronger autonomy for republics. The last Yugoslav government opted to accommodate some of these demands for political pluralization, with the hope of curbing the rise of nationalist politics.[32] Marković introduced the first multiparty elections in Yugoslavia in November 1990, hoping to deliver on the requests for pluralization and democratization that came from within the League of Communists, as well as from new political forces and civil society alike. Galvanized by the support he enjoyed in Bosnia, Ante Marković formed his own party, the multiethnic, antinationalist Union of Reform Forces of Yugoslavia (Savez reformskih snaga Jugoslavije, or SRSJ), in a bid to challenge the undercurrents of nationalist rhetoric that were getting louder day by day. In a multiethnic society like Bosnia, this appeared to be a sound political alternative to the loosening grip of traditional communist blocks, and indeed Marković enjoyed great popularity in the country. Yet, as Alfredo Sasso has noted, the SRSJ was "a government party in the opposition": the first multiparty Yugoslav elections had led Serbian and Slovenian leaderships to view the elections as a source of legitimacy for their own (opposing) views of the future of Yugoslavia and its republics; nationalist leaders had "identified in Marković an ideological rival and a credible threat for consensus."[33] Subjected to criticism from both the nationalist forces and the more orthodox and conservative wings of the Yugoslav League of Communists, Marković's SRSJ was not able to attract a significant number of votes across Yugoslavia—despite its leader's popularity.

The popular support in favor of reformist ideas led the conservative forces within state apparatuses to engage with nationalist rhetoric, in order to mobilize the population along ethnic lines and thus shift the focus of political discourse "away from issues of reform toward the threat of nationalism."[34] Threatened by opposition movements, the ruling Serbian Communist elite—led by Slobodan Milošević—found in an ethnonationalist framework of popular mobilization a way to secure its status, privileges, and legitimacy. At the same time, in neighboring Croatia new nationalist forces led by Franjo Tudjman fueled public fears of Serbia's expansionism and further exacerbated anti-Serb rhetoric. Tudjman and Milošević set in motion a propaganda machine that seemed to appeal to the economic grievances of many citizens: falling economic standards and political instability in each of the republics were the result of exploitation and political subordination by the hands of other republics. Croatian and Serbian leaderships shared the interest in polarizing ethnic oppositions to preserve power structures and conceal the elites' appropriation of formerly socially owned economic resources.[35] A reinterpretation of World War II history in terms of national victimization gained importance as a means through which nationalist elites legitimized ethnic diversity and subsequently argued for the impossibility of a peaceful and multiethnic coexistence, in a "clear case of manipulation of fears in the service of politics."[36] Appeals to ethnic victimization were engaged to spread a sense of historical injustice, construct a sense of national and ethnic solidarity, and supersede other aspects of social stratification.

In this climate, the first multiparty elections in 1990 signaled the victory of nationalist parties across the Yugoslav federation, which began to crumble under growing secessionist pressures from political elites in the different republics.[37] Croatia saw the victory of the Croatian Nationalist Party (HDZ). The Serbian Radical Party (SRS) won 13.5 percent of the Serb vote, gaining electoral mandates only in the region of Knin, where the Serbian minority (if compared to the whole Croatia, where the Serbs constituted the 12.2% of the total population) outnumbered the ethnic Croats. Croatian Serbs, in fact, still preferred the reformed Communist Party (SKH-SDP). During the summer of 1990, the Serb Democratic Party (SDS), guided by Milan Babić—the mayor of Knin—requested first cultural and then also territorial autonomy from Croatia; the so-called log revolution, where Serbs denied Croatian forces the access to the Knin area, saw for the first time the intervention of the Yugoslav National Army (JNA) alongside the Serbian rebels. The creation of a Serbian Autonomous Region in Krajina (December 21, 1990) was followed by the declaration of independence of the Republic of Serbian Krajina (RSK) in December 1991.[38] Violence broke out between Croat and Serb forces, who occupied almost one-third of the Croatian territory. This led to a major flight of more than thirty-three thousand Croats from Serb-occupied territories, mainly Krajina and eastern Slavonia.

Nationalist pressures did not leave Bosnia immune: in a country with a variegated and complex ethnonational composition (44% Bosnian Muslims, 31% Bosnian Serbs, 17% Bosnian Croats), political divisions mirrored the fracturing that had been occurring at the federal level. Newly formed nationalist parties stoked tensions between the three constituent nations. The SDS used the threat of Islamic fundamentalism to mobilize Bosnian Serbs into asking for further autonomy. One must then consider the particular insubstantiality of the fundamentalist threat in Bosnia, where the Muslim population was particularly secularized and at times characterized by widespread atheism; the population of practitioners calculated in 1985 was 17 percent.[39] On the other hand, the strong rhetoric of Croatian autonomy, combined with the perceived threat of Serbian expansionism and a Muslim majority, led Bosnian Croats to organize themselves into a separate party (HDZ). Muslim nationalism, though marginal in socialist Yugoslavia, gained momentum in Bosnia as the population became squeezed between Croat and Serb nationalisms. The elections in Bosnia-Herzegovina held in December 1990 recorded, in the percentages of support for the three main parties (the Bosnian Muslim nationalist Party of Democratic Action, or SDA, led by Alija Izetbegović; Radovan Karadžić's SDS; and HDZ, headed by Mate Boban), a substantial correspondence with the internal divisions, respectively between Bosnian Muslims, Bosnian Serbs, and Bosnian Croats.

"Workers Yes, Warriors No": Militarization and War Resistance

Despite being a comparatively small power in the global Cold War, Yugoslavia was a heavily militarized country, with one of the largest armies in the world. Its military industry was a significant part of its economy, and the country relied on its military exports for both economic and geopolitical reasons. Military service in the JNA was compulsory for at least twelve months for each adult male citizen aged eighteen to twenty-seven. The shared experience of compulsory military service, while heavily routinized and ritualized, created a space for affect, friendship, and a sense of supranational unity in difference. As Tanja Petrović has argued, the JNA's universal conscription also functioned as a vehicle for establishing and consolidating the Yugoslav multiethnic citizenship project.[40] In addition to serving in the military, workers in Yugoslav workplaces and factories were routinely trained as reserve forces in the Territorial Defense, the republican arm of the JNA. The Territorial Defense consisted of lightly armed local defense groups tasked with supporting army military operations in case of a foreign invasion of the Yugoslav federation.[41] Thus, while workplaces were sites of the socialization and strengthening of interethnic bonds through everyday interactions, they were also spaces of everyday militarization.

Companies like Energoinvest had their own sections of the Territorial Defense, which engaged workers in yearly training and celebrated commemorations of the partisan uprising and liberation of the country. On these occasions, the company journal would often sing the praises of the Territorial Defense as a defender of the homeland and the workplaces. For example, in 1988 the journal described the yearly celebration of the Yugoslav partisan uprising of 1941 (Dan Borca, or Day of the Fighters) as follows: "This is the day of the Yugoslav worker and warrior—everyone is a worker-warrior [*radnik-ratnik*]. . . . The army of workers in all republics and autonomous regions is an army of fighters for self-management, for higher productivity, but also to defend their country from potential enemies. This is a day where we must say that Yugoslavia is one and united!"[42] This excerpt highlights two important aspects of military discourse within workplaces: First, it refers to the hyphenated formulation of *worker-warrior*. This was commonplace terminology in Yugoslavia and other socialist countries. Following the Marxist-Leninist doctrine, countries such as the USSR and China had already constituted "Workers' and Peasants' Armies." During the later stages of the Cultural Revolution, hyphenations such as that of the *worker-peasant-soldier-student* were introduced by the Chinese Communist Party. While, since the nineteenth century, European states and the US had established military conscription through the citizen-soldier paradigm, in the socialist world this was conjugated in class and *worker-ist* terms.[43] With roots in the antifascist and partisan narrative, this rhetoric was also part of the wider socialist and non-aligned ideology that had guided Yugoslavia in its military support of liberation struggles around the world. Indeed, the Yugoslav global promise had also been one of solidarity with (workers') movements for liberation across the globe, fighting for economic as well as political independence.

Linked to the hyphenated *worker-warrior*, another important aspect that emerges from this quote is the overlap of workplace and homeland. In fact, workers who undertook compulsory military service or participated in the routine military exercises within workplaces were exposed to a rhetoric of patriotism that entangled the homeland with the workplace. Defending the integrity of the workplace by ensuring its prosperity was subsumed into the broader narration of the worker-soldier defending the homeland. This compression of space between the local workplace, the national homeland, and the international sphere would become a crucial aspect of the life of workers during the Bosnian War.

The pervasive militarization of Yugoslav society was not left unchallenged, particularly as new movements for democratization and demilitarization emerged parallel to the workers' mobilization. Demilitarization, pacifist, and antiwar movements in Yugoslavia developed in the 1980s as part of a much wider wave of pacifist activism than spanned across the Iron Curtain. In fact, since the Vietnam War, the Soviet invasion of Afghanistan, and the acceleration of the nuclear arms race that characterized the early 1980s, demilitarization, antiwar, and pacifist movements had emerged and gained momentum across Europe and beyond. Though locally embedded, these had a strong transnational and even global character and united youth activists, social movements, labor unions, and a broad band of progressive forces.[44] In several countries of socialist Eastern Europe, antiwar movements were characterized by complex articulations of top-down, state-sponsored movements as well as bottom-up movements that characterized a form of "détente from below" through several transnational formal and informal networks.[45] In countries like the German Democratic Republic, Poland, and Czechoslovakia, moreover, peace movements were also strongly connected to human rights movements and prodemocracy, antiestablishment activism; transnational solidarities with Western European activists gave further momentum to these mobilizations.[46] In Yugoslavia, too, the 1980s had been characterized by a surge in bottom-up mobilization, including students' protests against compulsory military service.[47] Here, several activist groups and social movements—from antimilitarist and green movements to feminist and democratization activists—merged within broader antiwar coalitions, which, even more than in the rest of socialist Eastern Europe, acquired significance and urgency given the immediacy of a potential conflict.[48] In this first period, activists in different countries managed to maintain contacts with movements in the other republics, which enabled them to coordinate protest activities and thus lessened the sense of isolation that would follow in the proceeding years.[49] Taking their protests to the streets, groups of citizens and activists across Yugoslavia were registering their vexation with the country's rapid descent into nationalist chaos.

As threats of military escalation intensified in 1991, so did antiwar and antinationalist mobilizations across the country: antiwar movements across Yugoslavia organized mass protests, street demonstrations, and other pacifist initiatives to stop the escalation to war—from petitions to antiwar campaigns and cultural initiatives. This kind of mobilization overlapped and merged with that of workers, who had been demanding better standards of living, higher wages, and more democratic relations within the workplace.

Alarmed by the looming escalation of the conflict and by the news that was coming in from Slovenia first and Croatia afterward, in 1991 and 1992 workers joined antinationalist protests across Bosnia in great numbers. Under the slogans "We will not let you divide us" and "Against the war, for peace, work, and bread," thousands of workers marched in Sarajevo between the end of 1991 and the spring of 1992.[50]

A banner (see fig. 4.1) that workers carried during a peace march in the spring of 1992 was particularly significant: it read "Workers Yes, Warriors No" (*Radnici da, Ratnici ne!*).[51] This banner held a significant political message: workers publicly and deliberately subverted the militaristic socialist jargon of *worker-warrior* with an antiwar framing. Through this banner, workers were strongly rejecting what they anticipated would become their

Figure 4.1. Workers marching to the parliament of Bosnia and Herzegovina, holding a banner that reads "Workers Yes, Warriors No!" on March 3, 1991. Credit: Milomir Kovačević

fate, the imposition of a role they refused to embody—that of fighters in a civil war. Here, workers invested their role as defenders of the workplace and homeland with a new political meaning: no longer a rhetorical term relegated to partisan commemorations but an appropriate political self-positioning toward the coming war. Particularly in urban spaces, the "socialist" legacy of pride in the workplace and the need to defend it as one's homeland remained strong.[52]

Workplaces were key sites of mobilization, antinationalist dissent, and popular demands for social and economic rights. In response, nationalist parties resorted to intensifying the radicalization of ethnopolitical discourses, ultimately leading to violence. Arben, a worker from a factory in Tuzla, recalls how he joined the protests of 1992: "It was roughly two hundred of us, we went to Sarajevo to protest against the war . . . we organized it with the union . . . we were beaten up by the police, pretty bad."[53] For the workers I spoke with, recollecting their opposition to the war brought up very strong emotions. In what were usually two-to-three-hour interviews, this was the moment where testimonies became the most fragmented, punctuated by long pauses. These events were very painful to recall and perhaps hard to comprehend since such events and their memory required the speakers to confront a trauma. The tone of voice and body language often changed as they reconnected to those memories. I was extremely careful not to overstep any boundaries and to let people tap into these experiences only insofar as they felt at ease. Not everyone was ready and willing to display fragility or comfortable with doing so, and thus I left the questions about the war as open as possible. Nevertheless, I was grateful when interviewees shared their memories, at a great sentimental cost to themselves. This part of the interview, I often felt, was a bonding moment. Some told me it was the first time they had spoken about some of these events and their feelings about them. Asim, a former blue-collar worker in an Energoinvest factory in Sarajevo, recalls with great sorrow:

> The majority of my colleagues, 90 percent of workers were soldiers [*borci*], warriors [*ratnici*], they did not have another choice; even in places where people did not want to fight, they had to. I know, when the first grenade fell, I did not want to . . . three nights, three nights I was in prison. In the beginning, I did not want to go, but it was not possible . . . you must. [*Long pause.*] I feel terrible when I think about that.[54]

Asim lamented that he had no choice but to participate in a war he did not support. It was important for him to remark that most soldiers were also workers and that recruitment had been imposed on them. For Asim, this went against what he treasured the most: the feeling of solidarity among workers within his factory.

The opposition to the war also meant that many workers tried to leave Bosnia as soon as they could. Many explained that they felt the pressure to "become Bosnians, Serbs, or Croats" and fight for the homeland, as part of different ethnic-based armies. Their view is perhaps best exemplified in the words of Mladen, an engineer from Energoinvest's information technology company IRIS, who fled Sarajevo at the end of 1992:

> If I stayed for one more day, I would probably . . . I would have been forced to join their forces [the Serb paramilitary] and to shoot at Sarajevo or to . . . I would have probably killed myself rather than join their forces and plans.[55]

Mladen chose to leave his factory, his home, and his family behind so he would not be conscripted within nationalist paramilitary groups or forced into war. He viewed the ethnonationalist division of the country as an imposition against which he would have resorted to a last act of self-destruction rather than accepting it. Similarly, the technician Branimir bitterly reflected that his own ethnic compatriots (Serbs) considered him a "deserter" after he managed to flee from Sarajevo thanks to the help of one of his Muslim colleagues at his factory in East Sarajevo.[56] Asim's, Mladen's, and Branimir's testimonies indicate that the rise of ethnonationalist politics was not met without unease, grief, and trepidation in the workplace. The interviewees want to remember workplace solidarity as untainted by ethnic divisions, and they want to affirm strongly their own personal views on the matter. The political background against which these interviews took place may have also colored these responses. This was immediately after the Bosnian antiprivatization protests of 2014–2015, where workers— many of whom were now unemployed—reasserted solidarity against the crony ethnonationalist parties deemed responsible for the corruption and bankruptcy of many companies. As a result, these interviews were another avenue for people to voice their dissent and distance themselves from divisive politics both now and in memory.

In Defense of Work: Workers as Soldiers after Bosnian Independence

When the JNA sided with Serbia and responded to Croatia's independence with an armed conflict, it was clear that the conflict would extend to multiethnic Bosnia, especially after the country held its independence referendum in March 1992.[57]

The recognition of Croatian independence had important repercussions on the political situation in Bosnia and Herzegovina. It was now clear that Bosnia too would have to follow Zagreb's example; otherwise, it would have remained in a Yugoslav federation de facto under Serb control. Bosnian Croats and Bosnian Serbs were increasingly vocal about independence. The European Economic Community (EEC), for its part, pressed for an internal referendum within the country as the only condition for the eventual recognition of independence.[58] Only 63.4 percent of those eligible to vote took part in the March 1, 1992, independence referendum; in fact, Karadžić's SDS prohibited Serbs from participating in the poll. Although more than 99 percent of those who voted were in favor of independence, their numbers were too small for a solid state entity to be founded.[59]

Soon after the referendum, the Bosnian Serb leadership declared the establishment of a Serb Republic of Bosnia and Herzegovina (the Republika Srpska), with its capital in Pale, a separatist Croatian community of

Herceg-Bosna, led by Mate Boban. On April 6, 1992, Bosnia was recognized as an independent state first by the EEC, then by Russia and the United States. However, Bosnia's path to independence was used by Milošević and Karadžić as a pretext to begin the military phase of its partition. As federal army columns began to withdraw from Croatia into Bosnia, heavy artillery positions were built around major Bosnian cities, including Sarajevo.[60]

Between April 5 and 6, 1992, Karadžić launched an offensive against Sarajevo, with the justification that it was necessary to defend the local Serbs, who, according to the Belgrade newspapers, were in danger of expulsion. Sarajevo was soon divided between the Bosnian forces, which were stationed mainly in the Muslim-majority suburbs and on the southwestern hills, and the Serbian forces, which controlled the suburbs that housed the supply of gas, water, and electricity to the entire urban area. The Bosnian Serb Army (BSA) was then positioned on most of the heights surrounding the city. A pattern of military aggression by the JNA and the newly formed paramilitary forces had emerged since the beginning of the conflict in Croatia: the JNA forces became implicated in numerous episodes of ethnic cleansing and mass murder. In Bosnia, the army had already started to arm Bosnian Serb paramilitary formations and had distributed an estimate of 51,900 firearms to them.[61] Sarajevo was, of course, not the only city to be under attack since the early days of the war. The JNA and Bosnian Serb paramilitary forces swiftly moved from the North and East of the country, attacking and occupying several municipalities and violently expelling non-Serb civilians. In Zvornik, the bottom-up civic initiatives organized within workplaces could unfortunately do very little against the sheer force of the JNA and Serb paramilitary forces' attack on the city, which started just a few days after Bosnia declared its independence. Zvornik's position on the Drina River, with a road bridge that crossed the border between Serbia and Bosnia, was of strategic military importance. A swift attack on the city caused it to fall under Serbian control. What ensued were war crimes, mass murder, and the violent expulsion of non-Serb civilians at the hands of Bosnian Serb paramilitary forces.

Unable to rely on an official army, parts of the official Bosnian government that did not side with the BSA or the Croatian Defense Council (HVO) struggled to mobilize forces into the Army of Bosnia-Herzegovina (ARBiH) and at first relied on the Territorial Defense (a remnant of the socialist military organization). The forces defending Sarajevo counted almost thirty-five thousand soldiers in 1995, around 80 percent of whom were working-class citizens of Sarajevo. This social stratification was similar for the over eighty thousand soldiers engaged in the ARBiH, where most conscripts were workers from the city and its surroundings. While the majority were ethnic Bosnjaks, there were also ethnic Croats and Serbs, though in smaller percentages.[62] Ismet recalls how the veterans of the Second World War and partisan struggle participated in the improvised defense forces at the beginning of the war in Sarajevo:

> They were in my section, from the antifascist council [former SUBNOR]. We did not know what grenades were, you know? They weren't mobilized, but they helped us and advised us, they were very useful. What would we know, what are grenades, what is shrapnel? I was hit by shrapnel, near the spine . . . it's a struggle . . . when they see a red star, five-pointed star, they tremble, they're incorrigible . . . they were really good people. But unfortunately, they gave up. They don't like it when I tell them, "This is your mistake, not ours." They haven't built it well. How could I be wrong, how could it be my fault? No, the system was made before. And they really don't like it when I tell them, "What did you do for 50 years, created a system and did not make it how it is supposed to be [*kako treba*]." They made the travesty of a system that turned against its people. The Yugoslav National Army was the fourth strongest in Europe, and turned against Slovenians, Croats, Bosnians.[63]

Ismet's reflection speaks to a cognitive dissonance—a way of reckoning with the collapse of Yugoslavia and his new role as a soldier. For him, the war demanded an explanation that he did not have because he did not belong to the generation that designed the Yugoslav project. While grateful for the contribution of Yugoslav partisans against fascists and Nazis, he believed the older generations had to be held responsible for creating a weak political order, the implosion of which he was enduring at the potential cost of his own life. Ismet's remark about the JNA turning against its own people—a frequent one among my interlocutors—reveals another important dissonance in the Yugoslav promise. The promise of military power and prowess, of relevance at home and abroad by virtue of its army and its military exports, clashed with the country's posturing as a leading example of peaceful coexistence among peoples and nations. When the war reached home and the army's claim to ethnonational neutrality disintegrated, people watched in horror at their own army's show of strength.

The rapid escalation of the conflict and workers' recruitment into opposing armies made it particularly difficult for them to maintain their antiwar resistance: workplaces became simultaneously spaces of resistance and places of division. Drawing from different experiences in the army or defense forces from the socialist times, workers self-organized into local military units. A group of Energoinvest workers, for example, coordinated actions in the Sarajevo borough of Dobrinja. This neighborhood was developed as a working-class residential area in the early 1980s in preparation for the Winter Olympic Games of 1984. Energoinvest owned many apartments in this area, and it was estimated that over two thousand employees were residing here.[64] A strategic post for both the Serbian and Bosnian forces—being close to the airport and giving access to a part of the Serb-controlled territories—this district saw violent clashes between the two factions and was partly regained by the ARBiH in late 1992.[65] Here, self-organized workers' defense was vital in the first months of the conflict.[66] As an example, an article titled "Today Warriors, Tomorrow Workers"—again using the trope *ratnici-radnici*—reported a phone conversation with workers isolated in Dobrinja, praising them for their courage in defending, primarily, their workplace: "You have proved yourselves in the fight today as you have yesterday in the workplace."[67] Once again, the synonymous use of *work* and *fight*—of defending the homeland and the workplace—demonstrates the mobilizing power of these two concepts and the ways in which workers were summoned to the battlefields. Hence, in the first months of the war, the workplace was a space of mobilization in which "old" ideas of socialist "workerism" and solidarity coexisted with new pressures for determining ethnic alliances.

Amid this tension and dissonance, workers interpreted their role as worker-warriors in different ways. For Dževad, a worker in the Armature factory in Sarajevo and a veteran, the socialist era still shaped the way he and his colleagues understood their role as worker-warriors:

> Each factory had its own keepers, firefighters, and those were people who had weapons. . . . So when the war started there were people in the workplace, and they protected the factory. Every year in Yugoslavia we used to go for two weeks for military exercises. We kept those weapons in the factory, in a warehouse. And in a moment during the war, we were in a tough situation, and we used those weapons. . . . So, people had that feeling for keeping the property, to fight for it.[68]

Fighting to keep the materiality of the workplace intact, to preserve what workers considered their property, reflected workers' long-term attachment to their factories. For Dževad, reflecting on the socialist roots of this impromptu defense was another way to signpost his distance from nationalist tropes. For him, it was important to remember the workplace as a site of

Figure 4.2. "We Don't Give Up!" is the title of *Energoinvest List*'s "war edition," November 1992–March 1993. Credit: Energoinvest, author

workerist solidarity, rather than remarking against whom those weapons were used. A workplace and its workers, rather than a nation and its (ethnic) citizens, were under attack.

As a company registered in the Bosnian territory, Energoinvest had initially provided logistical support (equipment and personnel) for the local Territorial Defense. In 1993, as the siege of Sarajevo reached its first year and a ceasefire did not seem to be in sight, the company's management abandoned its position of neutrality and notified its support for the ARBiH. Of the roughly 14,500 workers that Energoinvest employed in Sarajevo, more than 3,000 were deployed in the ARBiH.[69] While the war carried on, the Bosnian defense forces, and particularly those engaged in Sarajevo, became increasingly ethnically homogenized. This was the consequence of a political design implemented by the SDA, which had gained increasing influence after the beginning of the war and started "saying that the Bosniaks were the central nation in Bosnia," thus relegating local Serbs and Croats to their "reserve homelands."[70] This homogenization affected the way the company sought to position and represent itself. The same employees who only a few months earlier had organized a workers' defense of the Dobrinja borough were now conscripted in the army, where a more ethno-patriotic rhetoric prevailed.

Izmet Hadžić, a former engineer at Energoinvest and commander of the workers' defense unit, commended the role of worker-fighters in defending their workplace—which he defined with ethnonational tropes: "Energoinvest is worth fighting for; its workers want to return to their factories, they want their machines. This will be achieved with weapons, but it is certain that the Bosnian-Herzegovinian Energoinvest has an army of fighters."[71] This view is emblematic of the coexistence of *workerist* rhetoric (talking about factories, the unity of workers) and patriotic tropes (fighting for the freedom of factories and homelands); the socialist hierarchy of class over nation was being challenged, as national divisions superseded anything else. It also reveals a shift toward a nationalized view of the factory—a Bosnian, rather than Yugoslav, Energoinvest. With Yugoslavia breaking apart, the very notion of the "homeland" had changed: warring factions fought over borders, streets, and houses. The experience of Energoinvest suggests that the workplace too was a space of contention, where new ethnonationalist discourses challenged preexisting notions of internationalism and Yugoslavism. Fractured along new borders that shattered the socialist internationalist dream, Yugoslavia was not the homeland anymore.

However, visions of class solidarity as a counterargument to ethnonational divisions did not disappear from workplaces, even during the conflict. When the news first reported the looting of company material at the hand of Serb paramilitary forces, the management and unions tried to appeal to workers beyond the border. The president of the general union (Savez Sindikata), Sulejman Hrle, called for the mobilization of workers in the "aggressor states" (Serbia and Montenegro) to raise their voices against the looting of machinery, knowledge, and even trademarks that was allegedly carried out by their military forces.[72] The issue of materials and equipment being stolen from factories was particularly common and pressing throughout the conflict. Soldiers and groups from both sides would use stolen equipment, materials, and machinery for various purposes—mostly to fashion new military equipment.[73] Many directors lamented the lack of material and resources due to theft.[74] The company journal started to portray these events as the consequence of aggressive Serbian expansionism, which "Yugoslav" workers were encouraged to resist. The reasoning went that Bosnia was attacked by another state, but this was primarily a design of the nationalist elite that must be resisted in the spirit of workers' solidarity. As the war was increasingly discussed as an aggression toward the Bosnian territory by expansionist Serb forces, a supraethnic workers' identity was juxtaposed with these nationalistic tones.[75]

This view is perhaps most evident in an open letter addressed to Serbian and Montenegrin workers, calling for solidarity across borders. The journal editor wrote, "What the Četniks are providing you has been stolen from Bosnian factories, mines, institutes and laboratories. . . . Brothers in the collectives! We have fought for the same things, for an apartment, a salary, a pension. And today is the same; you do not have regular salaries, thousands of you are waiting for a job . . . or maybe the front? . . . And in the end, if your Četniks cannot be considered people, you, workers, remain people."[76] The use of the term Četniks (the ultranationalist and Nazi-collaborationist Serb formations during World War II) can be interpreted in two ways: first, to legitimize the Bosnian forces of defense against the Serbian aggressor; and second, to tap into the Yugoslav values of the partisan liberation struggle and mobilize workers around a common (socialist) set of values: class solidarity against nationalist divisions. Here, physical equipment transcended its material attributes, becoming a signifier for the fracturing of workers' unity across borders.

New Borders, No Bridges: Dividing the Workplace across the Front Line

Until almost one year into the war, the workplace newspaper kept mentioning Energoinvest's global and (pan-)Yugoslav connections as something that defined the company's ethos, which would guarantee its survival even after the conflict. For example, as the chief editor remarked in the second "war issue" (*ratno izdanje*): "The subsidiary firms of Energoinvest outside Bosnia are successfully working in Ljubljana, Maribor, Skopje, and Zagreb and have kept connections with our partners in the world. Energoinvest has to create the history of the business world and ensure the survival of its workers."[77]

The interplay between Energoinvest's internal structure as a supranational workers' collective and the global nature of its operations shaped its antinationalist discourse as the country plunged into war, threatening business. Mentioning successful agreements in Libya, Ethiopia, Tanzania, and Algeria, where Energoinvest was building electric power lines, was a matter of great pride for the company's continuing narrative of a multinational enterprise. The first year of the war, the company paper wrote, "has shown how we can still maintain our reputation successfully and acquire new investors."[78] However, maintaining a reputation as a reliable partner was increasingly difficult for a country at war. Investors and partners, though keen on Energoinvest to complete the projects it had initiated abroad, were unlikely to keep investing in it, and thus the war was leaving Energoinvest without vital partnerships and investments.[79] For a company whose corporate identity was based on its global partnerships, the conflict-induced isolation and the rupture of global networks caused by the dissolution of Yugoslavia constituted serious concerns.

While the situation for Energoinvest's foreign joint ventures and business deals might have been relatively untethered to the conflict, the situation at the domestic level was dire. The loss of contacts and industrial production worsened as the conflict proceeded and multiple front lines emerged across Yugoslavia. Parts of the former JNA and newly founded Serbian paramilitary forces seceded and occupied parts of Bosnia and Herzegovina after its independence declaration in 1992. Forces affiliated with Croat and Serb nationalist parties sought to establish influence in regions with similar ethnic majorities. Serb paramilitary forces violently occupied territories and carried out campaigns of ethnic cleansing in Bosnia and Croatia and put large cities like Mostar and Sarajevo under siege. In territories controlled by the Croatian HVO in the western part of the country (Herzegovina), the violent targeting of ethnic minorities was carried out extensively.

The consequences of the territorial fragmentation ensuing from the war were immense, particularly for the civilian population but also for the economy. The disruption of logistics and production affected the whole industrial milieu of Yugoslavia. Factories across Yugoslavia were temporarily closed or reconverted in the service of warfare production. Industrial facilities across the country produced only around 5–6 percent of their prewar capacity during the conflict.[80] This marked an immense loss of industrial jobs, which were not reinstated after the war, and commenced a process of deindustrialization that would accelerate after the war. One of the most immediate effects of the war on Bosnian companies was their "cantonization"—much like the rest of the country, they wwere divided into cantons. In fact, with the beginning of the siege in Sarajevo in April 1992, the company's headquarters remained isolated from many of their production and research centers, as well as from their partners across the country.

Some of Energoinvest's most important production factories were near or on the front line—particularly the industrial complexes built on the outskirts of the city.[81] The very space of the company, which functioned as a physical representation of its corporate identity as a Yugoslav company, came apart at the seams. The Yugoslav global dream of a company united by the spirit of "Brotherhood and Unity," much like the country that it mirrored, came crumbling down as the conflict ensued. Its global relationships shriveled up simultaneously, and as business dried up, new forces began to reshape the company.

Toward the end of the war, when it became evident that Bosnia's internal borders were there to stay, a new phase of fragmentation commenced. This transformation had profound repercussions for a company like Energoinvest, whose factories were now state property of two different entities: the Bosnian Croat- and the Serb-dominated areas. This top-down fragmentation of the company along ethno-territorial lines sanctioned its respatialization and realigned its corporate identity from supranational to national. In a transformation that mirrored Bosnia's, the company also developed a "Serb" and a "Bosnian" splinter.[82] Because of the country's territorial division, many of the company's refineries, factories, and research centers in Zvornik, Lukavica, Doboj, and Srebrenica (all in Republika Srpska) were no longer under the control of Energoinvest's headquarters in Sarajevo; they simply shared equipment, patents, and trademarks with their "Bosnian" counterparts.

The journal reiterated that despite its losses, Energoinvest had managed to maintain its core in its cadres, engineers, and knowledge: "There is another energoinvest (with small letters) that has been trying already for a thousand days to be Energoinvest [a reference here to the Serbian counterpart]. However, it will not be. . . . Energoinvest will keep working, it has something of the Bosnian stubbornness [*bosanski inat*] in it."[83] The newspapers at the time emphasized the importance of the mobilization of resistance against an external aggressor; here, the attributes of the "resisting nation" overlapped with those of the "resisting company," as Energoinvest increasingly ascribed itself specific national characteristics—the Bosnian defiance or stubbornness (*inat*) being the most representative.[84]

This reconfiguration of corporate identity also came after the appointment of a new general manager, Edib Bukvić, in 1994. Bukvić was a former vice president of the government and a prominent figure in the SDA.[85] A former employee of Energoinvest, Bukvić epitomized this "nationalist" turn in his acceptance speech in June 1994: "In the past two war years, those who had gained much from Energoinvest destroyed its image. This is the so-called Serbian Energoinvest. . . . We will benefit from the abandonment of a huge number of unnecessary cadres, especially those cadres which have rebelled in the hills [an indirect way of referring to Serb paramilitary forces], because if those people had wanted to work, they would not have fought."[86]

Henceforth, business contacts, patents, and cadre knowledge became increasingly part of a process of "ethnonationalizing" the company, as the fight for its legacy assumed nationalistic traits. Bukvić is regarded by many of his critics as a director who put his party's interests and orientation before the good of the company.[87] Under his presidency, the composition of the company's management board changed, and several Serb members were dismissed: a move that some of my interlocutors viewed positively as a rebalancing of power within the company. Presenting it as simply a managerial decision, the very blasé way the members of the new management commented on the dismissal of Serb coworkers is testament to the extent to which ethnonational discrimination had become commonplace and normalized. This kind of procedure was mirrored in Republika Srpska as well: by early 1998, the then prime minister (and current president) Milorad Dodik sacked seventeen directors of large state-owned enterprises (including Energoinvest's own oil production and distribution company Energopetrol) to replace them with political figures and technocrats closer to him.[88]

Bukvić decided to rebuild part of the production line in the Bosnian part of Sarajevo. The central branch in Sarajevo, in fact, had maintained all the international links and networks created in the decades of Yugoslav non-alignment. This project was supposed to revive the production of steel armatures for a projected value of USD 15 million.[89] As business restarted in the Bosnian-controlled Sarajevo, it created further difficulties for the remaining factories located immediately behind the lines of the Serbian-controlled territory, such as Lukavica. These factories saw their workforce, and the possibility of regaining part of their former production capacity, significantly diminished. It was impossible for many of those residing in the Bosnian Army–controlled territory to reach the workplace on the other side. Much like his "Bosnian" counterpart, the director of Energoinvest's former Research-Development Center for Electro-energetics (Istraživačko-razvojni centar za elektroenergetiku, or IRCE) in Lukavica (now "Serb" Energoinvest) was also primarily concerned with safeguarding his company and factories. I interviewed him in the central building of a closed industrial site, the only one that still hosted some daily activities. Along the empty corridors, a set of Energoinvest prizes and commemorative plaques hung on the walls. Near the entrance, a glass door opened into a room where flowers adorned the photographs of the former employees who had died during the war. During our discussion, Miro remained very matter of fact about the split, but at times a bitterness became palpable as we talked about the consequences it had for his workplace. He showed me around the empty place, explaining that the division from Energoinvest Sarajevo had commenced a decline for the firm:

> I constantly told my close colleagues that . . . we must keep and preserve this property. . . . But we kept it only as physical property . . . the market, the business partners, those were gone.[90]

Workers, engineers, and managers who had remained in Sarajevo—mostly Bosnjaks but also some Serbs and Croats—indeed used the documentation and know-how that had remained within the central branch to re-create in the federation what had remained in Republika Srpska.

Mirsad Kapetanović, an expert in electrical engineering at IRCE since 1977, recalls that in a matter of one night, barricades were built near his home in Dobrinja, which did not allow him to reach his workplace in East Sarajevo:

> Ever since, I have never been able to get any papers or materials from my old institute [IRCE]. Since Energoinvest had the right to the institute, we rebuilt it here, we as workers gathered and rebuilt IRCE and the factory just as it had been in Lukavica, and we restarted export with the contacts we had. So the one that remained there [in East Sarajevo] collapsed because it did not have any people.[91]

The war-related destruction of industrial sites and the dramatically changed workforce demographic were widespread issues that affected the Bosnian economy across entity borders. Although some production of aluminum kept functioning in the eastern part of Bosnia, under the control of the Bosnian Serb forces, the situation for Aluminij Mostar was rather dire. The facilities of Aluminij Mostar, much like most of the city's industrial and cultural heritage, were destroyed during the war. Mostar had Bosnia's only aluminum smelter, which was subject to severe damage when the fighting between government forces and the Bosnian Croats in 1993 shut off power to the facility.[92] The strategic nature of aluminum production in the region, with Aluminij Mostar being one of the largest facilities there, meant that much attention and investment was dedicated to rebuilding it. Meanwhile, worker shortages commonly resulted from ethnic cleansing and displacement and affected several industrial areas in the country. Even where the war had left most of the industrial infrastructure untouched, as was the case of Tuzla, the disruption of supply chains and market deliveries had put these companies under sometimes fatal stress. Factories stood empty of materials and workforces.[93] Oil refineries and pumps that belonged to Energoinvest's subsidiary company Energopetrol were also severely damaged, and only a few of those that remained in the Bosnian Serb territories, which were less affected by shelling, remained operational. Furthermore, Energopetrol had several gas stations on the coastline of Croatia; after the conflict, these remained under full Croatian control, while property and employment claims on those facilities are still ongoing.[94]

The facilities of Energoinvest in East Sarajevo were far from being the only example of a factory splintering alongside new borders. Tvornica Aparata (TAT) was a large thermoelectric factory that had an export of USD 110 million and employed over 1,200 workers before the war. The large industrial area of Stup in the southern outskirts of Sarajevo, where TAT was situated, had seen the fighting between the Bosnian, Croat, and Serb armies in 1992–1993, with several episodes of factory looting. After 1995, a "TAT" in East Sarajevo (Republika Srpska) existed in parallel with a TAT in the federation's part of Sarajevo, still bearing Energoinvest's trademark.[95] According to a commentator in the Bosnian newspaper *Dani*: "The Serbs got the machinery, the Bosnjaks the land and the collapsed buildings. All got something, but TAT lost everything: partners abroad, prestige, large contracts. There is work neither for those who took the machinery, nor for those who had the old location."[96]

As the very spaces that glued workers' communities together became divided, workers ascertained their dire situation. In many letters to newspapers, interviews, and comments from the time, workers expressed their concern regarding the crumbling of the physical and metaphorical bridges built by the project of global socialism. Their accounts indicate that the defense of the country and that of the workplace were one and the same for them. Their motivation was in great measure to preserve their workplace as a space that would give them the possibility of a prompt return to their jobs and livelihoods. After the war, workers trying to rebuild the factories and restart production struggled to restore their companies to past glories.[97] "In the first months," recalls Dževad, a veteran and former employee of Energoinvest, "we worked, and nobody even wanted to be paid, we only wanted to start the production. There was such enthusiasm!"[98] Many workers like Dževad envisioned a quick return to normality, to their workplaces and their colleagues, a shift away from the "normality of the abnormal"—as Ivana Maček has defined it—which was Sarajevo under siege.[99] Attempts at reconciliation and at piecing back the fragmented spaces of the workplace were hindered by the fractured nature of postwar Bosnia. With new borders limiting internal mobility, many Bosnjak workers who had remained in the besieged Sarajevo went to work for the "Bosnian" Energoinvest, while those in Lukavica went to the "Serb" Energoinvest. Ethno-territorial divisions crumpled workers' expectations of a swift reconstruction of their companies based on the prewar tenets of territorial unity.

5

LAYERS OF DESERVINGNESS

Ownership and Employment after the War

SINCE THE BEGINNING OF THE CONFLICT IN BOSNIA, proposed peace plans sanctioned a de facto division of the country along ethnic lines and further legitimized campaigns of ethnic cleansing aimed at homogenizing different areas.[1] By mid-1993, the UN Security Council had extended the mandate of UN forces involved on the ground to protect the safe areas where most displaced civilians had sought refuge; moreover, the North Atlantic Treaty Organization (NATO) had been authorized to conduct aerial military interventions, in particular against the Serb military forces.[2] After the UN repeatedly failed to mediate a peace deal, in April 1994 the Contact Group consisting of the US, Russia, the UK, France, and Germany took shape. This initiative aimed to set in motion a looser and, above all, faster negotiating process. Although this first proposed plan fell through because of Radovan Karadžić's Serb opposition, it constituted the blueprint for the following agreements, which established and reinforced an ethnonational division of the country.[3]

At the end of March 1994, Sarajevo government troops and Croatian Defense Council troops launched an offensive against the Serbs in northeastern Bosnia, in response to which they violently resumed bombing in Sarajevo. In the meantime, the UN forces present on the ground, because of their lack of internal coordination and of effective military power, were unable to effectively shield large groups that had sought refuge in the northeastern areas of Srebrenica, Bihać, Goražde, and Žepa, which saw the most heinous war crimes committed against the civilian population unfolding in the summer of 1995, culminating in the Srebrenica genocide. In August 1995, Operation Deliberate Force saw NATO engaged in effective air raids that forced the retreat of Ratko Mladić's troops.[4]

A few months later, in December 1995, the leaders of Croatia, Serbia, and Bosnia were taken to the military base in Dayton, Ohio (US), to reach an agreement and end the war. The treaty established the division of the Bosnian territory into two entities: the Republika Srpska, comprising the main Serb-dominated territories and the eastern part of Sarajevo for a total of 49 percent, and the Federation of Bosnia-Herzegovina (FBiH), covering the territories with a Bosnjak Muslim or Croat majority, for a total of 51 percent.[5] The FBiH was itself divided into ten cantons, most of which had a clear ethnic majority.[6] Bosnia also has an independent district (Brčko District), which is the only example of multiethnic self-governance in the country. To this day, most of the legislative and executive power in Bosnia and Herzegovina is held by the state parliament, which is governed by an ethnic quota principle, whereby the presidency rotates among the representatives of the three recognized ethnicities (Bosnian Muslims, Bosnian Croats, and Bosnian Serbs).[7] The governing principle coordinating these two entities was crystallized in a system where the three main ethnic groups and their representatives obtained the most political and economic leverage.[8] In 1996, the first national elections after the war cemented this demographic outlook.[9]

Dayton initiated a complex two-tiered citizenship regime, whereby Bosnian citizens would also hold entity citizenship. For example, citizens who resettled in Republika Srpska (usually Bosnian Serbs seeking to live where they were the ethnic majority) would automatically also assume citizenship of the Republika Srpska. The result of this policy was that citizenship regulations acquired ethnocentric traits.[10] Further, as Denisa Kostovicova and Vesna Bojičić-Dželilović have underlined, this system "allows ethnic elites to sustain the system of informal rule involving disregard for state-sanctioned rules and regulations, which is obfuscated by the ethnic elites' stature as guardians of a group's national cause."[11]

Postwar Property Reforms, Reemployment, and Exclusion

Property relations are an important and enduring dimension of civic conflict. Scholars have observed this in postconflict Sri Lanka and Zimbabwe, where land ownership has been demarcated unevenly for members of a majority ethnic group. South Africa offers another example of the ethnic-based distribution of land ownership rights, as nonwhite citizens were routinely excluded from accessing private property.[12] Similarly, postconflict reconstruction through privatization has entailed a sharpening of regional inequalities in Mozambique; in Cambodia, the revitalization of the private industrial sector was characterized by an overwhelming ethnicization of industrial and property relations in favor of ethnic Chinese entrepreneurs.[13] At the same time, in the case of several South Asian and, to a lesser extent, Latin American countries, ethnicity fared prominently in nationalization programs; thus, nationalization, as much as privatization, can work as an exclusionary measure toward minority ethnic groups.[14]

Besides postconflict countries, in multiethnic postsocialist nations such as Latvia or the former Czechoslovakia, access to private property—particularly housing—was linked to ethnic privileges.[15] This process of ethnicization spilled over onto new employment and ownership regimes, redefining deservingness in the postwar, postsocialist context. In his work on mobility trajectories in postsocialist East Germany and the Czech Republic, Till Hilmar highlights the importance of temporality—in his case, before and after 1989—as a significant feature in determining values of merit and deservingness or the justice beliefs generated through social comparisons.[16] In the case of postsocialist and postwar Bosnia, deservingness assumed a further layer, that of war compensation through ownership. Privatization reforms became a tool to reshape workplaces and their protagonists: changing ownership regimes reflected different ideas about societies, as well as the promises the state was making to deserving citizens about how these transformations would benefit them—promises made but not always kept.

The war of 1992–1995 dramatically changed Bosnia's demographic landscape. Though the numbers vary greatly according to sources and studies, it is estimated that between ninety-seven thousand (civilians) and two hundred thousand (including soldiers) people have disappeared or lost their lives in the Bosnian conflict, and almost 1.3 million people were granted the status of refugees.[17] About half of the prewar population had been displaced. Damages to the environment, cultural heritage, and urban and industrial landscapes were enormous. Just for the city of Sarajevo, which was heavily hit by bombardments throughout the conflict, the estimated loss was over EUR 14 billion.[18] Rebuilding the industrial infrastructure, and thus the labor market and employment opportunities, was going to prove an arduous task, as more than 25 percent of the prewar productive capital stock, infrastructure, and housing stock had been lost.[19] For returnees and internally displaced people, the process of returning to housing and employment was marked by hardship and discrimination. Studies on labor market outcomes in postconflict situations showed that refugees and internally displaced people in postconflict Bosnia found it more difficult to access employment than those who stayed, and this was particularly true for displaced men.[20]

These dramatic changes in the composition of demographics and geographical and employment structures after the war altered the very fabric of many companies across Bosnia. Since the beginning of the war, employment had been politicized into a tool of active ethnonational discrimination. At the beginning of the war, local and national governments ordered a termination of employment for those who remained absent from their workplaces without justification.[21] Although, ostensibly, this was an attempt to prohibit people from leaving their hometowns and joining paramilitary armies, it exacerbated divisions by burning bridges between those who stayed and those who left—namely, members of ethnic minorities who, feeling threatened during the conflict, decided to flee to their ethnic-majority areas. While for some the factory had been a space of resistance and recruitment, for others it became a place of exclusion. It left them with nothing to go back to.

As the war continued, minority communities faced unlawful mass layoffs that went unrectified in the chaos of war. A significant case was that of Aluminij Mostar, a major producer and refiner of aluminum, which was part of the Energoinvest group until 1991. Here non-Croat employees were excluded from reemployment.[22] Another major case was that of the mining complex in the town of Prijedor (Republika Srpska), where non-Serb employees were fired en masse after the beginning of the war.[23] The cities of Banja Luka, Mostar, and Livno also saw large dismissals of ethnic minority workers and of those in mixed marriages, as their loyalties were called into question.[24] Cases of the unlawful dismissal of workers like those of Mostar and Prijedor occurred across Bosnia and at the expenses of members of all ethnic or national groups. In an instance presented in front of the Human Rights Commission, for example, an applicant accused the authorities of Republika Srpska of denying him a fair trial concerning his unlawful dismissal.

The court ruling stated: "At the end of 1992, due to the outbreak of hostilities on the territory of Bosnia and Herzegovina, [his company] stopped working and the entire complex in which the applicant's business premises were located, was illegally taken over by Elektroškola Banja Luka. The applicant felt that he was forced to stop working on his business premises because he was of a different nationality. The applicant thereby lost his ability to use the business premises."[25]

Former employees of other companies in both entities presented similar instances to the court and claimed that their work had been illegally terminated, at times because of their ethnic and national origin.[26] In the FBiH, a total of 52,286 complaints had been filed with requests to be reinstated in previous working positions. The parliament of Republika Srpska opened similar tribunals and received "58,488 requests from people who believed that their employment had terminated illegally."[27] Thus, roughly 110,000 employees in both entities sued their former employers for unlawful dismissal on ethnic grounds. However, workers who were granted the right to sue for unlawful dismissal often reported their disappointment in the low compensations.[28]

In addition to the unlawful ethnic-based dismissal of employees, the question of (re)employment and compensation for war veterans became one of the main fault lines of division in postwar Bosnia. Already in socialist Yugoslavia, glorifying former combatants of the partisan struggle and rewarding them with privileges was a well-established praxis. Workplaces were spaces where these veterans would enjoy visibility and respect and where they would be celebrated on several occasions, such as July 4 (Day of the Fighters, or Dan Borca) and November 29 (Day of the Republic, or Dan Republike). New political forces drew on this glorification, though in a highly divisive fashion. In both Bosnia and Croatia, the reintegration of veterans "was largely left to the national and entity governments, leaving ample space for nationalist elites. [These] created policies whose aims were ambiguous, blending reintegration with compensation yet inevitably favoring the citizen-soldier."[29] Similar to Croatia—where veterans of the "losing" army (Serbs) were not entitled to any benefits—Bosnia also tied its reward policies to ethnicity.

In a society where, until a few years earlier, unemployment had been a social taboo and source of stigma for citizens, employment became a political pacifier in a context where financial compensations for veterans were deemed unfeasible given the lack of resources.[30] Employment itself became a prize for having shown loyalty to the ethnic community. Bottom-up pressure from unions and veteran groups contributed to the push for reemployment as a reward for a specific group of veterans. Already at the beginning of 1995, demobilized soldiers had started to demand solutions for employment issues in the community of veterans, those injured or incapacitated by war, and members of the families of fallen soldiers.[31] In their demands for reemployment, union representatives constantly stressed "the decisive role of workers in defending the country," which had to be rewarded by granting them "social and material security."[32] On many occasions, and particularly in parliamentary discussions with the government, workers' representatives expressed dissatisfaction with the slow pace of workplace reconstruction and stressed that this was particularly unfair to those "workers-warriors who had defended Bosnia."[33] The federation's general union advocated for giving the priority of return to those demobilized worker-warriors who were still waiting to be reemployed.[34] They also argued that demobilized soldiers ought to have priority in reemployment because "they had made the biggest contribution to their country's freedom."[35] Worker-warriors and their representatives had thus opted for a negotiation strategy that would emphasize their role *as patriots* who deserved to be prioritized above those who had not fought for their workplaces and homelands. This discourse was adopted by the scores of unions that emerged in post-Dayton Bosnia.[36] Across the country, these groups demanded the "development of priority employment schemes for vets."[37] Veteran groups, often divided along ethnic as well as political lines, generally operated at a "high level of synergy with the (respective) government and the municipal authorities," who in turn were eager to gain and maintain the support of these groups.[38]

Nationalist parties in the two entities that constituted Bosnia and Herzegovina promised reemployment to veterans and workers during the war and created a buffer system (waiting lists) that helped mitigate the optics of mounting unemployment by reassuring people that the system was slowly being restored and that they had not been forgotten. The labor laws discussed in both entities between 1997 and 1999 formalized this complex system. Companies unable to employ at their full capacity put their workers "on waiting lists" (*na čekanju*) until they could either reemploy them or dismiss them completely. This status guaranteed workers a percentage of their salary, to be provided by the employer while they were registered "on the waiting list" (for a maximum of six months).[39] In both entities, the parties that had advocated most strongly for compensations and rewards for worker-warriors sought to consolidate popular support by promising social guarantees of employment and severance pay to former employees, in accordance with their ethnicity and veteran status.[40] Granting this as a form of reward was meant to symbolically recognize veterans' efforts and consolidate the ethnonational discourse in rebuilt communities. Yet employment policies often became tools in the hands of new ruling elites who sought to homogenize communities and reshape the ethnonational social fabric of the workplace.

With pressure to ethnicize the workplace mounting, both Republika Srpska and the federation implemented regulations to favor the reemployment of veterans and demobilized soldiers.[41] In Republika Srpska, soldiers who had fought in the Army of Republika Srpska (predominantly Serbs) had employment priority. However, in the federation, where two armies—the Croatian Defense Council (HVO) and the Army of Bosnia and Herzegovina (ARBiH)—fought first against each other, then together against Serbian forces, reemployment policies were highly contested. Here, veterans of the HVO and ARBiH—separate factions at war between 1992 and 1994—were supposed to be included in the same federal regulations favoring veterans' reemployment. However, as the friction between the two constitutive nations of the federation (Croat and Bosnjak Muslims) did not appear to be winding down, disagreements between their respective veteran groups continued.

For example, the municipality of Sarajevo promoted veterans' return to the workplace, demanding collaboration from companies across the municipality.[42] According to the law, demobilized soldiers (roughly twelve thousand) would be guaranteed return to their workplaces. If the workplaces had been physically destroyed, the veterans would have to be employed somewhere else, in accordance with their qualifications. Further, enterprises that could not fill the workplace with their former workers had to employ demobilized soldiers from ARBiH.[43] However, representatives of the Croat Nationalist Party (HDZ) soon questioned these provisions, since they claimed these did not grant equal rights to veterans of the two armies. As they stated at a parliamentary meeting, the law resulted in "inequality for all those who were part of HVO—because at some point that was characterized as an enemy army. . . . Those who had the fortune to be in ARBiH had their workplace waiting for them, and have a priority in employment if they did not work; those who were in HVO . . . did not have any theoretical chance to think about the rights of demobilized soldiers."[44]

This issue remained unresolved, and companies in different cantons across the federation gave priority to the reemployment of veterans of their respective ethnonational majority. Although at the beginning of the war most workers in Energoinvest had demonstrated against the conflict, their recruitment under different "ethnic" armies had shifted their perspective. Understandably, the prospect of returning to a multiethnic workplace was viewed by many as problematic. While workers had overall positive reflections on the prewar workplaces—primarily because of a sense of community and security that, for some, was conjugated in multiethnic terms—their reflections on the immediate postwar years show an awareness of how unattainable and undesirable such an equilibrium could be. Wartime ethnic conflicts could not, and should not, be so easily dismissed in peacetime. Access to employment, much like many other aspects of daily life, became a formal and informal tool of separation—perhaps a requirement of the very complex and fragile postwar equilibrium. A period of adaptation was required, during which institutional, social, and economic rebuilding could not be exempted from reflecting the profound divisions of the war.

Many interlocutors reflected on this complexity by pushing against the notion that a postwar multiethnic workplace was viable, let alone desirable. Mate was a Croat blue-collar worker employed in the large company Aluminij Mostar. He recalls his return to work after his time as a soldier in the Bosnian Croat army HVO:

> I started to work again in 1999. I was a Croat soldier for five years; I carried the shotgun and fought for . . . for something, why I do not even know . . . I fought to survive like everybody else. And now, think: you are in the position as a director of Aluminij, which is in the territory that HVO and Croats controlled at the time. And now all of a sudden you cut the ribbon and you say, "OK, now those who were [employed] here will return." And those against whom I fought come to work, and I stay at home without a job. In a time when the situation was terrible, you can imagine. That was impossible. Do you understand? Muslims could not just come back. First, you had to pacify, to employ your people, and if there was space for the others, no problem. Do you understand? There was the war, and it was a catastrophe. And now [it was as if] I come and I say, "You cannot. You did not work here before. I will bring in him from there," but until yesterday I saw him through the gun sight.[45]

Many demobilized worker-warriors discuss their participation in the war in a similar way: the conflict itself was a matter of survival. Employment was the only way to secure that survival after the war, and in this reward, priorities were clear. Other veterans voiced similar opinions during our interviews, and the priority of reintegration for demobilized soldiers of the respective winning army was discussed in a matter-of-fact way. Dževad, a veteran of the ARBiH who worked at Energoinvest-Armature in Sarajevo, reflects:

> The policy after the war was the priority employment for demobilized soldiers, our workers who were in the defense forces. So we all received those

> demobilized soldiers back in the production in the factory. That was the prior-
> ity. It was almost an order, but it made sense. . . . After all, we were all men, we
> were all sent to war, so we all had the right to go back.[46]

This sentiment was mirrored across the new ethnic boundaries. Željko, a worker from Lukavica (Republika Srpska) and a veteran from the Serbian forces, said it made sense that "only the Serbs who lived in Republika Srpska and those who had fought for it during the war would have employment priority."[47] My interlocutors insisted that I understand this nuance: on the one hand, it was important to present this preference given to ethnic kin in the return to work as common sense, rather than a malignant or premeditated will to exclude. By presenting divisions as orders that came from above but that made sense, they may have wished to demystify what in their eyes is a common misconception that Westerners and outsiders have of Bosnians as a people deeply divided by ethnic hatreds. That politics "from above" rather than people "from below" causes rife divisions is a common narrative in contemporary Bosnia. On the other hand, speaking to a Westerner and an outsider, they wanted to highlight how unfair the expectations of a return to multiethnic "normality" and interethnic cooperation at work would have been at the end of the war. For some, this was the first time an outsider had asked them their opinion about the complex politics of return, and they wished to express their discomfort and frustration with a system of multiethnic power sharing that they felt had been imposed after Dayton. These tensions showed me how complex and ambivalent people's attitudes are toward life in contemporary Bosnia: they yearn to give space to reconciliation but are frustrated by how this has been undemocratically implemented.

While the workplace was a device for worker-warriors to encourage mobilization in defense of Yugoslavia, the war-induced fragmentation of the country into multiple homelands gave it a new connotation. The conceptual overlap of worker and warrior, of homeland and workplace that had once sustained the dream of a united workers' community took on a new meaning, turning work into the prerogative of one ethnicity over the other. The promise of employment, largely abandoned a few years after the end of the war, constituted the only hope for the symbolic recognition that many worker-warriors demanded.[48] When disattended, the promise of reemployment became a source of bitterness among veterans. Addis was one of the many workers who reflected with sarcastic bitterness on the (lack of) employment as a defining feature of his life and position within society: "You asked me if I am respected [as a veteran], but look at my situation, I am laughing now, but I am unemployed."[49]

The Voucher Route: Postsocialism and Privatization Reforms

The reconfiguration of Bosnia's political and social fabric in the postsocialist and postwar context went hand in hand with a profound transformation of economic and ownership rights. After the dissolution of Yugoslavia and the ensuing wars, each former republic had continued its own path toward privatization. Although with some differences, and with the exception of Slovenia, which was much less affected by the war of 1992–1995, the new political class of independent Bosnia, Croatia, and Serbia renationalized companies that had been socially owned. In November 1994 a decree of the Republic of Bosnia—initially aimed at gaining control over companies directly related to military production—approved a full nationalization of all property still listed as "social property."[50] What had been owned by workers in Yugoslav times would now be transferred to direct state control.[51] Republika Srpska proceeded, later on, to approve a similar law within its territory, and similar initiatives occurred in Serbia itself and in Croatia at the beginning of the 1990s.[52] Across eastern Europe, the turn toward neoliberalism coincided with this renationalization and privatization through recentralization, as Johanna Bockman shows.[53] Yet neoliberal transformation was, in many ways, an afterthought for new Bosnian elites. This legal transformation was an attempt at consolidating ethnonational control over industries, workplaces, production, and real estate within the entities. The final eradication of self-management and marginalization of workers was a byproduct of the ethnicization of ownership that came with the new post-Dayton system.

After the nationalization of social property in 1994, the Republika Srpska and the federation gained full control over national property (worth roughly BAM 10 billion) to be privatized.[54] In the years between 1994 and 1997, the Bosnian national government, as well as the entity governments of Republika Srpska and the FBiH, started debating and drafting privatization laws. The privatization of these resources constituted an important element in the postwar elites' consolidation of economic and political power. The nationalist leadership of both entities put strong pressure on both international representatives and the national governments to ensure that privatization would be under entity, rather than national, purview.[55]

The Peace Implementation Council (the international organ tasked with coordinating the Dayton Peace Agreement's implementation) and the major international donors (World Bank, European Bank for Reconstruction and Development, USAID, etc.) started to put pressure on the local governments to approve fast mass privatization. This transformation would be carried out under the supervision of the high representative, the EU envoy tasked with the implementation of the Dayton Agreement on the ground.[56] The institution building and privatizations were led by different expert communities: the former was supposed to be negotiated within parliamentary chambers, while the latter would be assigned to technocratic experts in the privatization agencies.

After months of political stalemate between representatives of the two entities over privatization, in July 1998, the former high representative Carlos Westendorp decided to impose a privatization law that recognized "the rights of the Entities to privatize non-privately owned enterprises and banks located on their territories."[57] Instead of a nationwide privatization law, each entity would regulate the process autonomously, and only in a few cases would they have to cooperate. This decision was presented as an initiative to unblock the political impasse and speed up the privatization process. Nevertheless, by deciding on two different privatization agencies for the Republika Srpska and the FBiH, ethnicity was built into the very institutions that would oversee privatization. The pressure to proceed quickly with privatization overruled the desire to maintain ethnic balance: each entity would now give privatization rights to its increasingly ethnically homogeneous community of citizens.[58] Similar to the case of privatization and economic reforms in postconflict Rwanda, in Bosnia too international advisers did not factor in the role that ethnicity would have potentially played in the phasing in of economic reforms.[59]

In the immediate aftermath of the war, a fast mass privatization program through the rapid distribution of ownership vouchers was launched. This was in line with what had been carried out across most of the former socialist countries of eastern Europe and the former Yugoslavia, where local policymakers and Western advisers alike deemed voucher privatization to be the most efficient way of redistributing ownership rights. In Bosnia, ruling nationalist parties with free-market aspirations proceeded with the distribution of ownership rights through vouchers as—allegedly—the most rapid way of creating private ownership under conditions of domestic capital scarcity.[60] The rationale for the new reforms through vouchers excluded any option for internal (i.e., workers') shareholding, as this would "unjustly advantage workers."[61] Following this logic, the architects of postwar economic reforms in Bosnia were of the opinion that voucher privatization would democratize property rights. Economists Stiepo Andrijić and Aleksa Milojević were the first directors of, respectively, the privatization agencies of the FBiH and Republika Srpska from 1996 to 1998. They both had an established academic career in Bosnian universities, although they had not been directly involved in the reforms of 1989–1990. Faced with the constraints of a new socioeconomic geography of property—whereby ownership rights were now linked to entity citizenship rather than work history—they promoted a model that would ratify new grounds for deservingness in the postsocialist society. Reflecting on this during our interview, Andrijić commented that in the previous system

> factory workers could obtain a higher level of ownership than university professors. So, in that sense, there was a certain kind of discrimination. [After privatization] all citizens got certificates to buy whatever they wanted in the territory of the federation.[62]

For him, the new laws further democratized the Marković model, by including those subjects who had been allegedly excluded in its initial formulation. In Republika Srpska the rationale was similar. Aleksa Milojević, the first director of the Privatization Agency of the Republika Srpska and a member of parliament in the immediate postwar years, noted that the voucher model was "following the fundamental principle that citizens are naturally owners."[63] The architects of the first postwar voucher reforms in Bosnia were thus motivated by a need to "democratize" ownership, assigning rights to a supposedly wider group of people (citizens) as opposed to a more restricted one (workers). For them, transferring capital from social and state ownership to private hands was meant to right the wrongs of a system that had created the "illusion of ownership" for the working class.[64]

With the new voucher system, every citizen was entitled to a basic certificate of BAM 1,900, with additional certificates in recognition of military service. These certificates allowed for the purchase of shares in enterprises (through a public offering of shares) in the newly created privatization investment funds or in the previously state-owned or company-owned apartments. This meant that they were not directly linked to a specific set of shares in a specific company but could in theory be used to purchase shareholding rights. Some workers viewed the distribution of shares in the form of vouchers to the general population as a dismissal of their prerogative as shareholders. Commenting on this, Ismet, the president of the Union of Metalworkers (Sindikat Metalaca Bosne i Hercegovine), one of the largest in the country, noted:

> This kind of privatization through shares was presented to us, and at first glance, we identified it as the Marković privatization. Only that with Marković you had internal shares, and now you had external shares or certificates. So with Marković, only the workers could be owners, and we thought that was the right way. . . . However, when the war finished, and they told us that we once again would get the shares and be owners, it turned out that even my mother-in-law, who never worked anywhere, could become the owner of the firm because they gave her certificates![65]

Ismet had expected to receive privileged ownership rights following the Marković model. He was outraged that someone who had never worked (in his words, his mother-in-law) could claim ownership rights to his factory or company as much as he could. This remark reveals a value system characterized by hierarchies of deservingness: only those who had worked could be owners of their own factories.[66] Ismet's expectations of postwar privatization were shaped by his experiences of reform in the self-managed socialist workplace.

This was not an uncommon trend among workers and union members across Bosnia. Danko Ružičić, the president of the textile branch of the Unions Council of Republika Srpska, also remarked on the injustices of a system that rewarded everyone with the same vouchers: "Those who worked for thirty, forty years were treated like my daughter who was six months old then, or my mother who was sixty at the time and never entered a factory and worked."[67] These considerations, frequent among my interlocutors, reveal an inner sense of hierarchy when it comes to ownership. No longer "nobody's and everybody's"—as was the slogan in socialist Yugoslavia—ownership was very much connected with a structure of (male) deservingness, justified through work in an industrial setting. The fact that these comments often referred to women also reveals the hierarchy of "productive" and seemingly "unproductive" or reproductive labor implicit in these narratives. That someone's mother never entered a factory seemed to automatically disqualify her from any claim to ownership.

As Katherine Verdery noted in her analysis of changing property regimes across postcommunist transformation, property has to be understood as a bundle of powers and rights that entails complex meanings and ideas about labor, community, and kinship and that shapes relations among people as much as relations between people and things.[68] In Yugoslavia, as in Verdery's analysis of the Romanian case, social ownership was characterized by a degree of fuzziness, as indeed it lacked (or challenged) "the clear edges of an ideologized notion of exclusive private ownership" that came with postsocialism.[69] While workers had criticized the official socialist jargon of "social property" (*društvena svojina*) as a fuzzy (legal) category—not private, public, or collective—they felt attached to it. They viewed property rights not just as a prerogative of the individual but as a social right of *individual workers belonging to a collective*. No matter how critical workers were of self-management, "nonwork," and unproductivity, they still approached "work" and "ownership" with a set of values embedded in Yugoslavism, socialist ideals, and a specific corporate culture. These values informed their criticism of the criteria of voucher distribution.

In addition, the timing and nonregulation of such a privatization model created discontent among the population, leading to its ultimate failure. In fact, both in the Republika Srpska and the FBiH, this first wave of voucher privatization happened in a context of deep impoverishment for citizens who had just come out of a war. In a situation of unstable equilibrium sustained by the informal economy, people started selling their shares on the illegal market in exchange for cash or primary goods. Thus, the shares' value substantially decreased, with more than 99 percent of certificates traded at 3 percent of their nominal value.[70] As the president of the national union explained:

> Workers sold their shares because they had nothing to live on. That is the darkest of pressures because anyone who wanted his family to survive, to buy a loaf of bread had to sell certificates which otherwise he could invest in a factory. And so they sold them on the black [illegal] market.[71]

Workers found themselves in the predicament of having to choose between bread and work—that is, between present and future sources of survival. Most of them did not fully understand that they were selling their shareholding rights in their own companies; they just traded certificates on the illegal market, as this was the fastest way to procure cash or primary goods. A few spots of illegal trade of shares emerged around their cities, where petty criminals and war profiteers bought shares from workers for 1–2 percent of their real value.[72] In many cases, war profiteers bought vouchers and certificates from the most vulnerable in such a manner, using them to buy up state-owned property and assets for a minimal fee.[73] By the end of 1999, the majority of certificates had been either used to purchase flats or sold on the illegal market for cash.[74] As a result, trust in this new form of privatization through certificates quickly dropped, as former workers and soldiers struggled more and more to give any value to these documents.

In various interviews collected by newspapers at the time, veterans showed their mounting dissatisfaction with voucher privatization, already noting how their expectations had been unmet in this transformation. A former soldier in a news interview declared at the time: "What should I do with my certificates, other than sell them? I fought for four years for this country, and I got this paper which I cannot use for anything, as I would need more money to buy some part in a company, and I do not have it."[75] On the same note, another veteran declared that he did not believe in the possibility of using his shares in the privatization of big companies, saying, "The government and new owners will again think of something so that normal people cannot buy anything."[76] Today, many workers and veterans report similar views on the value of vouchers assigned to them. Although they got these shares as "compensation because they fought in the war," they mostly perceived them as "useless" or even a "theft from the state, against soldiers and citizens."[77] Vouchers were perceived as a regression: a temporary solution to appease a desperate population rather than an aid for economic recovery. Dispossessed workers, aware that many of their companies were facing an inevitable decline due to the nontransparent process of privatization, did not associate the same kind of value with privatization vouchers as they had with the shares they bought during the Marković reforms.

In 2000, a public opinion poll conducted by the Faculty of Political Sciences in Sarajevo confirmed that only 6 percent of respondents were eager to use vouchers to invest in companies.[78] The majority of interviewees expected problems in the use of vouchers and attributed this lack of trust to either the fact that they were severely devalued (35%) or the fact that citizens did not have currency and thus sold them for it (50%). Further, the majority lamented that the government did not inform citizens about the financial value and prospects of the companies where vouchers could be invested (55%).[79] Whether devalued on the illegal market, sold for hard currency and primary goods, or used to secure ownership rights to formerly socially owned apartments, vouchers entailed a mismanagement if not full squandering of companies' assets. Workers' lack of trust in the new form of privatization through vouchers did not mean they were less eager to be owners of their factories. Here, the crucial difference with the much-appreciated Marković model was the fact that, in it, workers could claim direct shareholding in *their own* companies. The distribution of vouchers to the general population was problematic for them, as it superseded the hierarchy of deservingness codified in socialist times.

With voucher privatization, property rights were subordinated to ethnonationalist mechanisms of inclusion and exclusion, and this became a mechanism to rank and control different segments of the population—veterans and returnees in particular.[80] The exclusion of ethnic minority workers from property shareholding occurred in many large companies across the country. The most prominent case, though not the only one, was that of the aluminum giant Aluminij in Mostar, formerly a company of the Energoinvest group. In 1996, the HDZ took over the management of Aluminij and privatized it through a process whereby most shares went to Croat workers and management.[81]

This case has become an example of the controversial outcomes that privatization had in the country. Milan Jovičić, the most outspoken of the group of non-Croats who were excluded from Aluminij, took his experience as evidence of corrupt political interests in privatization. For him, members of Croat, Bosnjak, and Serb nationalist parties all had an interest in legalizing ethnic cleansing by privatizing companies according to partisan interests.[82] Aluminij Mostar exemplifies how employment and ownership regulations came to be entangled with ethnic discrimination. Although no legal provisions entailed the actual exclusion of ethnic minorities from property rights, the ethnic homogenization of many areas in the country led to a de facto ethnic-based distribution of certificates in many of these areas.

The postwar reforms—much like those that had preceded them—grappled with questions of productivity, motivation, and deservingness in society, though with different conclusions with respect to policy. In a matter of a few tumultuous years, Bosnia experienced many models of reform, from worker-based ownership to ethnic privatization. While emerging from very different political traditions, both reform models were about changing people's relation to, and understanding of, deservingness and motivation in society. The Yugoslav political tradition had created a specific model of ownership that corresponded to a certain respect for "workers" in the form of the democratic organization of workplaces, corporate values, privileged redistribution, and ownership rights. Even the national-ist parties, though with a different society in mind, still understood prop-erty regimes as a main tool to consolidate consensus and the promises of an (ethnically homogeneous) society. As expressions of different political traditions (from New Socialism to ethnonationalism), changing owner-ship regimes were nothing but a way of honoring the changing criteria of citizenship, belonging, and deservingness in Bosnia.

Reluctant Ethnicization

I had noticed that discussing Energoinvest and the workplace after the war brought up a certain tension in the verbal and physical language of workers I was talking to. I was curious to understand how ethnicity was mediated within workplaces and how, in turn, people may have wished to present to me their own narratives and counternarratives of the socialist past.[83] During our conversations, I sought to explore how they tried to reconcile their ostensible attachment to a workerist, supranational identity with what they viewed as an ethnicization of the postwar workplace. They showed a very complex relation with the issue of ethnicity in the workplace and the perceived higher relevance it assumed after the war. While they might regard themselves as victims of a situation that increasingly crystallized ethnonationalist logic within the workplace—a consequence of a fractured and highly nationalistic political system—there is also evidence that they accepted it as an inevitable consequence of the war. When it came to issues of reemployment, it was often mentioned within minutes of discussing the war and ethno-national divisions, a testament to the difficulty of coming to terms with such a radical transformation of one's surroundings.

I suspect that the relevance of ethnicity in the socialist workplace is often de-emphasized in contemporary recollections to mark a difference between "then" and "now"—perhaps as an expression of disillusionment with the very concepts of democracy and justice, which, as Ivana Maček has found in her anthropological account of Sarajevo under siege, were often as-sociated with Western countries and their inability to intervene during the war.[84] The workers I spoke with were mostly urban dwellers, socialized in an environment that promoted positive discourses of interethnic exchanges and were particularly hesitant in openly raising the issue of ethnicity as a divisive factor between them.[85] Downplaying the extent to which they thought of reemployment in ethnonationalist terms is another testament to the hierarchical shape that memory takes in this context. At the same time, interviewees frequently criticized the new management, institutions, and regulations as having become imbued with ethnonationalist and clientelist logics. "You cannot find a job if you are not of this or that nationalist party" is a pervasive complaint among workers. Munevera gave a striking example of this friction with the new management—de facto politically appointed by the Ministry of Industry. After the war, she pondered whether to return to her workplace in Energoinvest but decided against it because of the way the director behaved. She said:

> After the war, I went to visit Energoinvest only once, because I did not like the way in which they work, specifically the way they entered the building. The secretary of the director of my branch, she had to greet him with "Selam Alejkum." I did not like that he had to be saluted like that, and I saw that there was no place for me anymore.[86]

Munevera, who identifies as a secular Muslim, was annoyed at seeing religious expressions penetrating the daily life of her former workplace. New rituals openly marking the management's religious and ethnic affiliation clashed with the set of supranational values she associated with the prewar workplace. Even though Munevera recalled the years immediately preceding the war as characterized by a strange climate of interpersonal and inter-ethnic friction, she viewed ethnicity in the workplace as an anomaly.

Selective of their memories, interviewees would often describe ethnic frictions as something that entered the workplace from above, after the war years. Muamer was a metalworker in one of Energoinvest's daughter companies in Tuzla. He pointed out:

> MUAMER: Before the war . . . we were all like brothers. Nobody asked anyone what his or her name was.
>
> ANNA: And how was it after the war?
>
> MUAMER: Of course, many left for the Republika Srpska at the beginning of the war and fought from there. Then, they had the right to return here, but they did not. They were afraid, and we do not know what they thought. After the war, things started to be a bit more stable, over time. People started a bit to reason again . . . Politics, that is, it drowned people in their brain. I personally think that all those politicians who have stirred and brought to this war, they should be killed, and we should be a unified nation, and not think in national terms.[87]

Muamer's view of the transformations in his workplace is quite commonplace, as the unwillingness to return is viewed as being imposed by political factions seeking to divide citizens and the workforce. These reflections often stem from interviewees' current views of the Bosnian society as forcefully being kept divided by the interests of ethnonationalist political elites. This assessment is indeed a reflection on the present: many wish that this kind of pervasive ethnicization did not exist, as it taints their memory of a harmonious workplace symbol of the Yugoslav multiethnic promise. It is more important for them to remember the workplace as undivided, even as they find justifications for the current fragmentation of workplaces. While my interlocutors may have felt uncomfortable in raising personal ethnic grievances, it remains significant how they channeled them through a narrative of geographical division along ethnic-based boundaries, imposed by aggressive nationalist forces. At the same time, it is evident from these testimonies that the lack of minority returns to prewar workplaces has been somewhat normalized through the narrative of *being on the other side*. Much as in the instance of the worker being discredited as "a drunk" by his colleagues, discussed in chapter 4, here too assessments of ethnic frictions are somewhat downplayed as they do not support a wider need of workers to project their identity as undivided by ethnonationalist politics. In using a counternarrative to the dominant political discourse of ethnic friction and division, they themselves created a narrative of the past and crafted a certain sense of self to reaffirm a certain vision of their country as undivided—a vision crucial for me to understand and for them to preserve.

Making sense of the ethnic homogenization of the workplace brought up interesting perspectives on the perception of "the other" and their motivations. Marko was a machine worker in Energoinvest's daughter company Tvornica Transportnih Uređaja (TTU) in Tuzla. He reflected on the (ethnic) divisions in the workplace and the return to employment:

> Those who had left when the war started, they could not be reemployed. They had been fired because they had left their jobs without notice. Because I think that those who left Tuzla, those were considered traitors, but I think, maybe they did not leave to fight on the other side, maybe they went abroad, maybe they simply did not want to fight . . . they fled . . . but some people thought that they were traitors, so there were situations in which they could not be reemployed. People of all nationalities, Bosnjaks too, they fled. So when the war was over, they came back looking for employment, but they could not because they had been fired, because they had left the country.[88]

For Marko, the workplace is yet another place where the war and the issues of reemployment have made ethnicity into a critical factor in shaping social relations. Like many of his colleagues, he also views the "ethnicization" of the workplace as something that was enforced by geographical divisions during and after the war and by the difficulty of returning as an ethnic minority.

So, despite Yugoslavia's disintegration, its project of shaping workplaces into sites of cohesion through employment had taken root in the workers' value system. The hyphenated identity of worker-warrior that had once invoked solidarity in the workplace and undermined ethnic divisions was now tainted by a process of reconstruction that created layers and hierarchies of deservingness among worker-veterans. As the poet Veronica Forrest-Thomson wrote, hyphens connect disparate ideas and identities but also divide them for etymological reasons, creating paradoxes.[89] In the postsocialist state, work still held a crucial symbolic role in shaping lives and communities, this time to divide rather than unite. Workers made sense of the complexity of new social relations in the workplace by creating layers of deservingness: everyone had the right to be reemployed, but those who fought "on the right side" had priority. These testimonies highlighted not a clear perception of ethnic polarization within workplaces but rather a normalization of an ethnic discourse about reemployment.

Class and national identity could not reemerge unscathed from the rubble of the Bosnian War and postsocialism. In many locations, the postsocialist reconstruction of workplaces had to grapple with a physical, and not just metaphorical, tabula rasa: factories were fully or partially destroyed and had to be rebuilt fast. Here, more than in other countries in the region, the international community directly involved in reconstruction and peacekeeping promoted institutional reforms that, while designed to supersede ethnonationalist divisions, reproduced and reinforced identity politics.[90] The heavy-handed involvement in economic restructuring, which accompanied institutional rebuilding, profoundly altered the class-identity nexus within workplaces. The neoliberal promise of a classless, multiethnic or nonethnic society where the only values are those of competitiveness and deservingness collided with the reality of reforms, which deepened class *and* ethnic inequalities. Workplaces became spaces where privatization and liberal reforms further sewed together class and national identity.

Employment, work, and ownership relations were thus at the center of the ethnic refashioning of Bosnia in the immediate postwar years. The war acted as a catalyst for the ethnicization of workplaces, as work became an instrument of exclusion, after being a pillar of the Yugoslav promise of interethnic integration.[91] This is not to say that ethnicity did not exist in the socialist workplace; rather, the symbolic recognition bestowed on work had an eminently supranational connotation. The socialist workplace was imbued with Yugoslavist tropes. The ossification of ethnonational discourses, underpinned by the spatial division of the country into (aspiringly) homogeneous areas, reconfigured employment and ownership as a tool for the exclusion of the undeserving. Top-down and bottom-up pressures to compensate worker-warriors reshaped workplaces, introducing different promises of deservingness that gave new meaning to the discursive tropes and values of socialist Yugoslavia—the worker-warrior, the centrality of employment, the workplace as the homeland and basis for ownership. Even though postsocialist reforms were supposed to make a tabula rasa of socialist traditions, including workers' attachment to their companies, the discourse of deservingness in the name of ethnicity reinforced the tie that workers felt to their companies. Ownership and employment were further internalized as currencies of reward, at times dividing and at others unifying.

Yet people were reluctant to describe the workplace (and their position in it) as ethnically divided. Workers admitted that ethnicization became inevitable because of the way the conflict and the peace process unfolded, but they were careful to present themselves as victims or powerless bystanders who helplessly watched their workplace turn into ethnic monoliths. At the same time, this reluctance coexisted with a matter-of-fact recognition of the impossibility of returning to a (perhaps idealized) "nonethnic" workplace. While not oblivious to the presence of ethnicity in the workplace, these workers wanted to assert their distance from, or reluctance to, ethnicized modes of being. This self-positioning could be because "active" or "vocal" ethnic discrimination is frowned upon or actively contested in some parts of Bosnian society, particularly in urban contexts; at the same time, it could derive from an understanding of the workplace as antinational or supranational, an idea that still lingers in (post)socialist workers' groups. It might also be because of my own position as a young woman coming from Western Europe, to whom people want to give a certain impression of what Bosnia *really* is and to counter a stereotype of a country plagued by unsolvable ethnic tensions. Equally possible, they may have wished to point out, through a concrete example of their workplace, that the model of harmonious ethnic coexistence that the Dayton Peace Agreement so strongly promoted was nothing but a forceful imposition on a reality where ethnic conflict was still rife. The expectation that workers would lay down arms and restart production alongside those they may have considered former enemies could not remain in the reality of the postwar workplace.

Figure 5.1. Entrance of Energoinvest—Lukavica in East Sarajevo. Credit: Author

At the same time, this potentially romanticized recollection of ethnic solidarity in the prewar workplace should not be seen merely as a performance. Rather, it is an emotional device through which many people express their dissatisfaction with the current system. In a hierarchy of values, the memory of an idealized nonethnic workplace supersedes the one of a return to work made inaccessible by the logic of postwar nation building. The latter is not excluded or silenced but is (often inadvertently) made subordinate to the need of preserving the promise of unity through work. Layers of deservingness created hierarchies in the way my interlocutors remembered the workplace: it was important to remember it as an undivided space of work rather than a place of exclusion. This remembering was as much about dealing with past traumas as it was about creating hope for future coexistence—a belief that something could be salvaged from these memories, even if the utopia they represented was all but lost. It was a simple yet profound way of saying "If the past was different, then the present need not be the way it is." Whether the experiences of ethnic harmony were exactly as remembered or not, their persistence in collective memory represents a desire to reverse time *forward,* rather than backward.

6

EXPECTING THE GLOBAL

New Horizons of Development and the Fate of (Post)Socialist Corporations

THE SEQUENCE OF TUMULTUOUS EVENTS THAT SHOOK CENTRAL and eastern Europe—from the fall of the Berlin Wall in 1989 to the collapse of the Soviet Union two years later and the violent dissolution of Yugoslavia in 1991–1992—appeared to upend the promise of reformism. A whole world of alternatives seemed to vanish under the sheer force of the Washington Consensus. Much as in Eastern Europe, developing countries embraced market-oriented reforms. At the brink of the new decade, it looked as if a new global order had just emerged from the ashes of the bipolar one. History was over: markets had won. Less than two decades later, however, the global financial crisis put a dent in the seemingly inexorable triumph of market-led growth. Neoliberal models of development were not airtight but could be—and indeed had been—flawed.

I view the neoliberal turn not as an ideology that allowed governments to be legitimated in "breaking" the promises of their social contracts (as Fritz Bartel has argued) but rather as just another global promise.[1] This promise emerged as a "spectrum of ideas on how to create and preserve free markets in an age of popular sovereignty," derived from a multiplicity of ideational influences and domestic political power plays.[2] The global neoliberal promise came to associate growth and prosperity to market-led development as an alternative to state-led development.[3] The promise of new opportunities for global market integration came with the restructuring of the international division of labor, where new interdependencies were forged. In Southern and Central-Eastern Europe, new core-peripheral relations of dependency emerged from the neoliberal promise of equal integration, shaped by the shifts of high-value activities toward regional "core" countries and the reorientation of peripheral economies toward lower-value production under the threat of constant relocation elsewhere.[4] For Southeastern Europe, and for the Bosnian economy in particular, this was very much a case of deindustrialization through peripheralization. Not only were companies restructured but their geographies of production were transformed.

The neoliberal turn determined a shift away from Fordist modes of production and into an era of deindustrialization at the global level.[5] In this regard, the passage from Fordism to flexible accumulation saw a progressive decline in manufacturing output and employment—first in the richer countries of the Global North and then progressively in eastern Europe and the developing world as well. Although pervasive in its aspirations for market-led liberalized rationality and private enterprise, the promise of global integration under neoliberal terms accelerated the process of deindustrialization in the Global North, while the Global South did not eventually benefit from a transfer of manufacturing jobs to its economies. In Latin America, for example, the abandonment of old strategies of economic development for the neoliberal promise of growth and integration ultimately entailed a turn toward extractive industries, at the expense of labor-intensive manufacturing sectors—what some scholars define as premature deindustrialization.[6] The variegated ways in which the neoliberal promise was translated in different contexts produced multiple and at times diverging outcomes of deindustrialization, and thus diverse responses and countermovements.[7] A myriad of industrial closures, shutdowns, and bankruptcies have accompanied a shift away from what had been the preferred industrial growth strategies of emerging economies in the socialist and developing worlds: import-substitution industrialization and export-led growth. The promise of neoliberalism was indeed to do away with both old-school types of state-led development and industrialization and with the old structures of the international division of labor.

Development Goes Small

Neoliberalism established itself as a global trend to redefine the role of the state in development. As Corinna Unger contends, the conservative counterrevolution of the 1980s saw the emergence of a critique of top-down, state-centered development policies and the consequential emergence of neoliberalism as a development strategy.[8] In a global economic context that crunched states' spending capacities and where the role of structural adjustment and revised terms of trade became preponderant, state-led models of development assistance were abandoned in favor of smaller initiatives, often led by nongovernmental organizations.[9] Thus, development went small: as socialist states withdrew from their global development ambitions, state-led, large infrastructural projects of development assistance came to be substituted with smaller and more targeted initiatives.

Development going small also coincided with another crucial transformation in the way economic growth was to be pursued. Large enterprises—particularly state or publicly owned—appeared to struggle in a global market that demanded increasing agility and innovation. This was even more the case in socialist countries: analysts across East and West interpreted the economic crisis in the socialist world as evidence that (state-owned) large enterprises were less competitive, less prone to risk, and less innovative than smaller private enterprises.[10] In addition, new approaches to economic development privileged the diffusion of microcredit and microfinance as a new strategy for economic growth and poverty alleviation (particularly in the Global South). This was a phase of transformation in the very scale and horizon of development—from large projects to smaller-scale initiatives. As a result, economic development strategies relied increasingly on the expansion of small and medium enterprises (SMEs) and strengthened an understanding of development primarily driven by growth and innovation in the small private sector. Pursuing SME-led growth as a strategy for development was a political choice, one that reflected a turn away from larger, state-led projects of development. This was particularly the case in former socialist countries approaching market-led transformations. The underlying assumption was that the rapid innovation of the small private sector would lead to a faster path to global integration.[11]

Several international organization dedicated to international development, including the United Nations Conference on Trade and Development (UNCTAD), the United Nations Development Programme (UNDP), and the World Bank, espoused this turn toward small-business growth as a new mantra for development—not just in the Global South but also in the former socialist world.[12] Since the late 1990s and early 2000s, large international institutions like the Organisation for Economic Co-operation and Development (OECD) and UNCTAD had set up models of development for transitioning countries based on the growth of the small and medium private sector, while until then there had been a propensity to favor large (private) businesses.[13] In an increasingly globalized economy, the focus was on the quick growth of SMEs rather than the development of employment capacity.[14] Several analyses conducted by the World Bank or European Bank for Reconstruction and Development (EBRD) argued that a business-friendly environment grounded on SMEs would be the most attractive to private investment and would help develop local entrepreneurship in "transitioning" countries.[15] The growth of the small private sector was envisioned as a development strategy: these international institutions regularly established advisory groups for privatization in many of the "transitioning" countries where they were involved (from Argentina to the former Soviet Union, Pakistan, and Sri Lanka).[16] These bodies would generally coordinate assistance to, and cooperation with, local authorities involved in privatization. In this way, advisers could supervise more closely the implementation of privatization according to World Bank or OECD standards. While these advisory groups were created ad hoc for each country, they also contributed to a broader spread of neoliberal principles, as they often supported large-scale privatization and market liberalization.[17]

The influence of foreign advisers in the economic transformation of former socialist countries varied across the spectrum, as indeed local governments and experts revised, translated, and at times rejected foreign models. While the situation on the ground of "transitioning" economies looked much less uniform than what critics of the Washington Consensus believed, as indeed varieties of postsocialist transformation emerged across central and eastern Europe, international financial institutions did play a significant role in shaping market-oriented transformations.[18] This was particularly the case in the former Yugoslavia, and even more so in Bosnia and Herzegovina, where the promises of postsocialism clashed most evidently: on one hand, the promise of nationalism, of rewards and reform, of a new nationalist strong state, as we saw in chapter 5, pushed for a mass distribution of ownership rights. On the other hand, the neoliberal promise of doing away with the state, of rebuilding through the economy (rather than through the nation), proposed a radically different ownership framework for large enterprises.

The End of Alternatives and a New Global Promise

The wars of the 1990s had left Yugoslavia destroyed, indebted, and subjected to high rates of emigration. Conditions for economic recovery were very different from what had been the case for other socialist countries in the region. The utmost necessity was to secure economic stability as a further guarantee of the peacebuilding process. As a result, across former Yugoslav republics and in Bosnia in particular, foreign intervention for economic reconstruction—from donations to infrastructural projects and privatization programs—came to be ingrained in the peacebuilding process. After the ratification of the Dayton Peace Agreement in 1995, international institutions like the International Monetary Fund (IMF) and the World Bank implemented reconstruction programs of "liberal peacebuilding": a set of reforms that simultaneously sought to reestablish the rule of law, consolidate democratization processes, and ensure stable economic rebuilding. Empowered by the apparent success of the large-scale reforms implemented in Poland, Hungary, and the Czech Republic, international financial and development institutions like the EBRD, the World Bank, and the United States Agency for International Development (USAID) pursued a hands-on approach to the economic reconstruction package envisaged for the former Yugoslavia. Especially in Bosnia and Herzegovina, the institutions overseeing the peace implementation process became increasingly involved in steering economic reforms. Peacebuilding was construed not just as post-conflict stabilization but as a much larger operation of political and economic reforms.[19]

The imperative for the former Yugoslavia was to rebuild and "catch up" with the economies of a newly formed liberal order in eastern Europe. In this context, the role of advisers from key international financial institutions grew substantially, as they provided legitimacy to government-led privatization policies through their role as consultants or by directly being involved in the shaping of privatization measures.[20] The latter case was most evident in Bosnia and Herzegovina, where privatization was carried out under the supervision of the high representative, the EU envoy tasked with the implementation of the Dayton Peace Agreement on the ground.[21] After proceeding with the most urgent infrastructural reconstruction, the Peace Implementation Council (the international organ tasked with coordinating the Dayton Peace Agreement's implementation) and the major international donors (the World Bank, EBRD, and USAID) started to put pressure on local governments to approve fast mass privatization. The program of reforms followed a change of scale in the rationale for development: growth and reconstruction could be delivered by strengthening the small private sector. With international assistance, in 1998 Bosnia was granted a three-year USD 5.1 billion Priority Reconstruction Program, which called for financial and technical support for private sector development.[22] In drafting growth and development strategies, these institutions approached Bosnia's situation as they would other developing countries in need of humanitarian and economic aid. It was key for the country to exit poverty and restart its economic path to market-led transformation, following models brought from abroad.

The developmentalist ethos of international institutions like the World Bank or EBRD was evident in this approach: Bosnia's reconstruction could be mapped along development phases. Though in need of immediate aid, Bosnia's technological and economic infrastructure presented important differences from other small developing countries: strategic enterprises already existed, and the country could be integrated within a regional market. Markets and companies did not have to be built anew but needed to be radically transformed. A significant share of the World Bank's financial and technical assistance focused on creating a favorable environment for private sector development, privatizing socially owned and state-owned assets and supporting SMEs' growth.[23] The reconstruction program was thus meant to deliver on the new global promise of SME-led growth and development: Bosnia was to abandon the "étatist economic attitudes of the past" and get rid of large state-owned enterprises, which were seen as a source of economic inefficiency, corruption, clientelism, overemployment and noncompetitiveness on the world market.[24] Under the coordination of the Office of the High Representative, an International Advisory Group for Privatization (IAGP) was established in Bosnia.[25] This body, which included most international agencies and donors, had a strong mandate to coordinate and proceed with the privatization of strategic enterprises—in other words, companies of "significant importance for the Bosnian economy"—which would be sold to strategic partners and investment funds.[26] The majority of large formerly socialist enterprises, many of which had constituted the core of the Bosnian exporting sector, were selected as "strategic" for the Bosnian economy and were privatized under the supervision of USAID and the World Bank.[27] The primary objective of privatization in Central and Eastern Europe was, for the World Bank, to break the link between the public political apparatus and the economic or financial sphere. Large state-owned enterprises were the embodiment of such a link and therefore should be broken down and privatized. Only in this way, the World Bank and IMF still argue, is it possible to restructure these large complexes properly.[28]

The IAGP's first go-to solution was to break apart these large conglomerates and privatize them separately, thus supporting the development of SMEs. As state institutions did not have the capacity to invest in enterprises, and as the main objective was to delink companies from state support and find private capital to be invested in them, scaling down seemed like a good strategy to attract (foreign) direct investments to these companies. The smaller units would be easier to handle: the profitable ones would be privatized or restructured; the unprofitable declared bankrupt. This fragmentation was a common response in central and eastern Europe during and after transformation.[29] In fact, large state-owned companies symbolized the last stronghold of an old communist mentality, a widespread opinion among advisers at the IMF, World Bank, and Office of the High Representative. The Swedish diplomat and special envoy to Yugoslavia Carl Bildt wrote in his memoirs that in Bosnia "there was a tendency to believe that all the old companies and structures could function again, once their buildings and machinery were repaired. The war had destroyed the physical structures of the economy, but not always the mental structures of state planning and socialism."[30]

The aim of privatization reforms was thus not just to consolidate the private sector; rather, they were meant to have a much broader, transformative effect on people's mindsets and attitudes. Under the tenure of High Representative Paddy Ashdown (2002–2006), the breaking apart of large enterprises and their transformation into SMEs gained further traction. The former British diplomat and leader of the Liberal Democrats in the late 1980s was one of the main supporters of this turn: during his mandate, he created the so-called Bulldozer Initiative, a set of reforms drafted partly in collaboration with local businesses, aimed at creating a business-friendly environment for SMEs.[31] During a lengthy interview we recorded in his residence in London, Ashdown recalled:

> I was very influenced in this by what happened in my own community of Yeovil [United Kingdom] two years after I became an MP in 1985 . . . it is called the Westland crisis. Westland was a company which built helicopters, and my community was entirely dependent [on it]; this became the object of a political battle between Michael Heseltine and Margaret Thatcher . . . the effect was that this firm lost eight thousand jobs . . . so as a young MP I went around working with the district council, working with others to create small businesses into which they could go. And instead of unemployment rising, unemployment stayed stable, and we began to generate a whole new basis for our economic success . . . so in a way what I was trying to do was replicate

> that . . . We began the process to make Bosnia and Herzegovina's economy
> a European style economy rather than a post-communist one . . . so I found
> myself doing in Bosnia what I had opposed under Mrs. Thatcher's govern-
> ment. But she was right, so [in Bosnia] I had to tear down the old communist
> business-destructing structures.[32]

This quote gives us an insight into the rationale of one of the central orga-
nizers of privatization in the early 2000s. For Ashdown, large enterprises
in Bosnia were a malfunctioning legacy of the communist period, much as
those in the UK had been a legacy of the nationalizing labor governments:
both eras were characterized by business-unfriendly regulation, which he
set to change. As a middle-income country in need of economic development and transformation, Bosnia could look to the UK as a form of inspiration or a model. Ashdown recognized that Bosnia, in his view, had
the potential to achieve economic growth and progress if it revitalized, or
transformed, its economic structures. In his view, the only way of effectively replacing large inefficient enterprises was through the development
of private SMEs. This juxtaposition of *European* and *postcommunist* is quite
telling of the international advisers' understanding of the Bosnian economy. The mentality that tied a vision of growth, development, and employment to large enterprises had to be dismantled here as in the rest of eastern
Europe. The structures, experiences, or legacies of each country were dismissed in the face of the need for rapid reform. This was not the case just
in the Office of the High Representative: by its own admission, the World
Bank did not hold a great deal of specialist knowledge of the workings of
centrally planned economies, nor did it employ specialists to take part in
advisory missions in "transitioning" countries.[33]

Despite recognizing that Bosnia had a robust industrial sector, international advisers understood it as a legacy of the socialist system subsidizing
its industries, which were now unable to compete on a global market that
had changed greatly since the late 1980s. After the war, as much had to be
rebuilt, Bosnian industries were not thought of as able to compete on the
global market. Bosnia was now in the periphery of the world economy, occupying "simultaneously a peripheral, marginal, and post-colonial position":
whatever preexisting international contact its enterprises had established
was not valuable in this new context.[34] Indeed, several consultants and institutions viewed state- and socially owned enterprises as "ill-equipped"
to participate in the market economy.[35] As the former high representative
Carl Bildt remarked in his memoirs, "It was important to make it clear that

our efforts did not involve reconstruction, as many aspects of the economy that had been destroyed by war would have been demolished in any case by international competition in the global economic transformation process. It proved difficult to gain acceptance of this idea."[36] Again, this reflection reveals an understanding of Bosnian enterprises' global aspirations as nothing more than a leftover of the socialist mentality, something that did not fit the new promise of prosperity and growth through the small, private, local sector as envisioned by international advisers.

As the US ambassador and deputy high representative Donald Hays stated in 2004, the orientation of economic policymakers in postwar Bosnia was mistakenly centered on seeking to revive production in the large industrial conglomerates that had been the pillars of Yugoslavia's economy: "Pre-war Bosnia and Herzegovina enjoyed a kind of heavy-industry golden age—or at least the illusion of one. People whose careers were built in that golden age naturally wanted to recreate it—so they channeled their energies into getting the old industrial combines back on their feet. They failed, of course, because history had moved on and left this industrial network disconnected and irrelevant."[37]

A sense of teleological predetermination comes through in this speech: history had moved on (and away) from a former socialist country like Bosnia, which had to catch up on the path to modernization, now paved with new ideas of (small) development. The underlying assumption was that socialist "giants" were neither technologically advanced nor apt to compete on the global market: only privatization and scaling down would improve their competitiveness.[38] While it is true that these companies were much less profitable than other large Western companies even at the time of socialist Yugoslavia, the fact that they had covered market niches in the developing world, in which they often had held a competitive advantage over their Western counterparts, was not considered to be an asset: the Global South, after all, was itself in need of development and so was not considered a reliable economic partner.[39] While some development agencies recognized that "Bosnia's economy was closely integrated with the other Yugoslav Republics, and had strong external ties with trading partners in Europe, the U.S., and the former USSR," they also noted that most of these ties had been disrupted as a consequence of the war and should not be a priority in enterprise reconstruction.[40]

Global aspirations did not belong to the economic landscape of a small peripheral country like Bosnia, which now had to focus on "small" development. As a result, the destiny of the few large export-oriented enterprises like Energoinvest was not to be reintegrated as competitors in the world market but to be restructured and privatized as smaller companies of a small economy in the European periphery. The promise of new growth and development entailed a tension between global market integration, which implies the ability to scale up and be competitive, and privatization needs, which imply fragmenting and getting rid of unproductive parts. The result for many large enterprises was a shrinking of their global horizon, a peripheralization of their market aspirations, as they could at best aspire to gain a presence in the regional market.[41] Bosnia's European future—which, in the words of Fedja Burić, was "frequently promised, but always delayed"—stood firmly on the country's reconstruction as a small regional economy.[42] Therefore, the very construction of the socialist "global" or "internationalist" project as intrinsically flawed was thus crucial to the way the country's economic reconstruction was conceptualized. When advisers at the World Bank, USAID, and the Office of the High Representative considered the economic collapse of the late 1980s as evidence of the socialist regime's inability to adapt to new developments in the global economy, they came to accept the de facto reperipheralization of the Bosnian economy and its major exporters as part of a new natural world order. Returning (post)socialist Southeastern Europe to its condition of semiperipherality in the capitalist world system also meant pushing its citizens into a condition of marginality: a "return to Europe," yes, but as peripheral subjects.[43] As much as in Poland, Russia, or Romania, viewing the collapse of socialism as an opportunity to return these economic systems to the "normality" of Europe was a conscious, political choice, and one that had very real consequences for millions of people.[44]

Deindustrialization and Postwar Reforms

The Yugoslav "global" promise clashed with the "neoliberal" one on several aspects; the most fundamental difference pertained to the intended fate of core enterprises after the collapse of state socialism. These conflicting models of reform significantly shaped Energoinvest and its reconstruction after the war. The company had been severely damaged during the conflict: by 1995, roughly 90 percent of its physical capital was destroyed, and it employed less than 10 percent of its prewar capacity.[45] The priority for the management was the absorption of its large unemployed workforce and the subsequent reconstruction of factories and research centers. At the start of privatization in December 1999, the overall capital of Energoinvest amounted to roughly BAM 240 million, with a state capital share of 94.77 percent.[46] Energoinvest was organized as a core company taking care of engineering and marketing, with nineteen subsidiary companies where Energoinvest held a capital share of 30 percent, 60 percent, or 70 percent (the rest being in state hands). In these years, the company was restructured so it could adjust to market orientation and secure a higher degree of independence for single companies while centralizing some functions in the central company in Sarajevo. Although they were technically Energoinvest's property, the firms that had been part of the corporation but whose legal location was in Republika Srpska were no longer under Energoinvest's direct jurisdiction.[47] The then prime ministers of Republika Srpska and the Federation of Bosnia-Herzegovina (FBiH), Gojko Kličković and Edhem Bičakčić, respectively, reached an informal agreement that the co-ownership between the FBiH and Republika Srpska would be written off.[48] The strategic subsidiary companies of Energoinvest were offered to foreign investors via tender privatization for a value of roughly BAM 140 million. The reason for this choice was primarily connected to the difficulty in finding internal bidders with sufficient capital available for the privatization of such large enterprises.[49] Most of the buyers were collective or privatization investment funds (PIFs), foreign banks, or private citizens—usually with some political or management role. Workers participated only indirectly in this process, by investing their shares in privatization funds.[50]

The ethnicization of property did not just pertain to the realm of individual ownership rights; it also shaped how large conglomerates like Energoinvest were privatized.[51] In fact, by mid-1998 two separate privatization frameworks were implemented in Republika Srpska and the FBiH, with decision-making being fully decentralized.[52] This meant, for example, that Energoinvest's most profitable oil refineries and extraction facilities in Republika Srpska (Rafinerija Bosanski Brod and Birač-Zvornik), which amounted to the value of approximately BAM 160 million, were under the control of the Republika Srpska, while the central engineering company and much of its extraction factories remained in the FBiH.[53] Thus, former workers of Energoinvest could expect to receive vouchers corresponding to shares of the overall entity capital only insofar as they were citizens of either entity. Then, they could invest such vouchers solely in those Energoinvest daughter companies that had remained under the jurisdiction of the entity of which they were residents. Several instances of exclusion from property rights on the basis of ethnicity emerged in Energoinvest and its former factories. In the case of the aluminum factory Birač in Zvornik (Republika Srpska), which in 1989 belonged to the Energoinvest group and could count on an export of USD 312 million, the shareholding rights of Bosnjak workers (4.5% of capital) purchased before the war simply disappeared in the company's postwar privatization.[54] During interviews and informal conversations, these cases were brought up as evidence of how entangled local nationalist interests were with corrupt privatization practices. These were discussed, not as examples of ethnic discrimination per se, but as additional evidence of political interests in denying workers their shareholding rights.

In the following years, numerous attempts at privatization failed because of a combination of mismanagement, corruption, and a lack of investment flow. A variety of factors converged on this failure: First, some of the core profitable companies set to be privatized according to the IAGP plan went bankrupt and were liquidated for a fraction of their original value; during the process, thousands of workers lost their jobs.[55] Second, corruption scandals had tainted these sales, as local buyers did not restore production as promised but rather sold the land to construction developers.[56] Third, there had been a significant misreading, on the side of international advisers, of what was necessary for these factories to start production again. For example, one of Energoinvest's subsidiary companies produced switchgears for electric and nuclear power plants for partners in Libya and Cuba. It relied on the central branch to maintain trade relations, place its orders, update research and technology, and so forth. Breaking this link with the mother company, as decided by international advisers, made it extremely difficult to continue production for the foreign market. While unprofitable subsidiaries were indeed in dire need of restructuring and owed years of unpaid salaries to their workers, their privatization as single units detached from the central branch signified for them a loss of global networks and partnerships.[57] As a result, this kind of privatization did not reverse the deindustrialization of Bosnia's export sector but instead deepened it. Whatever had not been wiped out by the war quickly decayed at the hands of privatization.

Enduring Reforms and the Resurfacing of Global Ties

As a prerequisite to obtain World Bank assistance, international experts specialized in tender privatization ("dealmakers") were hired by local governments to assist in selling state-owned enterprises to strategic local and foreign investors and would have the power to steer privatization reforms toward outcomes more agreeable to donors.[58] A group of independent economists from the Universities of Sarajevo, Banja Luka, and Mostar—who had been involved in the Marković reforms—were vocal in criticizing Bosnia's development strategy, and they challenged the unquestioning acceptance of unemployment, the stimulation of export, privatization, and financial liberalization as the only solution to the country's economic woes.[59] Economic and legal experts contested the unclear privatization process, which they claimed did not take into account the fact that workers' shareholding was in many ways the "most acceptable model of privatization" because it considered and valued the contribution of workers in creating what had constituted the social property.[60]

In an op-ed in Bosnia's mostly widely circulated newspaper, *Oslobodjenje*, Professor Momir Čečez of the University of Sarajevo argued that "the state should be involved in the market. Not a single country has developed without the help of the state, not even the U.S.A."[61] Though they had been critical of an excessive involvement of the state in economic affairs in the 1980s, local experts were equally wary of a complete withdrawal of the state from the economic sphere. Professor Anto Domazet, the dean of the Economics Faculty and a former manager of Energoinvest, was involved in a research project with UNDP and worked closely with both local governments and international advisers. At the end of our lengthy interview in his Sarajevo study, he concluded bitterly:

> All in all, the basic problem in Bosnia and Herzegovina is that the governments always relied on the international community for consultations. We [local experts] have been treated like waste. "We have our consultants," they said, "who are a product of the market economy. They have experience. Why risk it with the local people?"[62]

For local economists, postwar neoliberal reforms came to signify a loss of intellectual and political autonomy and prestige. These economists were embittered by their exclusion from political life in general and from a rather influential position in the reforms project.

Clashes between international advisers and local experts did not just pertain to the realm of macroeconomic policy but affected the very transformation of Energoinvest. The IAGP's promotion of the fracturing of the company into smaller units—a profitable core of three or four companies and a multitude of unprofitable factories—alarmed Energoinvest's management, and its members began criticizing the international community's privatization plans. The management board, with the support of the union and the workforce, proposed a different kind of restructuring of the company as a whole instead of smaller units and denounced that the IAGP had intervened and ignored this crucial insight.[63] Managers employed all kinds of health metaphors and corporeal analogies to point out the shortcomings of the IAGP's plan.

In one of the first public meetings between the government and the management board in 1996, Božidar Matić, a former managing director, declared, "We want to show that the biggest value of Energoinvest is *its position in the world market*. In the process of privatization, Energoinvest should be accepted as a whole, as one organism that has grown for 45 years. Like an organism, it can carry diseases, but a cure can be found. However, a body cut into pieces cannot be brought back to life."[64]

Health metaphors described Energoinvest as a unified body whose success was destined as long as its corporeal integrity was preserved. Matić often employed these health metaphors, defining nationalism as the cancer of society. In an interview right after the IAGP proposition to dismember Energoinvest in September 2000, Mesud Čaušević, the deputy general director of Energoinvest, declared, "That would destroy us. It would be the same as if someone cut off one of our legs and made us run."[65] The rest of the management was also outraged by this decision, commenting that the separation of subsidiary companies was "as if a doctor suggested the amputation of the heart to a patient that had just suffered a heart attack."[66] The management of smaller factories was mostly in favor of either internal privatization—in other words, the purchase of shares by employees—or sale to foreign investors. The latter option was viable only insofar as the investors had enough capital to restructure and revive production, with the condition that they would remain within the Energoinvest's consortium.[67]

Managers' dissatisfaction with the IAGP's planned privatization was, much like that of economic experts, articulated on two levels. First, this form of privatization entailed a loss of decision-making power and relevance in the company and threatened the status, benefits, and control of the "old guard" of managers. Privatizing Energoinvest as a unicum rather than a set of splintered companies would have left managers like Božidar Matić at the center of decision-making and control. As was the case in other postsocialist countries, the fragmentation of companies dislodged managers from elite positions; even if they maintained leadership, as Vlahovljak did, this was within much smaller and less important enterprises than in socialist times.[68] Second, and in conjunction with this, party influence (or lack thereof) was a key element in the criticism of the new management, which was installed directly by the government. Much as local economists' criticism of privatization entailed a reevaluation of the state as a key actor of macroeconomic development, managers found themselves with an ambivalent position toward the role of state control within the company. Although they had criticized the clunky mechanism of socialist self-management and the overbearing presence of the party-state, they reconsidered this presence as orderly and expectable in comparison with the volatile political pressures of the postsocialist system.

For some, like former director Džemajl Vlahovljak, the higher degree of control exerted by the Communist Party in combination with the institutions of self-management fared better than what, in his view, was the overbearing presence of political parties in the postwar company:

> [In socialist times] you had a workers' council that appointed the director and to which the director answered. You had a so-called self-governing worker control that supervised all of this together within the company. You had a trade union that also saw all that as its own, so it's not that, that means the members of the trade union were at the same time the owners of all that, of course you also had a party organization that was all that, at that time the League of Communists, that controlled all that. So the director was under constant, so to speak, some monitoring of those organs . . . I'm not saying that ownership was more efficient, that's another story, but in any case, the management was better controlled and supervised than in state ownership [what it is right now]. Now you have a combination of management, supervisory board, and political party.[69]

Vlahovljak's political orientation as a former Communist and part of the social democratic, antinationalist wing of Bosnian postwar politics of course informed this consideration. At the time of our interview, Energoinvest was mostly state owned and influenced by the then Party of Democratic Action (SDA) ruling majority. His comments reveal an awareness of the paradox of transformation: in the postsocialist context, the complex structure of semi-privatized companies under partial state ownership entailed a less transparent and more volatile political influence on the companies' management. His assessment echoed the clash, typical of the socialist era, between the political and the technocratic as sources of influence and advancement within the company. For the managers who did not hold political positions within the new ethnonationalist parties, the main problem was not only the political control coming from an opposing government but the fact that this would come without checks and balances and without the relevant technocratic expertise that the managers could embody. The marginalization of a corporate culture that valued them as beholders of the technical skills necessary to steer the company through privatization overlapped with the sense of loss for a society that valued different modes of political patronage.

In the years after the IAGP-led privatization of the company, workers became increasingly dissatisfied with their conditions. In June 2008, roughly eight thousand of them protested the precarious living conditions caused by the process of privatization and the bankruptcy of their firms.[70] Dževad recalls his motivations as follows:

> We wanted to stay in Energoinvest because we did not have our own system for the foreign market, so we needed people who could sell our product. . . . And they took that away from us, like when they cut the umbilical cord that keeps a baby tied to the mother.[71]

Much like managers, workers too employed health and family metaphors to illustrate the kinds of transformation their companies had endured. Many referred to "transition" (*tranzicija*) as having signified the death of their companies, which were deprived of their "lifeblood" in the form of access to the global market. Mladen, an engineer for Energoinvest's information technology branch, bitterly noted that his company had been "killed with a purpose" by new owners only interested in its real estate value.[72] These references and metaphors reveal the sense of attachment that bound employees to the microcosm of work life in the former Yugoslavia. Grappling with the very real prospect of financial and material ruin, workers and managers reverted to a language of visceral trauma, a testament to the significance that deindustrialization (and peripheralization) had in their lives. They had learned to cherish Energoinvest's competitiveness in the global market, as it entailed experiences of international prestige and domestic prosperity. The promise of global relevance and integration still resonated among workers and managers; it carried such an imaginative power that people likened it to the lifeblood of their company, a collective body of which they felt an integral part.

Contrary to what international advisers in the USAID viewed as a company with no market future, managers in the Sarajevo central branch valued Energoinvest's international contacts and sought to revive them through the central branch. This was a much smaller company, with about five hundred to a thousand employees, roughly ten times less than its prewar workforce. The resurfacing of global ties was a necessity for two reasons: first, to recuperate what the company was owed from before the war and, second, to restart trading and production with world partners. Several managers of Energoinvest tried to establish consortia with local and regional banks to claim back the debt the company was owed from several developing countries, such as Congo, Cuba, Iraq, Ethiopia, and Syria. As many of these countries had defaulted on their debts several times or experienced civil war and unrest, it had been particularly difficult for Energoinvest to enforce their claims. At the same time, investigations have shown that the postwar directors of Energoinvest sold the debt for a fraction of their value to international "vulture funds" or simply settled them to recuperate a much smaller sum than what was owed.[73] When asked about this during our interviews, directors and finance experts from Energoinvest became particularly defensive or visibly uncomfortable if not slightly hostile. They often diverted the question to the issue of the financial and economic instability of the debtor countries. According to Dževad Ganić, the former assistant for financial affairs to the general director, Nedžad Branković, it had been difficult to reclaim debts from Cuba, as by the mid-2010s the country had still not repaid the billions in Bosnian currency in commercial loans it had borrowed since the 1970s.[74] Even in instances when Energoinvest did win court cases against indebted countries, there was little room to actually enforce such decisions, director Džemajl Vlahovljak complained. Nevertheless, the rather fuzzy ways in which these debts were handled, and the accusations of corruption that came as a result, significantly compromised the trust that workers had in their management, contributing to a wider sense of despair and distrust toward the new outlook of Energoinvest after the war.

In terms of recuperating trading ties, Energoinvest fared a little better. Between 2002 and 2005, the central management secured agreements for the construction of electrical substations and power lines in Libya, Algeria, and Ethiopia for EUR 25 million, 6 million, and 2 million, respectively.[75] Using the business contacts Energoinvest had established as a Yugoslav company in the 1970s, they signed new business deals in North and Central Africa and Iraq. At the end of 2003, for the first time since the war, they had a positive balance with a net profit of roughly EUR 50 million, with contracts including the General Electric Company of Libya and Electrical Project Company (ELPCO), which was a joint company in which the Libyan government owned 51 percent and Energoinvest owned 49 percent, established in the mid-1970s.[76] These contracts were maintained throughout the late 2000s, with new electroengineering construction contracts in Congo and Tunisia. By the end of 2009, Energoinvest had a net profit of EUR 3.5 million and employed 843 people, half of whom were highly qualified.[77] To reach these results, connections built in times of Yugoslav internationalism resurfaced: they served as the main currency of Energoinvest's global relevance. Their resurfacing as a tool for business purposes and a foundation for the company's reconstruction exemplified the desire to return to the promise of globality as conceived during its initial international expansion. Several directors of postwar Energoinvest whom I interviewed remarked on the importance that the few joint ventures with foreign partners had for the company's international business and contacts. Often, international conferences and meetings were also occasions for rekindling with foreign partners after the hiatus of the war. The former director Džemajl Vlahovljak recalls:

> Many people had come [to Yugoslavia] to study with stipends in our universities. So we created many friends in those countries . . . they returned to Iraq, Syria, Tanzania, Congo, so afterward we had someone who speaks Bosnian over there. The source of our knowledge and connections were these big international conferences, symposia, etc., and above all for that was the International Council on Large Electric Systems [CIGRE]. And there we met every year with many representatives of different countries, and of course people from the Third World countries came, to see how to develop energy and power lines. So even now we use this conference as a platform for our exchanges.[78]

Some of the business connections that had been created during the socialist times were indeed conducive to the restarting of these partnerships. Working in tandem with other partners in the region, Energoinvest was able to retrieve some of its former outreach in Africa and the Middle East by virtue of the long-term contacts it had established in the past. In 2017, the company brokered business deals with partners in Algeria and Tanzania for the construction of power plants and power connections, each of which was estimated at around EUR 50 million.[79]

These were remnants of the concrete implications of the Yugoslav global promise as it took shape within enterprises. Workers and managers had been deeply invested in the project of constructing relatively functional alternatives that would reconcile markets with people while maintaining options for global integration. They felt pushed away from this sense of global centrality in the context of postwar, postsocialist reforms, and it was the denial of a globality they once had that constituted one of the main foundations of their identity. Rejecting privatization and neoliberal reforms was, in a way, a rejection of a world without alternatives.

7

BOUND BY PROMISES

Narratives and Experiences of the Workplace Across Reforms

Tʜɪs ᴄʜᴀᴘᴛᴇʀ ᴇxᴀᴍɪɴᴇs ᴛʜᴇ ʀᴇsɪᴅᴜᴀʟ ɪɴᴅᴜsᴛʀɪᴀʟ sᴛʀᴜᴄᴛᴜʀᴇ ᴏғ expectations that emerged in my interlocutors' accounts as they reflected on, and made sense of, the transformation that consumed their company and working lives. In the case of Energoinvest, this (industrial) structure of expectations is molded by the constant tension between the promise of globality, the argument for reforms, and the experience of deindustrialization. The global promise constructed by Energoinvest's vision of the world, shaped through its global aspirations and non-aligned connections, defined not only the space of experience but also the horizon of expectation for those employed there. Similarly, the prospect of transformed ownership regimes refashioned people's visions of their role in the "reformed" workplace. These sentiments informed and constructed people's expectations and extended well into the postindustrial period as a linking factor within the community of workers.[1]

To understand how people mediate between the lost socialist values and the sense of decay associated with postsocialism, it is important to consider the role of expectations and promises in generating narratives of change. It was not just the legacy of life under state socialism but its promise of prosperity that created tensions between experiences and expectations during the period of transformation. Similarly, a cognitive dissonance between what was expected of market transformation and the experience of it characterizes most accounts of this period. This tension between the promises of change and the experience of transformation, I argue, generates a specific "structure of expectations." This notion builds on that of the structure of feeling—a set of sentiments shaped by a distinct historical experience that "gives sense to a generation or a period."[2] This structure of expectation reflects the historically contingent beliefs or projections of how change and transformation should pan out and which expectations are formed and acted upon.

Remembering and Reviving a Socialist Corporate Culture

During our first interview, Jakob Finci quoted a motto that, as he noted, workers at Energoinvest "all respected and were proud of": "We are Energoinvest's, and Energoinvest is ours."[3] This motto echoes the Yugoslav Communist Youth's "We are Tito's, Tito is ours" (*Mi smo Titovi, Tito je naš*) and is an excellent example of the diffusion of Yugoslavist ideas in the company. In the socialist period, in fact, it was common for workers to identify themselves with the name of their factories (*Tamovci* in the factory TAM, for example).[4] To this day, many workers still define themselves as *Energoinvestovci* (Energoinvest men). Zdravko, head of propaganda during the socialist period, defines what it meant for him to be an Energoinvestovac:

> It is that man who expresses loyalty toward his firm, for whom it is not irrelevant where he works, what's the name of his company . . . it was always like that, and it will always be.[5]

Here, Zdravko expresses an important view of the atemporality of the structure of expectations he associates with being part of this working collective. For most workers, historic time is clearly punctuated by a fault line—a "before" and "after" the fall of state socialism. They also reminisce fondly about the prevalence of certain values that defined their workplace and imbued their work with a deeper, almost spiritual, meaning and ethics. His remark highlights the need for a different kind of temporality, one that demands a sense of immutability in time passing, a desire to reaffirm an element of continuity in the face of change. Indeed, the pride they derived from it remains pervasive in the way workers and managers refer to their memories at Energoinvest. When asked what it meant to be an Energoinvestovac, Dževad replied:

> Oh, that was an honor. And still today it is an honor to be an Energoinvest man, only that today we behave differently, there is not the same morality and quality of people that there was before.[6]

Dževad's remark shows the importance, for him, of a set of moral values that he sees being marginalized in his workplace today—although only in part. His account memorializes a relatively stable workplace culture, intelligible to its members. However, workers' reflections on the moral quality of their former workplaces don't come without criticism. They do not necessarily claim that "this was a static or indeed perfect world. Rather, that relative stability and order gave the workplace a predictability that allowed a certain moral order to emerge and be reproduced."[7]

Most of my interlocutors connected the feelings of domesticity, security, and commonality to another important feature of their company: its position in the global market. Non-alignment was very much an actor's category, one that contained a mnemonic overlap between one's work and the contribution this made to the global socialist project. Feelings of pride and security were linked to the company's stability and notoriety as a global player. Having orders coming in from abroad and producing something for the foreign market created more of a sense of prestige among workers, who saw their role as carriers of the socialist project further legitimized: having foreign companies or states request their services and products, signing contracts and deliveries for several years, gave my interlocutors a sense of security and stability in their work and, as many commented, their lives. The more specialized production was—as in the case of TDS-Sarajevo, a company that produced components for power-transmission lines, over 90 percent of which were destined for the foreign market—the more workers manifested pride in being connected to this world.[8] The fact that these components would be destined for the electrical and petrol-chemical industries across the globe, as well as nuclear power plants in the Soviet Union, was associated with a sense of prestige: in the words of my interlocutors, it was "Yugoslav workers solving Soviet problems."[9]

Asim, a shop-floor worker at TDS, added that he felt proud because his job and livelihood were guaranteed:

> You know, when you have the market, it means you have a job. Your own salary is guaranteed. . . . If you have a market to deliver, that means you are provided with a five-, ten-year plan to do some work in advance. . . . Do you know what it means when you have a job in advance for two, three years? . . . When you have five months now, it's enough, but you won't have five years of a job guaranteed in advance.[10]

These kinds of reflections reveal two important features of the industrial structure of expectations shared by the workers I interviewed for this research: First, the stability and prosperity of one's job are immediately linked to the international outlook of one's workplace. Second, the market is associated with expectations of stability for one's job and one's very existence. Referring to the market as a bringer of stability and prestige may seem contradictory here: after all, markets fluctuate and are much more volatile than planned economies. In their reflections, workers often mentioned "the market" and "plan" almost interchangeably—as Asim did. For him, the market was understood in its literal sense: a global arena where the goods he produced would be circulated. The laws guiding this circulation, however, were very much those of planning, as his factory delivered most of its goods to partners in countries predominantly organized as planned economies. In a few sentences, Asim's remark encapsulates the complex dynamics of Yugoslavia's business operations: its companies walked a fine line between market and socialism, operating with a degree of independence within a system that was coordinated by planning and intrastate bilateral agreements. Producing for the foreign market was perceived to be a prestigious activity because it depended more on a market demand that they perceived to be less artificial than what the socialist state would impose in a purely planned economic system. Thus, Asim and his colleagues' understanding of "the market" was twofold: they saw it as a signifier of prestige and competitiveness and also a provider of security. Both the space of experience and the horizons of expectations were marked by the geographical reach of the company as a marker of stability. It was with these kinds of projections in mind that many workers approached the market reforms of the 1990s as something that would propel them toward stability rather than uncertainty.

Many interviewees associated their memories of stability in the workplace with socialist values and practices, in which they felt united in cooperation rather than divided by competition. Amila, an electrical engineer and then a cadre at Energoinvest, recalls the moments spent at Energoinvest with a sense of great affection for the socialist system that cemented unity within the collective:

> We were like a big family; I mean that we liked Energoinvest more than our own family, really! It was one collective, relaxed atmosphere, no competition. We were always together; we held sports games and other activities. . . . It was really a socialist system, in which we were happy.[11]

Here, Amila makes explicit the association between a sense of collective unity and the socialist system that fostered it. As several studies on workplace cultures in (post)socialist contexts have shown, workers used kin metaphors to describe labor relations in the firm, which was often depicted as a home or a mother with familial and benevolent attitudes, a provider of food, work, subsistence, and security for its "children."[12] This feeling of domesticity in the workplace, of being in one's second (or even first) home, was peppered throughout almost all of my conversations with former employees of Energoinvest. Even the pronouns workers used—*my* factory, *my* Energoinvest, *us* workers, *we* did, *we* worked, and so forth—denote the extent to which they were (and still are) attached to their workplace and its memory. For many of my interlocutors, the connection to their workplace fostered in them a strong attachment to the collectivist principles of Yugoslav socialism. "I must return to *our* socialism," explained Munevera, a technician in Energoinvest Sarajevo. She continued:

> This socialism means help, friendship [*drugarstvo*], and something similar, caring for other people. . . . I think it is difficult for young generations to understand what socialism is. I do not talk with nostalgia, but I talk about my own experience. . . . Back then you first looked at a person like a person [*čovjek kao čovjek*].[13]

Munevera's comment here is particularly interesting as she discusses a very personal understanding of socialism. We see here that her affect and attachment to her company are also intertwined with the virtue of its embodiment of Yugoslav socialist values, as she interpreted them. Mentioning nostalgia in a critical way, Munevera distances herself from those criticisms that would dismiss her recollection of socialism as "nostalgic." Her reflection could be viewed as what Fred Davis defined as "interpretative nostalgia," as she objectifies her sentiment and reflects on the emotion of nostalgia itself.[14] Furthermore, her reflection contains an implicit condemnation of an overly divided society, where ethnonational markers are what distinguish people. Her need to see "people as people," and not as ethnonational kin, is associated to a set of values that she views as minoritarian now but that was once (in socialist times) the norm.

Munevera was not dismissive of the party-state's role in shaping work and everyday life under socialism or its political control over internal company hierarchies. And yet, by explaining how important socialism was to her in overcoming political and ethnonationalist differences and seeing "people as people," she is making a profoundly political argument, a critique of the new post-Dayton order. In an extensive analysis of nostalgic cultures and practices in postsocialist Hungary, Maya Nadkarni has noted that feelings of nostalgia are associated with the longing for the absence of politics itself. Implicit in the nostalgia for the everyday life and material culture of socialism, she argues, is a reproduction of Hungary's ideological distinction between the private domestic sphere and the public world of politics.[15] Although in Yugoslavia this distinction was perhaps more implicit, Munevera's reflection partly hints at a desire to return to a workplace and everyday life that appeared devoid of politics.

The demise of the socialist workplace as a site of collective identity formation and as a point of reference for people's social structures has sparked important academic reflections on social memory and nostalgia.[16] In the post-Yugoslav context, as Tanja Petrović has noted, practices of recalling the socialist past under a positive light are often dismissed or delegitimized as irrational, unpatriotic, reactionary, and immoral; workers' fondness for the socialist "modernizing" project that provided welfare, job security, and a sense of dignity in work is dismissed as an inability to adapt to new circumstances.[17] Instead, workers' nostalgic narratives are partly an expression of despair at present conditions in which economic and social precarity prevail, partly a demand for normality and the expression of a need for continuity, and partly a strategy of the self to make sense of the present.[18]

This sentiment of nostalgia for a lost past of prosperity and community is not unique to the postsocialist condition, of course. Deindustrialization in the company towns of capitalist countries in western Europe and North America also sparked similar sentiments among working communities. Nostalgia for the kind of corporate culture based on industrial democracy and welfare capitalism that entered a phase of crisis and erosion in the 1970s has sparked important reflections on critical memory in these communities. Working communities, as Alice Mah observes, often have a feeling of "ambivalent nostalgia" for their working lives: they fondly remember having good jobs while being cognizant of the shortcomings of previous industrial structures and systems.[19] By reflecting a plurality of memories of the industrial golden age as a time of conflict and negotiation between corporate management and labor, for example, nostalgia becomes a source of community pride in the progressive values that shaped the industrial age, a vehicle to transcend the past and affect the future.[20] Moreover, nostalgia is not just a phenomenon that characterizes the junctural transformation to postindustrial societies. Rather, as Hannah Skoda's study of fourteenth-century Europe highlights, nostalgia is provoked by the perception of the "social acceleration of time" and by a sense of rupture and discontinuity. Nostalgic responses to cataclysmic changes can be "underpinned by societal resilience and by the sense that it is worth the mental effort to reimagine the future."[21] In this sense, it is important to consider contemporary nostalgia as a sentiment rooted in the major transformations of transnational capitalism, as something that emerges not only from the ruptures in the old industrial world order but also from its counterpoint, the transformations and accelerations of global capitalism. As Yanqiu Rachel Zhou notes, nostalgia is rooted in the time-space compression that results from globalization, as a source of major political and economic transformations that affect communities transnationally. In a way, the very fluidity of global changes invites a nostalgia for secure forms of world orders.[22]

Hierarchical Memories

Though passionate about the socialist collectivist values that underscored life in the Yugoslav workplace, my interlocutors were not uncritical of the many drawbacks of a self-managed workplace. After all, they belong to that "last Yugoslav [working] generation," who experienced the starkest contrast between expansion and contraction of their country's economy and its global project.[23] They recalled the effects of the economic crisis on their company, on their working lives, and on the dramatic trajectory of dissolution their country took as a result. At the same time, they talked fondly about the market reforms introduced by the last socialist government of Ante Marković as the apex of socialist reformism in their country and as a sincere opportunity to change their workplace for the better. Indeed, there is an ambivalent sense of nostalgia for a moment of great transformation and great potential: the late 1980s are, in people's memories, a moment when the gap between "what was" and "what could have been" is at its narrowest. Alfredo Sasso has termed this as "Antestalgija," a combination of Ante (Marković) and *nostalgia*—to indicate an "idealized projection of what a democratized Yugoslavia could have become."[24] Beyond propagandistic aspects, for a moment people touched firsthand what the reforms could have meant for them. Rather than being mere spectators of the crisis unfolding, workers had agency in making sense of the crisis and choosing consciously where to direct their support or criticism. It is through this sense of agency and relevance, I argue, that people find the most affinity with the Yugoslav reformist project. Glossing over the internal friction that emerged during the economic crisis may be a meaningful choice on the part of interviewees and should not be seen as simple false consciousness. Rather, it reveals a selective element in people's recollections, a process of hierarchical memory making in which certain aspects of the past occupy a more salient position as reference points for people's current values and demands.

Workers' ambivalence toward the socialist system of self-management is evident in their contemporary accounts as well and reveals an ongoing process of hierarchical memory making. Many of my interlocutors reserved critical or ironic remarks for the system of self-management. Šaban, a factory worker in an Energoinvest foundry in Tuzla, recalls:

> That system too had its defects. We would discuss for three hours in the workers' council, then we would receive a call from the top, and we would be told what decision to make. It would come from the [party] committee. The decision would be made already, and that would be it.[25]

Many recollect that workers' councils did not have real decision-making power when it came to management decisions: some workers were unhappy with self-management, and others thought that the working class never had any real power. Dževad remarked:

> I am telling you that was . . . That was the illusion of self-management, you know? And always in the firms there were people who [behaved] in this or that way, but the system functioned, you know? The system functioned, that hierarchy was known, that technological discipline was known, and there was a relatively small percent of those who, well, who dragged their feet in this or that way.[26]

Dževad's rendition of self-management as a well-operating and functional illusion is telling of workers' critical take toward the socialist system of self-management. Much as the promise of Yugoslav global socialism captivated workers, so did the illusion of equality provided by self-management contribute to establishing an orderly hierarchy within the workplace. Dževad's remark communicates that, even at that time, workers were aware of the superficial bindings of workplace democracy. Noting the powerful hierarchical structures that existed within the socialist workplace serves a double purpose: first, it was a way for him to take distance from a system that was heavily shaped by the party-state well within factories and workplaces; second, it is a way to recognize that, though problematic, such hierarchy was dependable, understandable, clear to everyone, and thus easy to read and navigate. In several interviews, the criticism of the lack of representation and convoluted decision-making in the system of self-management came always with words of praise for its capacity to foster a sense of community and collegiality among workers, as well as for its varying degree of influence over decisions on salaries and housing. Often in the same sentence, workers I interviewed expressed frustration as well as satisfaction with self-management. Words of critique were always subordinated and excused, as if to signal an existing hierarchy between what was more and less important to remember and to transmit to me.

To stress the importance of community and a shared feeling of ownership in today's postsocialist workplace, workers chose to recall their support for the Marković reforms, praising his proposal of workers' shareholding. These reforms codified their sense of attachment to their workplace and recognized it in legal terms. Munevera, for example, notes:

> At that time, we felt that the company was ours. Because that is where we collaborated, where were worked, and there we had the right to show our dissatisfaction and satisfaction. So it was normal that we cherished it as ours, basically as our workplace.[27]

Workers had been encouraged by the socialist definition of *social ownership* to view themselves as partakers of the factory ownership. This transformation was a step further, a legal recognition of their role as collective co-owners not only of the means of production but also of the capital produced. Thinking about the Marković reforms, Asim, a machine worker in TDS-Sarajevo, reflects:

> And that [reform] was OK because it was a contribution from the workers. Because we made these factories, I have made this factory myself, it has been built while I was working here. We allocated a part of our salaries for the construction of these factories, for their development. And so it was normal that I should have some participation in it, and that is why I got those shares.[28]

For them, it made sense that workers would be co-owners of their factories, as this resonated the most with their understanding of what social ownership was meant to be and what, in turn, workers' role in the workplace was. Mustafa had been a member of the company's union since his first employment in Energoinvest in the mid-1970s. He remembers that the Marković model

> was a very positive step. We accepted that in Energoinvest, and we registered the shares; we took part of our salary and took share participation in Energoinvest. That was a good solution, of course. The worker, the householder [*domaćin*], will be better at keeping his own house [than the state]. It would have been better like that.[29]

This kind of remark is persistent among workers reflecting on that period, and it reveals a common narrative of the Marković reforms as a transformation that gave factories to their rightful owners. Regardless of management rights, the past understanding of Energoinvest as belonging primarily to Energoinvestovci lingered. The workforce saw in shareholding an opportunity to accumulate additional resources in a context of significant financial instability. As Dževad, an engineer in a profitable Energoinvest factory, remarked:

> People thought that they would receive some benefits in a certain way, that they will be owners, and that they would be richer. It was not really whether a director or the state would be in a management position; they rather thought that through their ownership they would be a bit richer.[30]

To his eyes, then, Marković's project of "New Socialism" was the right combination of innovation and tradition. It gave breadth and legitimacy to their views as late-socialist worker-owners: critical of the dogmatisms of self-management and yet unwilling to demolish it completely. The promise of reformism, of a gradual progress toward a New Socialism—embodied in the Marković program—reduced the gap between the experience and expectation of ownership. Furthermore, Marković's formulation of market reforms as an opportunity to rejoin the global market from a position of reinvigorated strength broadened workers' horizons of expectations. Further integration into the global market, sustained by a reformed production and ownership system, seemed the most viable solution.

The tension emerging from the overlap of the promises of reform, the expectations of globality, and the reality of deindustrialization culminated in workers' narratives of marginalization and resistance. Workers still believed in the underlying principles of internationalism and collective ownership that had guided their economic aspirations. What they sought was, perhaps, not to throw the baby out with the bathwater but to simply change and improve the plumbing. These narratives constituted the core of that structure of expectations and sense of affect toward their company that had so vividly shaped their working lives. Workers might not have felt like managers, but they felt like owners. They might have feared the consequences of an unstable global market economy, but they did not wish to be removed from it. The promise of market reforms was also one of many adjustments to the new rules of the global market, where Energoinvest would have a renewed position as a holding corporation, a shareholders' company. This would attract foreign investors and partners, meaning potentially advantageous opportunities for workers. Hence, the promise of a reformed market socialism building a "new way" out of the crisis dovetailed with workers' feeling of ownership, their experiential affect toward factories, and their expectations of geopolitical relevance. As a result, the promise of reformism as a reboot of Yugoslavia's global aspirations has become the point of reference for many workers of the "transition" generation, shaping their recollection of the socialist and postsocialist period in a hierarchical fashion: the memory of what could have been with the Marković reforms, a combination of experiences and expectations, supersedes any ambivalence toward socialist self-management.

Fighting Back: Shares, Employment, and the Fleeting Global Promise

Retrieving workers' memories should not mislead one into viewing them as just witnesses of history and of the "end of work" that underscored the neoliberal turn. Rather, they were active participants in the historical transformations that affected their workplaces. The world of work and the narratives, values, and expectations associated with it were deeply transformed. Dominant narratives of deservingness and reward for war participation reshaped workplaces but also created ripples of contestation and rebellion against this transformation. Workplaces were at the same time the site of antinationalist and antiwar resistance, of divisions, of combatants, exclusion, and return. Although Energoinvest was an experiment designed in the internationalist and unifying image of the Yugoslav project, the Bosnian War did eventually pierce into the microcosm of the workplace and rip its fabric as well. After the war ended, workers returned to their workplaces, desperate to reconstruct their lives. Asim, a specialist worker in one of Energoinvest's industrial hubs in the Sarajevo suburb of Stup, remembers one of the first things he did after the war:

> So, after the war, there were around fifty of us, we went to clean up, to see if anything was left there. . . . There were the walls, some archives and papers, things that were not necessary. We cleaned everything from the garbage as well. "Come on," I was thinking. "We will go back; we will start working again."[31]

In the wake of unspeakable trauma and destruction, Asim and his colleagues hoped to revive a semblance of normalcy through the reconstruction of their workplaces. These industrial landscapes, though ruined, constituted for them the physical remnants of their working selves, but they also represented a symbolic order and meaning disrupted by the war. The experience of destruction, deindustrialization, and transformation was entangled with expectations of rebirth. Holding on to the physical space of the enterprise—within which people's sense of belonging had been interwoven through a narrative of industrialization first and resistance afterward—was often a way to mitigate or reverse a pervasive sense of loss.

It was in the spirit of hope and return, of rebuilding their lives, that workers began claiming their ownership rights again after the hiatus of voucher privatization. Although three and a half years of conflict had irreversibly changed companies, workplaces, and the socioeconomic landscape around them, workers had not forgotten that a property transformation had been initiated before the war. At a session of the parliament of the Federation of Bosnia-Herzegovina (FBiH) in 1996, for example, the president of the Trade Unions of Bosnia and Herzegovina remarked that workers—and especially demobilized soldiers—were "exceptionally interested in the privatization of companies . . . which they have built as workers during their whole working life."[32]

Many of those who had purchased their factory shares with the Marković reforms found out only upon return from the front line that their factories had been nationalized and that the record of previously purchased shares had in many cases been lost because of the war or negligence from the management's side. Although, in theory, the new privatization laws were supposed to guarantee the recognition of shares purchased under the Marković program, the state and the new management had little interest in acknowledging workers' shareholding, as it was deemed a messy and unprofitable solution. The lack of proper records of the reforms in 1990–1991 made the continuation of the shareholding model even more unlikely.[33] Expectations of reward for one's involvement in the war were reinforced by the first postwar privatization reforms, which distributed vouchers among the population.

When the Bosnian government renationalized most of its companies, the process included all property still listed as "social ownership." Often, this meant workers' own shares.[34] This policy created much resentment among workers, who saw in this shift the first of many betrayals on the side of the new postsocialist government. Sakib was an unemployed union member and veteran in Tuzla. He remarked:

> The social property was everyone's, yours, mine, his, and everybody's. The government changed it in 1994 in a very mysterious way. We were on the front

line, and they stole it from us workers. And when we came down from the mountains, the stealing continued; that was an economic war.[35]

Sakib's words here, his likening of what happened after the war to another kind of "economic war," reveal the shock and indignation he felt at seeing his shareholder's rights bulldozed. He felt deceived by a transformation that had happened behind his back while he was out on military conscription. Some workers even sent letters to the local privatization agency—the institution tasked with overseeing the privatization process—explaining that they had invested something to the tune of BAM 95,000 in the renewal of their company and asking for it to be converted into shares of the firm. As a way of further legitimizing their requests, they remarked that they were all demobilized soldiers seeking to buy their own company.[36] Asim, who used to work in TDS, one of the most successful factories in Energoinvest, recalls:

> [The Marković shares] disappeared; they simply were not there as if they had never existed. . . . It had all been transformed into state property. . . . While we worked and fought, they switched from social to state property so that they could sell our factories for peanuts.[37]

Much as in Sakib's recollection, in Asim's remark the anger toward the new political administration is palpable. Workers had mobilized in defense of a country that had promised to compensate them for their effort, to return their lives to the workplaces and communities they were jettisoned from.

The kind of postwar rhetoric of compensation and praise for veterans of the war that we saw in chapter 6 had created further expectations of reward, cementing workers' understanding that they were entitled to ownership of their factories. This rhetoric was adopted similarly in the two entities that constitute today's Bosnia, the FBiH and the Republika Srpska. Most workers I spoke to hold the state and the government accountable for not having fulfilled their promise. Omer, a factory worker in Energoinvest-Gradačac, said that he felt "horrible" when he thought about the relation of the state to soldiers and workers. He continued:

> It is like a stepmother that does not love her children. Most people who were in the war were workers, and they are still right now. They left their firms saying "Let's go and defend the country," and this is how they are repaid.[38]

Omer's metaphor illustrates the way many disenfranchised workers saw their relationship to the postwar state: the new state (i.e., independent, postsocialist Bosnia) was to him like a stepmother—that is, an acquired, nonbiological parent. His words indicate a distance but also an understanding of the state as a parental figure. However, the new state did not represent to him the bonds of care and trust associated with most parent-child relationships. It represented the absence of a parent, a lack of trust and common goals. It characterized the traumatic vulnerability that comes from estrangement in filial spaces. Moreover, he found it important to remark that most soldiers were workers. This reveals an implicit hierarchy that he views among those deserving of respect and compensation: already a pillar of the socialist society, the worker-fighter gained even more merit as he defended the country and the workplace. He found bitter disappointment in seeing those who left their companies seemingly spontaneously ("Let's go and defend the country") not being adequately compensated or having those companies snatched away while they answered the call to fight. He expected veterans *as workers*, and workers *as veterans*, to be better compensated, in terms of salaries, veteran pensions, and shares. This perhaps symbolizes another shock: that of realizing that the war had irreversibly changed people, communities, and places and discovering that returning to the life they had before the war was now impossible. These accounts highlight that shares are the materialization of an industrial structure of expectations, a tangible manifestation of the sentiments that shaped workplaces. Shares were a symbol of what tied workers to their sense of self, their place in society, and their glorification as veterans. As Elizabeth Dunn noted for women workers in a privatizing factory in Poland, invoking and mobilizing kin terms (workplace as a family, factory as a mother) was a way for workers to bring forms of social personhood into the workplace; this was an attempt to revalue their labor and reassert the primacy of work, jobs, wages, and autonomy over the new anonymized and exploitative forms of work, to reaffirm themselves as subjects of work rather than objects, as persons whose values and needs should be at the center of working lives.[39] Through emotional recollections of the postwar privatization years, my interlocutors expressed grief for the loss of both the legacy of past experiences and the futures they had hoped for. They were mourning the physical space of the workplace, seeing its ruins as a fading monument to their former status in the social order; at the same time, they lamented the ways in which their expectations of the future, which stood on the foundations of the past, went up in smoke, along with their fair share of decision-making power.

When the second phase of privatization commenced in 1998, international advisers recommended a fracturing of large conglomerates like Energoinvest, which would be privatized through the participation of private investors and privatization investment funds alike.[40] This meant that those workers of Energoinvest interested in becoming shareholders of their own companies could not use their vouchers to directly purchase shares. Instead, they had to invest their vouchers in privatization investment funds, which would then buy shares in specific companies. This kind of indirect ownership through investment funds, decoupled from specific factories, did not attract small shareholders, who expected to have direct shareholding rights in their former workplaces. Investment funds were often dubiously managed, and workers had virtually no control over where their vouchers would be invested. The strong presence of international advisers imposed a rather different relationship with the global, one made of interactions with faraway global institutions and their representatives, which made them feel completely powerless.

The fact that workers mostly valued direct ownership rights is perhaps most visible in the case of Energoinvest-Automatika, a producer of measuring instruments used in industrial production. This instance was one of the few where a collective of workers legally disputed privatization and claimed ownership of the shares they had bought during the Marković reforms (roughly 40% of the total capital). By mid-2002, the privatization agency sold 100 percent of the capital—a little over BAM 1 million—to investment funds (MI Group, PIF Bosfin) and to some prominent families linked with the Bosnian Muslim nationalist party (SDA) and with Energoinvest's top management (the later general director Enes Cengić or the then director of another of Energoinvest's subsidiary firms Osman Zec).[41] As workers repeatedly claimed in court, this sale did not recognize their rights as shareholders, which they acquired during the Marković reforms of 1990–1991. Moreover, the company had not paid workers' retirement contributions for the period between 1997 and 2000.[42] Asim, one of the workers who sued the company, explained his motivations:

> Those are my shares! I fought for those shares I bought before the war because they are mine and they are registered in court. Seventy percent of us workers bought those shares before the war, and we have filed a court case against the company; we have been involved in this for the past seven years or so, but we still have not managed to get our shares or our contributions back.[43]

In the end, this privatization deal was concluded without consideration of the shares previously bought by workers during the Marković reforms. An ad hoc commission set up in the early 2000s further determined that the postwar privatization reforms canceled, "with a stroke of the pen," the shares workers had acquired in 1990 under the Marković model.[44] Many of the records of workers' shareholding had been destroyed during the war, and the number of shares previously purchased varied greatly—from 40 percent in some companies to less than 5 percent in others.

In Republika Srpska, the situation was not much different. Here, the International Advisory Group for Privatization was less influential in the privatization of former factories of Energoinvest, since the companies had already been separated from the central branch in Sarajevo and were thus easier to privatize or liquidate. A smaller size allowed a potentially faster sale or a quicker liquidation. Much like their colleagues in the FBiH, however, Energoinvest workers here were equally enraged by a privatization model that did not recognize their rights as shareholders or that sold their companies to enterprises that did not revive production.

Workers of the Energoinvest factory RAOP, which produced switchgears in Lukavica (East Sarajevo), repeatedly went on strike in 2009, protesting months of unpaid wages and an unclear privatization contract that involved the entity government and the Serbian marketing company Jugotrade.[45] During the process of privatization, the fate of 36 percent of the company's capital, which belonged to small shareholders, remained unclear. Branimir, a white-collar worker employed in the company since 1970, recalls that workers like him had purchased those shares before the war, and some had even invested the vouchers they were given as veterans. As he comments, they believed that "Energoinvest would be like it was before the war. There was trust in the company, that it would revive production and that [they] would all get dividends from that."[46] Branimir spells out a common expectation among his colleagues: that his company would return to its prewar grandeur. He uses the word *trust* to describe the kind of bond that tied him to his factory. The prospect of reaping benefits from shareholding had widened this horizon of trust in the company's future and compelled former employees to take on a legal battle to claim those rights. In the end, however, the majority of state-owned shares were sold to a foreign company that did not revive production. As of 2016, workers of this company were still protesting to demand their rights and arrears.[47] In several other instances, Energoinvest employees accused the state and the company management of having denied them their property rights. They appealed to the Constitutional Court claiming rights over wages in arrears and company apartments and asked to be compensated in shares of their own factories.[48]

As these testimonies show, the postwar reformative project did not manage to create trust in the new property and ownership system. Workers in Energoinvest and elsewhere had remained attached to a different form of ownership, one that would be directly linked to their companies. They rejected new privatization reforms on the grounds that other forms of transformation were possible. For them, privatization came to be closely associated not only with the loss of jobs but also with the loss of their "working lives." In contrast with their experience of the Marković reforms, they viewed the postwar privatization as a process that callously excluded them from a space from which they drew their identity—as workers, veterans, shareholders, and Yugoslavs. Again, the promise of reformism occupied a higher position of importance in their hierarchy of memory, and they mobilized this to act against measures that disregarded their lived experiences.

Reclaiming ownership in court was not the only strategy that workers adopted to rebuild their companies and reclaim control over the fate of their workplaces. In several factories across the country, workers tried to reorganize from below and pulled together their resources to restart production. Perhaps most famous is the case of the DITA factory in the eastern city of Tuzla, where workers tried to invest their remaining vouchers and savings in an attempt to repossess their company and save it from bankruptcy.[49] This was one of the few instances in which workers had managed to keep their nominal vouchers, rather than being convinced to invest them in large funds that, as they would find out later, did not give them direct ownership rights in their factories. In 2001, as the government initiated DITA's privatization, workers bought the majority of shares. After a series of shady deals carried out by the new management, however, workers lost control over their factory. Asset devaluation and underselling orchestrated by the emerging local political-economic oligarchies brought DITA to the brink of bankruptcy. At this point, workers sought to take matters into their own hands and physically occupied the factory to protect it from looting and to restart production.[50]

"Protesting for production" was a key strategy for workers' collectives across the country, as they sought to counter the material and symbolic ruination of their factories.[51] Workers in the Energoinvest-Novi TNNO in Doboj (Republika Srpska), a producer of low-voltage equipment, bought their own factory after it had been declared bankrupt and managed to revive production after one and a half years. In 2006, after having been on strike since the first privatization in 2004, 330 worker-owners were able to reach a production of 25 percent of the prewar standards. In Bosnia, this was the first case of workers purchasing their factory after the mass privatization of the early 2000s.[52] Crucially, workers sought to maintain and revitalize the factory's relationships with its foreign partners. Building on the collaborative foundations established in the early 1980s under Energoinvest, the company started exporting to the Korean market.[53] Workers viewed this as a promising step toward the restoration of the company's past glories on the global market. Afterward, however, the issue of property became even more controversial, as an entrepreneur from a nearby town purchased the majority of the company's shares. According to workers, this was conducted under intimidating circumstances, as they were threatened with mass firings if they did not sell the shares. Though workers repeatedly went on strike, the company was finally declared bankrupt.[54]

The fear of bankruptcy and of losing one's job led workers of the Energoinvest factory TAT (producer of thermo-regulation equipment) to describe their postprivatization situation as "worse than in 1992," when the war started.[55] The desire to remain anchored to the feeble prospect of a revived production, rather than accepting the certainty of bankruptcy, led these workers to buy the machinery necessary to restart work. Similarly, workers of the factory TDS (transmission pipelines and electricity poles), most of whom were in precarious employment, remarked that they were paying the factory's energy bill to keep a minimum of production going and prevent their workplace from being completely shut down. "In the wake of postsocialist privatization," Larisa Kurtović notes, "workers had no choice but to assemble a future out of the ruins."[56] Furthermore, workers of TDS had strongly expressed their will to return to the central branch, especially after it had struck a USD 5 million deal with Libya for the building of electrical power lines.[57] This was the only case where the Privatization Agency and the Advisory Group for privatization initially sought to maintain the factory within the Energoinvest group after they saw that it would not be able to stand alone on the world market, as it needed strong coordination with the central branch.[58]

Mobilizing a Residual Structure of Expectations

Reclaiming the prospect of a global presence and working to resurrecting it were crucial aspects in the struggle for production. It was with the global promise in mind, with the relatively fresh memory of a past where they were (in)direct participants in a global project, that workers pursued actions to revive their factories. This adds a further layer to the affect workers have toward the materiality of their workplaces (equipment, buildings, products) as well as those objects that indirectly embody such materiality (shares and vouchers). This affect for the material is entangled with the experience and expectation of a workplace projected toward the outside world: objects assume an immaterial dimension as they become portals to (imagined) global futures. Reestablishing international contacts and restarting export-oriented production were key to fulfilling a double expectation: first, of going back to normalcy, signified by the company's revived activity and the prospect of stable work; and second, of returning to that vision of global relevance, status, and interconnection that propelled workers toward imagined futures. Seeking a place of relevance on the global market might seem impossible given the dire circumstances these companies find themselves in, a vision that lies beyond what can be empirically expected.[59] Yet this vision derives from actual dreams and hopes and reflects "the historical tension between factual states and distant goals."[60]

In postsocialist Bosnia and Herzegovina, much as in other postindustrial societies, change is "slowed and redirected by pre-existing industrial cultures," which live long after industrial practices have ceased to be productive.[61] Within workplaces, different actors debated and reframed categories related to the world of work (competitiveness, ownership, productivity, deservingness, efficiency) across the post/socialist, post/industrial divide. The process of negotiating these categories against the backdrop of (new) global promises produced disconnections between expectations and experience of change.

The resilience of what Susan Bayly has called the "global socialist ecumene"—in other words, the endurance of socialist-era values of internationalism and solidarity—is evident in the aspirations and expectations of those involved in the transformation of Energoinvest.[62] Although postsocialism, ethno-liberal reforms, and deindustrialization contributed to the erosion of spaces of working-class socialization, my interlocutors did not let these spaces go so easily, because they constituted a portal to their imagined futures. Reclaiming ownership of the material representation of that global promise was an important strategy to revive a feeling of agency in framing the future. Thus, claiming back shares and attempting to revive production were not acts of hopeless nostalgia for the socialist workplace of yore. Rather, keeping alive the memory of "what could have been" is a way to make sense of change by radically challenging the idea that it is an immediately positive thing. Indeed, postsocialist transformation has widened the gap between experience and expectation and heightened the dissonance between the present and the imagined future. The ruined workplace is, for many, a constant reminder of this dissonance, a space marked by incoherence: a "what *will* have been" sort of question.

Although factories and combines were subjected to constant erosion during the postsocialist transformation, this did not mean an obliteration of the world of work or a dissolution of the affective ties binding their employees together. On the contrary, even as these spaces disappear and are fragmented by multiple cycles of privatization, workers and managers hold on to them as significant for their socialization. Mobilizing a residual industrial structure of expectations, one that implies actively giving priority to certain aspects of one's memory and past (the promise of reformism and ownership, over the dysfunctions of self-management or the fracturing of the war) means not letting go of a vision of change radically different from what one has experienced so far. Grieving for the destruction of workplaces "as they once were" is a critique directed at a certain kind of change that marginalized workers and destroyed their workplaces. Mourning the loss of shares and of the potential of revived production is an attempt to keep alive the possibility that the old system will become new. Workers don't want to let go of the utopia that is so ingrained in their value system—one in which they are central protagonists, agents of change, rather than powerless witnesses. It is this feeling of powerlessness in the face of ruination that Miro notes here as he points to the broken-down walls and empty rooms of his factory:

> It is difficult for us to look at that. I'm not an owner of anything, but still it is so difficult for me to look at it. It would be best for me to leave at last. I should have left before, had I thought about my personal interests, the interests of my family, had I been smart. But I was not smart, and I stayed here . . . just to close the door.[63]

His reflection on his own naivete mirrors Mladen's at the beginning of chapter 4: He did not think for himself, for his own personal interests did not consider the reality of the imminent war. Instead, he stuck with a possibility, a promise, a dream—which he now protects behind a closed door.

Figure 7.1. Esad holding the bust of Tito he crafted in his garage. Credit: Author

Many workers I interviewed were visibly distressed by the collapse and fragmentation endured by their factories and often became emotional when reflecting on these transformations. Esad, a blue-collar worker I visited in the small town of Živinice, was a former employee of Energoinvest's steel foundry in Tuzla, one of Bosnia's industrial heartlands. This was a long and very emotional interview, during which he reminisced about his factory and colleagues and about the traumatic events of the war. Although at times he appeared self-conscious, he was very open about his feelings toward his factory and community of workers. Like many of his colleagues at Energoinvest, he also perceived his team as family and the factory as a place he built and fought to preserve—together with the values of solidarity that had been poured into the space. Later in the interview, he recalled that he felt like crying when he visited "his" factory after it was privatized (in the mid-2000s), to see it completely run down and dilapidated. During the interview, he compared this grief for a lost company to the one he felt when he lost a close friend during the war. His emotional attachment was so strong that he sought to preserve a physical memory of his factory: the vest he used every day when he went to work. Similarly, many of my interlocutors had held on to the objects that were products of Energoinvest's material corporate culture—small plates, pins, desk flags—all branded with the insignia of the company. Holding on to the physical materiality of industrial ruination, as Lisa Taylor argues, is another strategy for people to assuage their feelings of loss.[64] At the same time, it is a reminder that they, too, were part of a corporate culture that now excludes them.

Esad did not just preserve objects that connected him to his past workscape: he crafted new ones, thus giving a physical representation to the very motion of crafting and shaping his own past. With leftovers of scrap materials recuperated from the shop floor, he crafted a small bust of Marshall Tito—the embodiment of the Yugoslav dream—which he kindly gifted to me as a souvenir of our conversation. I often wonder what the gift was meant to represent. Through this small artifact, Esad resurrected the symbols, values, and history that had imbued a space—now reduced to rubble—where he had felt part of something bigger, a reality greater than the sum of its parts. Here, affectivity assumed a spatial dimension: the shop floor embodied for him the dream of Yugoslavist internationalism. It was a source of pride and purpose, something Esad sought to salvage from the ruins; to give those feelings a tangible form, a legacy that could be communicated and entrusted to others; to remind others that what he had experienced was a real moment in space and time and not just a dream.

CONCLUSIONS

This book has traced the long trajectory of a globally oriented Yugoslav enterprise as a microcosm of the broader socialist internationalist project with which Yugoslavia had carved out a name for itself. It followed Energoinvest through the tumultuous years of Yugoslavia's dissolution, the Bosnian War, and the subsequent decades of postwar and postsocialist reconstruction, where the aspiration to create a third-way economy, the trauma of a bitter war, new contentious identities, and the triumph and collapse of the free-market dogma, all collided in a condensed moment of time. Yet this is not just a story of rags to riches to rags again or a parable of corporate expansion and demise. It is also a tale of how Yugoslavia cultivated different ideas about social and corporate enterprise that sought to reconcile markets with societies at a time when they seemed mutually exclusive. These ideas crystallized into a hope, a promise, that workplaces could be democratic and prosperous by virtue of being global. More tangible than a social contract and less ephemeral than an imagined community, the socialist global promise was shaped by history as much as it made history.

For Yugoslavia, engaging in the project of non-aligned world making through economic partnerships with the developing world was a tool of both foreign policy and domestic development. Through globally engaged enterprises, the global socialist promise entered and shaped the everyday lives of thousands of workers, who were not isolated in backward socialist regimes. Indeed, export industries were the most exposed to the world market, in terms of business exchanges, joint ventures, and institutional connections. Their presence in the global market was construed as a factor of economic exchange, as well as an imagined space of transnationality. There was a very practical side to this world making, one where companies like Energoinvest played a role as spaces of the diffusion and consolidation of the socialist global project.

Energoinvest is emblematic of Yugoslav histories of transition. It was at the forefront of reforms that were aimed at transforming the world of work following newly emerging models of economic transition. Its size and strategic importance for the country's industrial sector meant that reforms were conceptualized bearing in mind the needs of the company and its workforce. To realize new promises of change and progress, enterprises—the gatekeepers of economic growth and market integration—had to be radically refashioned. Yet, within them, visions and expectations of change through global integration already existed and found their roots in socialist societies' embeddedness in transnational networks.

Remnants of the socialist global promise became enmeshed with a process of ethnic homogenization that accompanied the company's multiple phases of privatization. In a country like Bosnia at the turn of the twenty-first century—where a process of postconflict *re*construction overlapped with the *de*construction of socialist structures, institutions, and ownership practices—privatization determined a juncture between worker- and ethnic-based visions of ownership and citizenship. Yet, rather than fading into the background of a postsocialist, postwork society, the "global" workplace constituted an important tool for making sense of the transformations that occurred in late- and postsocialist Yugoslavia. The criteria for ownership distribution became based on ethnic citizenship, though this did not supplant previous understandings of worker ownership. Rather, this overlapped and led to complex frictions within workplaces. The pervasive and yet malleable nature of the global promise, and its role in cojoining work, ownership, and deservingness, allowed for visions of workerist and ethnonationalist citizenship to exist simultaneously under the same company roof. This juncture would not have been possible without all the complex prior formulations of socialist ownership and the attempts at transforming it.

Even in 2025, Energoinvest shapes and constitutes the social fabric of (post)socialist Bosnia. It is a miniature representation of the country's economic and social history throughout the second half of the twentieth century. It accompanied the country's socioeconomic developments and moments of crises, and it shaped its urban, social, and cultural landscape—from Bihać to Zvornik, from Mostar to Sarajevo. To tell the story of Energoinvest is to tell the history of Bosnia, and vice versa. Through it, we can see not only how national identity becomes incarnated within (national) enterprises but also how, in turn, national enterprises can support or challenge processes of nation building. Scholars eager to further explore questions of economic nationalism may find that the case of Energoinvest sparks new reflections on the role of nationality in business and corporate cultures.

The economic transformations traced in this book highlight the unwavering importance and relevance of the work-ownership-identity nexus, which has come to increasingly shape European and international politics. Indeed, a counterpoint to the neoliberal globalization enthusiasm has been a retraction toward illiberal or populist politics that has capitalized on the racialization or ethnicization of the world of work. Ethnic or racial identity (and citizenship) and its association with issues related to the scarcity of work are familiar political tools in the hands of far-right politicians in Europe and beyond and are particularly prominent in contexts of deindustrialization. In this, Bosnia appears now much less of an outlier than it might have seemed twenty years ago, as cultural, political, and economic identities have become increasingly ethnicized. To quote the sociologist Helmuth Berking, ethnicity is, indeed, "everywhere."[1]

To the workers of Energoinvest, the Yugoslav project promised a prosperous workplace democracy integrated into the world market as an agent of innovation and development. Energoinvest was an expression of the promises of Yugoslav internationalism, as encapsulated in the lyrics of its celebratory hymn: a story of ambitions, global economic entanglements, and business opportunities in the non-aligned world. With the twenty-first century came a new promise of postmodernity: one that championed a particular vision of global integration and a new world of work. Yet the promises of a postindustrial future seemed hazy and undefined, if not outright terrifying, for those whose jobs were going to decline. Besides promises of more efficiency and prosperity to be delivered by the market, there did not seem to be any vision for the postindustrial future in Europe, especially in its eastern parts.

In the postsocialist context, a fast track to mass privatizations and economic deregulation meant a marginalization of those actors that had, up until that moment, set their own terms for the rules of engagement with the global market. For many Yugoslavs, this autonomy—often expressed in the form of social ownership, job safety, and sociopolitical privileges bestowed on workers—was a distinguishing, dignifying, and indispensable feature of the Yugoslav political economy. For others, it was an impediment to growth and productivity that needed a revision, but seldom did anyone ask for a complete overhaul of the system. These opinions shaped the debates over the size, reach, and ownership regimes of companies like Energoinvest, but the cornerstone of alternative economics that had marked Yugoslavia as a global force went untouched. Thus, studying long-term transformation in a (post-)Yugoslav corporation illuminates the legacy of historically overlooked strains of globalization. These alternative formulations of global integration between the 1970s and 2000s compel us to view the postwar transformation—carried out under the hammer of a triumphant neoliberal order—in a different light: a shift between different framings of the global rather than a jump from isolation to interconnectedness.

Yugoslavia and the successor states are not the only case where local formulations of socialist reformism coexisted with or supplanted neoliberal principles. The post-2003 so-called Pink Tide in Latin America was another example where the New Left drew on a local formulation of social-ist reformism in response to a neoliberal-oriented transition.[2] Here too re-formers introduced social-democratic alternatives to neoliberal principles, embracing a turn to privatization with social-democratic values. Thinking about the (unintended) peripheralizing and deindustrializing consequences of neoliberal globalization should further the dialogue between scholars of eastern Europe and the Global South.

In addition, understanding the significance of a global imaginary opens the recent history of labor and resistance in postsocialist societies to new interpretations. Workers' discontent did not just arise from their inability to cope with globalization or from their longing for a nonproductive indus-trial world that will never return. Rather, workers understood and advo-cated for the need for reform, viewed themselves as globally integrated, and thus projected expectations of reform based on an understanding that they were active subjects in globalization reforms. For the people I interviewed, globalization is something that is simultaneously desired and feared, de-pending on how it is defined and who defines it: Would it mean a restora-tion of the business ethos and corporate culture that granted Energoinvest its place in the sun or a reinforcement of its status as a small regional player? In our quest to "frame the global" as a concept, a category, and an experien-tial space, it is important not to forget that the global is not something that just *is*—it's rather something that is interpreted and redefined in different ways, through different perspectives and different ambitions.

Not only did postwar neoliberal reforms infantilize and marginalize a workforce that had spent decades considering the merits and flaws of mar-ket reforms, but the promise of turbocharging an economy through eth-nicization, deregulation, and privatization failed to deliver any prosperity. Urban transformations, as well as the environmental, socioeconomic, ra-cialized, and gendered consequences of deindustrialization, have radically reshaped communities in the Global South and the postsocialist world, and not just as a consequence of delocalization away from the richer Global

North. For the workers of companies like Energoinvest, neoliberal globalization entailed removal and marginalization rather than connectivity, a reorientation toward narrower horizons. Whether this will be the fate of working peoples in the developing world who are witnessing a case of premature deindustrialization while experiencing firsthand the crumbling of capitalism's illusion of prosperity and its failure to deliver on its promises and myths is yet to be determined. It may well be, though, that the unmet expectations of globalization and industrialization will cause unrest and discontent or lead to a search for alternatives in the local pasts.

To an extent, neoliberalism seemed to promise the world to those who already had it. In doing so, it disregarded one key element: that their world was already made of alternatives; it was created as an alternative. The lingering power of alternatives, and of the idea of alternatives, suggests that neoliberalism's power of disembedding the economic from the political sphere was constrained by the weight of history, as experienced on the shop floor of Energoinvest. Notions of collective ownership, socialist corporate culture, and workplace democracy (in some shape or form) remained relevant guiding forces for workers who expressed their desire to participate in their countries' economic reconstruction. However, the war had produced its own divisive memories, the legacies of which contributed to fracture the cohesion of the country, its sense of shared history, and thus a sense of shared futures. The institutions that were entrusted with designing an economic system that would maintain ethnic peace ended up exacerbating the ethnic separation of working lives, creating an ethnocracy that offered little in the way of material comforts or national unity. The space of a company, thus, constituted a repository of overlapping and at times clashing memories—of work, of war, of socialism and internationalism, and of ownership. All these memories, the past lives of this company and its workers, are looking for recognition and significance in the postsocialist, postwar context.

The transformations that have occurred in Bosnia—and on the shop floor of Energoinvest—have taken turns in giving momentum and meaning to the memories of the socialist past, third-way reformism, the war, nostalgia itself. This has created an ever-changing hierarchy of transformation narratives, competing and contradicting each other, generating demands for ethnicity-based compensation for veterans and workerist solidarity against ethnonational division in the same breath. Even if the protests of 2014 waned down as quickly as they flared up and perhaps did not produce the lasting and radical transformation of the post-Dayton regime that activists wished for, they nevertheless gave a sense of there being a need for alternative formulations to the work-ownership-citizenship nexus. That alternatives are not just emerging ex novo but are grounded in people's memories should motivate historians to uncover and recover more histories of such alternatives. After all, to imagine alternatives is the first step to demand new promises.

For a long time, it might have appeared that there were no alternatives to the neoliberal world order. People in the socialist world were chewed up and spat out by the transformation period, which entailed a loss of employment, deindustrialization, and a realignment of production and market reach. The neoliberal developmental promise actually meant redacting state-led development aspirations in favor of smaller, private-led formulations and a reorientation toward small enterprises. In recent years, however, there has been a new drive to think of alternatives. New geopolitical dynamics and a reconfiguration of geopolitical balances are on the rise, with China prompting new formulations of state-capitalist development strategies in the economically and technologically developing world. At the same time, more than a decade after the financial crisis of 2008, considerations of the problematic consequences of austerity measures have sprung a renewed (scholarly and political) interest in heterodox ideas of economic growth and globalization. Also, climate change and its intersection with questions of economic (de)growth have foregrounded the importance of thinking about alternatives. Reflecting on the entangled nature of the multiple globalizations emerging from socialist and capitalist models helps us further to advance our insights into the history of capitalism by problematizing its linear trajectory of global expansion. Challenging the very notion of the intrinsic capitalist nature of globalization further encourages us to reflect on the manifold ways in which the socialist project, its history, and its legacy are crucial to our quest to "frame the global" as a space for alternatives. This book has shown how important it is to hold on to the memories of alternatives as catalysts of hope and roots of resistance.

NOTES

Introduction

1. Larisa Kurtović, "'Who Sows Hunger, Reaps Rage': On Protest, Indignation and Redistributive Justice in Post-Dayton Bosnia-Herzegovina," *Southeast European and Black Sea Studies* 15, no. 4 (2015): 639–59.

2. Feng Chen, "Between the State and Labour: The Conflict of Chinese Trade Unions' Double Identity in Market Reform," *The China Quarterly* 176 (2003): 1006–28; Feng Chen, "Privatization and Its Discontents in Chinese Factories," *The China Quarterly*, no. 185 (2006): 42–60, 43; Dario Azzellini, ed., *The Class Strikes Back* (Brill, 2018).

3. Dejan Jović, "Communist Yugoslavia and Its 'Others,'" in *Ideologies and National Identities: The Case of Twentieth-Century Southeastern Europe*, ed. John Lampe and Mark Mazower (Central European University Press, 2006), 277–302, 281http://books.openedition.org/ceup/2438.

4. Cristofer Scarboro, Diana Mincyte, and Zsuzsa Gille, eds., *The Socialist Good Life: Desire, Development, and Standards of Living in Eastern Europe* (Indiana University Press, 2020). On tourism and leisure in Yugoslavia, see Hannes Grandits and Karin Taylor, eds., *Yugoslavia's Sunny Side: A History of Tourism in Socialism (1950s–1980s)* (Central European University, 2010).

5. Looking at consumer culture in Yugoslavia, Patrick Hyder Patterson defines as the "Yugoslav Dream" the distinctive, homegrown version of the good life provided by the socialist state. Patrick Hyder Patterson, *Bought and Sold: Living and Losing the Good Life in Socialist Yugoslavia* (Cornell University Press, 2012), 322.

6. Radina Vučetić and Paul Betts, eds., *Tito u Africi* (Belgrade: Muzej Jugoslavije, 2017); Nemanja Radonjić, "A Non-Aligned Continent: Africa in the Global Imaginary of Socialist Yugoslavia," in *Socialist Yugoslavia and the Non-Aligned Movement: Social, Cultural, Political and Economic Imaginaries*, ed. Paul Stubbs (McGill-Queen's University Press, 2023), 302–31.

7. Theodora Dragostinova, *The Cold War from the Margins: A Small Socialist State on the Global Cultural Scene* (Cornell University Press, 2021).

8. Hilary Kahn, introduction to *Framing the Global: Entry Points for Research*, ed. Hilary Kahn (Indiana University Press, 2014), 2.

9. Rachel Harvey, "The Persistence of the Particular in the Global," in Kahn, *Framing the Global*, 182–205, 184.

10. James Mark and Tobias Rupprecht, "Europe's '1989' in Global Context," in *The Cambridge History of Communism*, ed. Juliane Fürst, Silvio Pons, and Mark Selden (Cambridge University Press, 2017), 203–23; Oscar Sanchez-Sibony, *Red Globalization: The Political Economy of the Soviet Cold War from Stalin to Khrushchev* (Cambridge University Press, 2014).

11. Besnik Pula, *Globalization under and after Socialism: The Evolution of Transnational Capital in Central and Eastern Europe* (Stanford University Press, 2018), 78.

12. Odd Arne Westad, *The Global Cold War: Third World Interventions and the Making of Our Times* (Cambridge University Press, 2005); Sara Lorenzini, *Global Development: A Cold War History* (Princeton University Press, 2019). For a comparison with the American vision of modernization and development, see David Ekbladh, *The Great American Mission: Modernisation and the Construction of an American World Order* (Princeton University Press, 2011).

13. James Mark, Artemy M. Kalinovsky, and Steffi Marung, eds., *Alternative Globalisations: Eastern Europe and the Postcolonial World* (Indiana University Press, 2020); James Mark, Bogdan Iacob, Tobias Rupprecht, and Ljubica Spaskovska, *1989: A Global History of Eastern Europe* (Cambridge University Press, 2019). Several authors have focused on East-South exchanges; here are just a few examples: Łukasz Stanek, *Architecture in Global Socialism: Eastern Europe, West Africa, and the Middle East in the Cold War* (Princeton University Press, 2020); Cole Roskam, "Non-Aligned Architecture: China's Designs on and in Ghana and Guinea, 1955–92," *Architectural History* 58 (2015): 261–91; Quinn Slobodian, *Comrades of Color: East Germany in the Cold War World* (Berghahn Books, 2015); Marcia C. Schenck, "From Luanda and Maputo to Berlin: Uncovering Angolan and Mozambican Migrants' Motives to Move to the German Democratic Republic (1979–1990)," *African Economic History* 44, no. 1 (2016): 202–34.

14. Although, of course, tensions and frictions existed within the movement, as historian Tvrtko Jakovina has shown in his volume *Treća Strana Hladnog Rata* (Fraktura, 2016).

15. See Jürgen Dinkel, *The Non-Aligned Movement: Genesis, Organisation and Politics (1927–1992)* (Brill, 2019); Christopher J. Lee, *Making a World after Empire: The Bandung Moment and Its Political Afterlives* (Ohio University Press, 2010); Svetozar Rajak, "No Bargaining Chips, No Spheres of Interest: The Yugoslav Origins of Cold War Non-Alignment," *Journal of Cold War Studies* 16, no. 1 (2014): 146–79; Changavalli Siva Rama Murthy, "Non-Aligned Movement Countries as Drivers of Change in International Organisations," *Comparativ: Zeitschrift für Globalgeschichte und vergleichende Gesellschaftsforschung* 23 (2013): 118–36; Hennie Strydom, "The Non-Aligned Movement and the Reform of International Relations," *Max Planck UNYB* 11 (2007): 1–46.

16. Paul Stubbs, ed. *Socialist Yugoslavia and the Non-Aligned Movement: Social, Cultural, Political, and Economic Imaginaries* (McGill-Queen's University Press, 2023).

17. Johanna Bockman, "Socialist Globalization against Capitalist Neocolonialism: The Economic Ideas behind the New International Economic Order," *Humanity: An International Journal of Human Rights, Humanitarianism, and Development* 6, no. 1 (2015): 109–28.

18. Béla Tomka, "How to Conceptualize State Socialist Globalization?," in *Globalization in State Socialist East Central Europe* (Palgrave Macmillan, 2024).

19. Here are just a few examples from the vast historiography of management and entrepreneurship in the socialist world: Philip Scranton, "Managing Communist Enterprises: Poland, Hungary, and Czechoslovakia, 1945–1970," *Enterprise & Society* 19, no. 3 (2018): 492–537; Max Trecker, "Entrepreneurs as Saviours of Socialism? The Complicated Relationship between East German State Socialism and Entrepreneurship," *Business History* 65, no. 7 (2023): 1209–25, https://doi.org/10.1080/00076791.2020.1781818; Valentina Fava and Volodymyr Kulikov, "Recent Trends in the Business History of Russia: The Blurry Borders of the Discipline," *Business History Review* 96, no. 2 (2022): 325–51, https://doi-org.ezproxy2.lib.gla.ac.uk/10.1017/S0007680521000386; Alexander I. Ageev, Mikhail V. Gratchev, and Robert D. Hisrich, "Entrepreneurship in the Soviet Union and Post-Socialist Russia," *Small Business Economics* 7, no. 5 (1995): 365–76, http://www.jstor.org/stable/40228791; Tibor Kuczi and

György Lengyel, "The Spread of Entrepreneurship in Eastern Europe," in *Transformations in Hungary: Contributions to Economics*, ed. P. Meusburger and H. Jöns (Physica, 2001), 157–72.

20. Phil Scranton and Patrick Fridenson, *Reimagining Business History* (Johns Hopkins University Press, 2013), 47; Vladimir Unkovski-Korica and Saša Vejzagić, "Business History Goes East: An Introduction," *Business History* 65, no. 7 (2023): 1119–36.

21. For an early summary of "organizational culture" literature, see Toyohiro Kono and Stewart R. Clegg, "Concept of Corporate Culture," in *Transformations of Corporate Culture* (De Gruyter, 2017), 1–24, 2, https://doi.org/10.1515/9783110807318-002; Luigi Guiso, Paola Sapienza, and Luigi Zingales, "The Value of Corporate Culture," *Journal of Financial Economics* 117, no. 1 (2015): 60–76, 61–62, https://doi.org/10.1016/j.jfineco.2014.05.010.

22. Terrence E. Deal and Allan A. Kennedy, *Corporate Cultures: The Rites and Rituals of Corporate Life* (Addison-Wesley, 1982); Michael Rowlinson and John Hassard, "The Invention of Corporate Culture: A History of the Histories of Cadbury," *Human Relations* 46, no. 3 (1993): 299–326; Oriol Iglesias, Nicholas Ind, and Majken Schultz, "History Matters: The Role of History in Corporate Brand Strategy," *Business Horizons* 63, no. 1 (2020): 51–60, https://doi.org/10.1016/j.bushor.2019.09.005; Dinah Rajak, "Corporate Memory: Historical Revisionism, Legitimation and the Invention of Tradition in a Multinational Mining Company," *Political and Legal Anthropology Review* 37, no. 2 (2014): 259–80, http://www.jstor.org/stable/24497490; James W. Cortada, *Inside IBM: Lessons of a Corporate Culture in Action* (Columbia University Press, 2023), http://www.jstor.org/stable/10.7312/cort21300.

23. Kenneth Lipartito, "Connecting the Cultural and the Material in Business History," *Enterprise & Society* 14, no. 4 (2013): 686–704, 702, http://www.jstor.org/stable/23701759.

24. Charles Dellheim, "Business in Time: The Historian and Corporate Culture," *Public Historian* 8, no. 2 (Spring 1986): 9–22.

25. Peter Dahler-Larsen, "Corporate Culture and Morality: Durkheim-Inspired Reflections on the Limits of Corporate Culture," *Journal of Management Studies* 31, no. 1 (January 1994): 1–18.

26. For interesting insights into varieties of capitalism and corporate nationality, see Eric Godelier, "The Corporate Nationality: A Question of Culture and Community?," *Journal of Modern European History* 18, no. 1 (2020): 28–47, https://doi-org.ezproxy2.lib.gla.ac.uk/10.1177/1611894419895228.

27. Béla Tomka, "Globalization in Socialist Eastern Europe: A Turn in Research and Its Discontents," *European History Quarterly* 53, no. 4 (2023): 685–96, 693, https://doi-org.ezproxy1.lib.gla.ac.uk/10.1177/02656914231200215.

28. For similar shares for imports from developing countries, see "Trends in Cooperation, 1954–1982," in *Yugoslavia: Economic Cooperation with Developing Countries* (Research Center for Cooperation with Developing Countries, 1983).

29. Anson Rabinbach, "The End of the Utopias of Labor: Metaphors of the Machine in the Post-Fordist Era," *Thesis Eleven* 73 (1998): 29–44.

30. Cristofer Scarboro, "Socialist Life and Its Discontent," in Scarboro, Mincyte, and Gille, *Socialist Good Life*, 207.

31. As suggested by Nina Vodopivec, "Yesterday's Heroes: Spinning Webs of Memory in a Postsocialist Textile Factory in Slovenia," in *Negotiating Normality: Everyday Lives in Socialist Institutions*, ed. Daniela Koleva (Transaction, 2012), 43–63.

32. Stef Jansen, Čarna Brković, and Vanja Čelebičić, eds., *Negotiating Social Relations in Bosnia and Herzegovina: Semiperipheral Entanglements* (Routledge, 2017), 12; Srećko Horvat

and Igor Štiks, eds., *Welcome to the Desert of Post-Socialism: Radical Politics After Yugoslavia* (Verso, 2015), 87.

33. George Lawson, "Introduction: The 'What,' 'When,' and 'Where' of the Global 1989," in *The Global 1989: Continuity and Change in World Politics*, ed. George Lawson, Chris Armbruster, and Michael Cox (Cambridge University Press, 2010), 1–24.

34. Michael Burawoy and Katherine Verdery, eds., *Uncertain Transition: Ethnographies of Change in the Postsocialist World* (Rowman & Littlefield, 2000); Sabrina P. Ramet, "Trajectories of Post-Communist Transformation: Myths and Rival Theories about Change in Central and Southeastern Europe," *Perceptions* 18, no. 2 (2013): 57–89; Chris Hann, "Beyond Otherness: With Reference to Hungarian Villagers, Academic Colleagues, Gypsies, Eastern Europe, Socialism, and Anthropology at Large," working paper 132 (Max Planck Institute for Social Anthropology: Halle (Saale), 2011), 1–19. See also Norbert Petrović, "Framing Criticism and Knowledge Production in Semi-Peripheries: Post-Socialism Unpacked," *Intersections* 1, no. 2 (2015): 801–2. On critical assessments and evaluations of "backwardness" as problematically associated with (socialist) Eastern Europe, see, among others, Neda Atanasoski and Eleonore McElroy, "Postsocialism and the Afterlives of Revolution: Impossible Spaces of Dissent," in *Reframing Critical, Literary, and Cultural Theories*, ed. Nadia Pireddu (Palgrave Macmillan, 2018); Maria Todorova, "The Trap of Backwardness: Modernity, Temporality, and the Study of Eastern European Nationalism," *Slavic Review* 64, no. 1 (2005): 140–64, https://doi.org/10.2307/3650070. For a compelling consideration of socialism's own understanding of backwardness, see Chris Hann, "Backwardness Revisited: Time, Space, and Civilization in Rural Eastern Europe," *Comparative Studies in Society and History* 57, no. 4 (2015): 881–911.

35. Rajesh Venugopal has critically addressed neoliberalism's ability to be everywhere and nowhere at the same time, in "Neoliberalism as Concept," *Economy and Society* 44, no. 2 (2015): 165–87, https://doi-org.ezproxy1.lib.gla.ac.uk/10.1080/03085147.2015.1013356. See also James Ferguson, "The Uses of Neoliberalism," *Antipode* 41, no. 1 (2009): 166–84, 173; Terry Flew, "Six Theories of Neoliberalism," *Book Eleven* 122, no. 1 (2014): 49–71; Stephen J. Collier, "Neoliberalism as Big Leviathan, or . . .? A Response to Wacquant and Hilgers," *Social Anthropology/Anthropologie Sociale* 20, no. 2 (2012): 186–95.

36. Denisa Kostovicova and Vesna Bojičić-Dželilović, "Europeanizing the Balkans: Rethinking the Post-Communist and Post-Conflict Transition," *Ethnopolitics* 5, no. 3 (2006): 223–41, 232; Fikret Čaušević and Merima Zupčević, "Case Study: Bosnia and Herzegovina," Centre for Developing Area Studies—in *Peace and Development: Democratization, Poverty and Risk Mitigation in Fragile and Post-Conflict States*, ed. Philip Oxhorn (McGill University and the World Bank, 2009), 10–50; Isa Mulaj, "Redefining Property Rights with Specific Reference to Social Ownership in the Successor States of the Former Yugoslavia: Did It Matter for Economic Efficiency?," *CEU Political Science Journal*, no. 3 (2007): 225–79.

37. Richard A. Dello Buono, "Latin America and the Collapsing Ideological Supports of Neoliberalism," *Critical Sociology* 37, no. 1 (2011): 9–25.

38. Philipp Ther, *Europe since 1989: A History* (Princeton University Press, 2018). Zsuzsa Gille rightly underlines that a critical understanding of postsocialism in central and Eastern Europe demands relating its transformations with the former "First" and "Third" Worlds. Zsuzsa Gille, "Is There a Global Post-Socialist Condition?," *Global Society* 24, no. 1 (2010): 9–30, 15.

39. Kristen R. Ghodsee and Mitchell A. Orenstein, *Taking Stock of Shock: Social Consequences of the 1989 Revolutions* (Oxford University Press, 2021), 16.

40. In approaching subjectivities, I found inspiration in poststructuralist and constructivist approaches that see subjectivity as "a nexus of relations with others and with a life-world"

that determine "the figuration and refiguration of identity." See Couze Venn, "Identity, Diasporas and Subjective Change: The Role of Affect, the Relation to the Other, and the Aesthetic," *Subjectivity* 26 (2009): 3–28, 3.

41. For recent studies of Yugoslavia's labor history, see Rory Archer, "Social Inequalities and the Study of Yugoslavia's Dissolution," in *Debating the End of Yugoslavia*, ed. Florian Bieber, Armina Galijaš, and Rory Archer (Routledge, 2014), 135–51; Rory Archer, Igor Duda, and Paul Stubbs, "Bringing Class Back In: An Introduction," in *Social Inequalities and Discontent in Yugoslav Socialism*, ed. Rory Archer, Igor Duda, and Paul Stubbs (Routledge, 2016), 1–35; Sara Bernard, *Deutsch Marks in the Head, Shovel in the Hands and Yugoslavia in the Heart: The Gastarbeiter Return to Yugoslavia (1965–1991)* (Harrassowitz, 2019).

42. Kristin Roth-Ey, "Introduction," in Socialist Internationalism and the Gritty Politics of the Particular: Second-Third World Spaces in the Cold War, ed. Kristin Roth-Ey (Bloomsbury, 2023), 7, quoted in Tomka, *Globalization in State Socialist East Central Europe*, 69.

43. Katherine Verdery, "Privatization as Transforming Persons," in *Between Past and Future: The Revolutions of 1989 and Their Aftermath*, ed. Sorin Antohi and Vladimir Tismaneanu (Central European University Press, 2000), 175–97.

44. Jason Read, "A Genealogy of Homo-Economicus: Neoliberalism and the Production of Subjectivity," *Foucault Studies*, no. 6 (2009): 25–36; Gal Kirn, "A Critique of Transition Studies on Post-Socialism, or How to Rethink and Reorient 1989? The Case of (Post)Socialist (Post)Yugoslavia," in *Beyond Neoliberalism, Social Analysis after 1989*, ed. Marian Burchardt and Gal Kirn (Palgrave Macmillan, 2017), 43–69, 54.

45. The literature on this topic is vast. As a point of reference, see David Ost, *The Defeat of Solidarity: Anger and Politics in Postcommunist Europe* (Cornell University Press, 2005); David Kideckel, "The Unmaking of an East-Central European Working Class," in *Postsocialism*, ed. Chris Hann (Routledge, 2002), 114–32; Al Rainnie, Adrian Smith, and Adam Swain, eds., *Work, Employment and Transition: Restructuring Livelihoods in Post-Communism* (Routledge, 2002); Piotr Žuk, "Employment Structures, Employee Attitudes and Workplace Resistance in Neoliberal Poland," *Economic and Labour Relations Review* 28, no. 1 (2017): 91–112; Ruth Mandel and Caroline Humphrey, eds., *Markets and Moralities: Ethnographies of Postsocialism* (Berg, 2002); Elizabeth C. Dunn, *Privatizing Poland: Baby Food, Big Business, and the Remaking of Labor* (Cornell University Press, 2004). For the specific literature on Yugoslavia, see, among others, Mihail Arandarenko, "Waiting for the Workers: Explaining Labor Quiescence in Serbia," in *Workers after Workers' States*, 159–79 (Rowman & Littlefield, 2001); Mladen Lazić and Slobodan Cvejić, "Working Class in Post-Socialist Transformation: Serbia and Croatia Compared," *Corvinus Journal of Sociology and Social Policy*, no. 1 (2010): 3–29; Miroslav Stanojević, "Workers' Power in Transition Economies: The Cases of Serbia and Slovenia," *European Journal of Industrial Relations* 9, no. 3 (2003): 283–301; Marko Grdešić, "Mapping the Paths of the Yugoslav Model: Labour Strength and Weakness in Slovenia, Croatia and Serbia," *European Journal of Industrial Relations* 14, no. 2 (2008): 133–51.

46. See, for example, Benedikt Korf, "Ethnicised Entitlements? Property Rights and Civil War in Sri Lanka," ZEF—Discussion Paper on Development Policy 75 (2003), 1–34, 2; James Ahearne, "Neoliberal Economic Policies and Post-Conflict Peace-Building: A Help or Hindrance to Durable Peace?," *Polis Journal* 2 (2009): 1–44, 37. See also Michael Pugh, Neil Cooper, and Jonathan Goodhand, *War Economies in a Regional Context: Challenges of Transformation* (Lynne Rienner, 2004).

47. Andy Storey, "Economics and Ethnic Conflict: Structural Adjustment in Rwanda," *Development Policy Review* 17 (1999): 43–63.

48. Lynn Abrams, *Oral History Theory* (Routledge, 2010), 105; Alessandro Portelli, *The Death of Luigi Trastulli and Other Stories: Form and Meaning in Oral History* (State University of New York Press, 1991), 53.

49. David Byrne, "Industrial Culture in a Post-Industrial World: The Case of the North East of England," *City* 6, no. 3 (2002): 279–89, 287, https://doi.org/10.1080/1360481022000037733; Tim Strangleman, "Exploring an Industrial Structure of Feeling: Creating Industrial Gemeinschaft in a Twentieth-Century Workplace," in *Stretching the Sociological Imagination*, ed. Michael Dawson, Ben Fowler, David Miller, and Andrew Smith (Palgrave Macmillan, 2015), 25–42; Tim Strangleman, "Deindustrialization and the Historical Sociological Imagination: Making Sense of Work and Industrial Change," *Sociology* 51, no. 2 (2017): 466–82, 471.

50. Chiara Bonfiglioli, *Women and Industry in the Balkans: The Rise and Fall of the Yugoslav Textile Sector* (I. B. Tauris, 2019); Chiara Bonfiglioli, "Post-Socialist Deindustrialisation and Its Gendered Structure of Feeling: The Devaluation of Women's Work in the Croatian Garment Industry," *Labor History* 61, no. 1 (2020): 36–47, https://doi.org/10.1080/0023656X.2019.1681643.

51. Reinhart Koselleck, *Futures Past: On the Semantics of Historical Time* (Columbia University Press, 2004), 257.

52. Tanja Petrović, *Utopia of the Uniform: Affective Afterlives of the Yugoslav People's Army* (Duke University Press, 2024), 5.

53. Sherry Lee Linkon, *The Half-Life of Deindustrialization: Working-Class Writing about Economic Restructuring* (University of Michigan Press, 2018), 5.

54. Maya Nadkarni and Olga Shevchenko, "The Politics of Nostalgia in the Aftermath of Socialism's Collapse," in *Anthropology and Nostalgia*, ed. Olivia Angé, David Berliner, and Jonathan Bach (Berghahn, 2015), 61–95, https://doi.org/10.1515/9781782384540; Veronika Pehe, "An Artificial Unity? Approaches to Post-Socialist Nostalgia," *Tropos* 1, no. 1 (2014): 6–13; Dominik Bartmanski, "Successful Icons of Failed Time: Rethinking Post-Communist Nostalgia," *Acta Sociologica* 54, no. 3 (2011): 213–31.

55. Kinga Pozniak, *Nowa Huta: Generations of Change in a Model Socialist Town* (Pittsburgh: University of Pittsburgh Press, 2014), 46.

56. Svetlana Boym, *The Future of Nostalgia* (Basic Books, 2001), 41.

57. Because of the kind of production in heavy industry, it was estimated that women constituted only 10 percent of the workforce. *Energoinvest List*, November 10, 1986.

58. Sandy Q. Qu and John Dumay, "The Qualitative Research Interview," *Qualitative Research in Accounting & Management* 8, no. 3 (2011): 246; Helen B. Schwartzmann, *Ethnography in Organizations* (Sage, 1993); Carl Ryant, "Oral History and Business History," *Journal of American History* 75, no. 2 (1988): 565; Niamh Dillon, "From Market Trader to Global Player: Oral History and Corporate Culture in Tesco, Britain's Largest Supermarket," *Oral History* 43, no. 1 (2015): 52–62.

59. Christina R. Lubinski et al., "Humanistic Approaches to Change: Entrepreneurship and Transformation," *Business History* 66, no. 2 (2023): 347–63.

60. For a broader discussion of workplace periodicals as a source of investigation in Yugoslav labor studies, see Rory Archer and Goran Musić, "Approaching the Socialist Factory and Its Workforce: Considerations from Fieldwork in (Former) Yugoslavia," *Labor History* 58, no. 1 (2016): 44–66.

61. For example, *Ekonomski Glasnik*, the publication of the Economic Faculty of Sarajevo; *Ekonomska Analiza*, the journal of the Yugoslav Institute for Economic Research in Belgrade

and Zagreb, which also published the records of annual conferences of the Council of Yugoslav Economists; *Naše Teme*, the journal of the Economic Faculty in Zagreb; and *Ekonomska Politika*, a weekly magazine like the British *Economist*.

1. Shaping the Global Promise

1. *Tito bez protokola Energoinvest* (Sutjeska Film Sarajevo, 1966), https://www.facebook.com/watch/?v=2593509930690559.

2. On developing countries' own agency in development strategies, see Jeffrey James Byrne, *Mecca of Revolution: Algeria, Decolonization, and the Third World Order* (Oxford University Press, 2016); Priya Lal, *African Socialism in Postcolonial Tanzania: Between the Village and the World* (Cambridge University Press, 2015); and Jodie Yuzhou Sun, *Kenya's and Zambia's Relations with China, 1949–2019* (Boydell and Brewer, 2023).

3. Adom Getachew, *Worldmaking after Empire: The Rise and Fall of Self-Determination* (Princeton University Press, 2019).

4. Alessandro Iandolo, "De-Stalinizing Growth: Decolonization and the Development of Development Economics in the Soviet Union," in *The Development Century*, ed. Stephen Macekura and Erez Manela (Cambridge University Press, 2018), 197–219; Anna Calori, Anne Hartmetz, Bence Kocsev, James Mark, and Jan Zofka, eds., *Globalization Projects East and South: Spaces of Economic Interaction during the Cold War* (Munich: Oldenbourg, De Gruyter, 2019); Christopher R. W. Dietrich, *Oil Revolution: Anticolonial Elites, Sovereign Rights, and the Economic Culture of Decolonization* (New York: Cambridge University Press, 2017).

5. Alvin Z. Rubinstein, *Yugoslavia and the Nonaligned World* (Princeton University Press, 1970), 170.

6. "Savezno Izvršno Veće—SIV," Fond 130, folder 607–1003, 1965, 1967–1970, p. 23, Arhiv Jugoslavije.

7. "Savezno Izvršno Veće—SIV."

8. Vladimir Unkovski-Korica, *The Economic Struggle for Power in Tito's Yugoslavia: From World War II to Non-Alignment* (I. B. Tauris, 2016), 67.

9. Zdravko Petak, "Ekonomski Federalizam U Socijalističkoj Jugoslaviji," *Politička Misao* 49, no. 4 (2012): 212–27.

10. Christian Michel, "It Is Not a Question of Rigidly Planning Trade: UNCTAD and the Regulation of International Trade in the 1970s," in *Planning in Cold War Europe: Competition, Cooperation, Circulations (1950s–1970s)*, ed. Christian Michel, Sandrine Kott, and Ondřej Matějka (De Gruyter Oldenbourg, 2018), 285–314.

11. Resolution of the Third Conference of Non-Aligned States, Lusaka, September 1970, p. 33.

12. As defined by Enrique Oteiza, Argentinian scientist and later director of the United Nations Research Institute for Social Development (UNRISD). Enrique Oteiza and Francisco Sercovich, "Collective Self-Reliance," *Social Science Journal* 28, no. 4 (1976): 664–71.

13. Gamani Corea, "Unctad and the New International Economic Order," *International Affairs* 53, no. 2 (1977): 177–87.

14. "Yugoslav News," Yugoslav Press and Cultural Center, New York, March 25, 1977, 1.

15. Ljubica Spaskovska, "Building a Better World? Construction, Labor and the Pursuit of Collective Self-Reliance in the 'Global South,' 1950–1990," *Labor History* 59, no. 3 (2018):

331–51; Ljubica Spaskovska, "Constructing the 'City of International Solidarity': Non-Aligned Internationalism, the United Nations, and Visions of Development, Modernism, and Solidarity, 1955–1975," *Journal of World History* 31, no. 1 (2020): 137–63.

16. Johanna Bockman, *Markets in the Name of Socialism: The Left-Wing Origins of Neoliberalism* (Stanford University Press, 2011), 93.

17. J. J. Hauvonen, "IMF Staff Papers," *IMF Staff Papers* 17, no. 3 (1970): 563–601.

18. "Savezni zavod za međunarodnu naučnu, prosvetno-kulturnu i tehničku saradnju," Fond 465, folder 5, 1979–1980, Arhiv Jugoslavije.

19. Jeffrey James Byrne, "Beyond Continents, Colours, and the Cold War: Yugoslavia, Algeria, and the Struggle for Non-Alignment," *International History Review* 37, no. 5 (2015): 912–32; Aleksandar Životić and Jovan Čavoški, "On the Road to Belgrade: Yugoslavia, Third World Neutrals, and the Evolution of Global Non-Alignment, 1954–1961," *Journal of Cold War Studies* 18, no. 4 (2016): 79–97.

20. "Energoinvest," lyrics by Alija Hafizović, music by Kemal Monteno, Yugoton, 1982. Author's translation.

21. Kemal Monteno is perhaps best known for the song "Sarajevo ljubavi moja," recorded in the same year. Alija Hafizović was a musician and artist, once a member of the Sarajevo prog-rock band Indexi. See also "Poslušajte kako e Kemal Monteno pjesmom slavio Bh. privredni gigant Energoinvest," Radiosarajevo.ba, accessed March 11, 2018, https://www.radiosarajevo.ba/metromahala/teme/poslusajte-kako-je-kemal-monteno-pjesmom-slavio-bh-privredni-gigant-energoinvest/216087.

22. Emerik Blum, "The Director and Worker's Management," in *Yugoslav Workers' Self-Management*, ed. M. J. Broekmeyer (D. Reidel, 1970), 172–92.

23. Dubravka Sekulić, "Constructing Non-Alignment: The Case of Construction Enterprise Energoprojekt, 1961–1989, Architecture, Construction Industry and Yugoslavia in the World" (PhD diss., ETH Zurich, 2020), 122.

24. *Oslobođenje*, November 11, 1971, quoted in Izudin Filipović, *Emerik Blum: Monografija* (Šahinpašić, 2002), 152.

25. "Proizvodnja aluminija veća od planiranje," *Energoinvest List*, January 12, 1987, 1.

26. "JUBMES—Jugoslavenska Banka za Medjunarodnu Ekonomsku Saradnju" [JUBMES—Yugoslav Bank for International Economic Cooperation], 1988, Fond 782, Fasc. 1791 (2832), Arhiv Jugoslavije; *Energoinvest List*, November 28, 1988, February 13, 1989.

27. "Savezni Sekretarijat za Ekonomske Odnose sa Inostranstvom" [Federal Secretariat for Foreign Economic Relations], 1979, Fond 751, Fasc. 1625, Arhiv Jugoslavije.

28. Š. Vučijak, "Značajan rast izvoza," *Energoinvest List*, January 25, 1988, 2.

29. Gilbert Burck, "A Socialist Enterprise That Acts like a Fierce Capitalist Competitor," *Fortune*, January 1972, 82–86.

30. Faruk Šarić, "Svijet cijeni poslovnost i kvalitet," *Energoinvest List*, December 12, 1988, 2.

31. "10 Najvećih proizvodnih organizacija udruženog rada u oblasti industrija i rudarstva poljoprivrede i šumarstva i građevinarstva," *Ekonomska Politika*, September 7, 1987, 5, 45; "U reformu—bez odlaganja," *Energoinvest List*, November 21, 1988, 2.

32. M. Barjaktarević, "Osrednjost kao sudbina," *Ekonomska Politika*, December 11, 1989, 18.

33. Viktor Meier, *Yugoslavia: A History of Its Demise* (Routledge, 1999), 46.

34. "Consensus for Market Economy, Legal State and Democratic Society," statement by Ante Marković on the occasion of the review of the Program of Economic Reform and measures for its implementation in 1990 at the joint session of the Federal Chamber and

Chamber of Republics and Provinces of the SFRY Assembly on December 18, 1989, in *Yugoslav Changes*, ed. Federal Executive Council Secretariat for Information, 94.

35. Nejboša Šavić, "Prestrukturiranje, razvojni ciklus i privatizacija u Jugoslaviji," in *Prestrukturiranje, Razvojni Ciklus i Privatizacija*, ed. Nejboša Šavić, 1–15; *Zbornik Radova Jugoslovenskih Ekonomista Za Savetovanje, 8–10 Maj 1990, Brioni* (Savez Ekonomista Jugoslavije, 1990), 5.

36. Energoinvest (engineering and power plant construction), UNIS (metal processing and engineering), and Šipad (wood and furniture manufacturer) benefited from Yugoslavia's policy of significant growth in the export sector in developing countries. These companies were respectively the third-, sixth-, and tenth-biggest producers in Yugoslavia in terms of revenue, and together they employed 190,000 workers across the country. "140 Najvećih proizvodnih preduzeća industrije i rudarstva, poljoprivrede, šumarstva i građevinarstva prema ukupnom prihodu u 1989. Godini," *Ekonomska Politika*, September 24, 1990, 4.

37. Republički Komitet za Odnose sa Inostranstvo, Izvještaj o Radu u 1988, Godini, Sarajevo, Januar 1989 godine, pp. 14–15, folder 47, "Zapisnici sa sjednice RSMO (1–6)," Državni Arhiv Bosne i Hercegovine. Here, Energoinvest is mentioned together with UNIS as the largest company responsible for cooperation and export.

38. UNIDO, Support Programme for Industrial Recovery and Private Sector Development in Bosnia and Herzegovina (1996), 7.

39. Božidar Matić at the meeting of the workers' council, "Energoinvest u vremenu i ispred njega," *Energoinvest List*, June 20, 1991, 3.

40. "Idejno-politički stavovi o organizovanju Energoinvesta u uslovima privredne reforme," *Energoinvest List*, December 12, 1988, 3.

41. Faruk Šarić, "Praktična primjena ideje nesvrstanosti," *Energoinvest List*, July 13, 1987, 2. See Ljubica Spaskovska and Anna Calori, "A Nonaligned Business World: The Global Socialist Enterprise between Self-Management and Transnational Capitalism," *Nationalities Papers* 49, no. 3 (2021): 413–27, https://doi.org/10.1017/nps.2020.27.

42. Hakija Turajlić's speech at the meeting of the workers' council, quoted in Faruk Šarić and Liljana Korjenić, "Kako ćemo poslovati u novim uslovima," *Energoinvest List*, January 19, 1987, 5. Turajlić would go on to be a prominent political and institutional personality in the early 1990s, when he became Bosnia's deputy prime minister of the first independent government (1992); he was then assassinated in 1993 near Sarajevo's airport during a diplomatic standoff between Serbian paramilitary forces and the United Nations Protection Force (UNPROFOR).

43. Božidar Matić, interview with author, Sarajevo, March 9, 2016.

44. Džemajl Vlahovljak, interview with author, Sarajevo, March 4, 2016.

45. Milorad Lazić, "Arsenal of the Global South: Yugoslavia's Military Aid to Nonaligned Countries and Liberation Movements," *Nationalities Papers* 49, no. 3 (2021): 428–45, https://doi.org/10.1017/nps.2020.6. See also Milorad Lazić, "Comrades in Arms: Yugoslav Military Aid to Liberation Movements of Angola and Mozambique, 1961–1976," in *Southern African Liberation Movements and the Global Cold War "East": Transnational Activism 1960–1990*, ed. Lena Dallywater, Chris Saunders, and Helder Adegar Fonseca (De Gruyter Oldenbourg, 2019), 151–79.

46. This is further discussed in Anna Calori, "Losing the Global: (Re)Building a Bosnian Enterprise across Transition," *Business History* 65, no. 7 (2020): 1226–41, https://doi.org/10.1080/00076791.2020.1819242.

47. Gilbert Burck, "A Socialist Enterprise That Acts Like a Fierce Capitalist Competitor," *Fortune*, January 1972, 82–86.

48. Unkovski-Korica, *Economic Struggle for Power*, 85, 94.

49. Branko Horvat, *The Yugoslav Economic System: The First Labor-Managed Economy in the Making* (International Arts and Sciences Press, 1976), 19.

50. Horvat, *Yugoslav Economic System*, 21.

51. These reforms gave nominal power to workers' councils, even though they did not entail any actual strengthening of workers' decision-making beyond their factory. See Goran Marković, "Workers' Councils in Yugoslavia: Successes and Failures," *Socialism and Democracy* 25, no. 3 (2011): 107–29, 116.

52. Peter Quinnan Wright, "Between the Market and Solidarity: Commercializing Development Aid and International Higher Education in Socialist Yugoslavia," *Nationalities Papers* 49, no. 3 (2020): 462–82.

53. Jakob Finci, interview with author, Sarajevo, March 8, 2016.

54. Together with Dervo Sejdić, Jakob Finci has sued the state of Bosnia and Herzegovina for discrimination in a case brought and won at the European Court of Human Rights in 2009. The Constitution of Bosnia and Herzegovina, sanctioned after the Dayton Peace Agreement of 1995, established a tripartite mechanism of shared presidency between what are considered "constitutive" ethnic groups: Bosnian Serbs, Muslims, and Croats. Sejdić and Finci, respectively citizens of Roma and Jewish descent, are automatically excluded by these provisions.

55. Catherine Baker, *Race and the Yugoslav Region: Post-Socialist, Post-Sonflict, Post-Colonial?* (Manchester University Press, 2018); Catherine Baker et al., *Off White: Central and Eastern Europe and the Global History of Race* (Manchester University Press, 2024).

56. Peter Wright, "Are There Racists in Yugoslavia? Debating Racism and Anti-Blackness in Socialist Yugoslavia," *Slavic Review* 81, no. 2 (2022): 418–41, https://doi.org/10.1017/slr.2022.150.

57. As, for example, the exchange between Yugoslav and Zambian delegations (including joint ventures between Energoinvest and the Zambian Industrial Development Corporation [INDECO]) shows. Federal Executive Council informative on the third meeting of the Yugoslav-Zambian Joint Committee for Economic Cooperation, held in June 1976 in Lusaka, Archive of Yugoslavia, Fond 574, folder F60.

58. Dubravka Sekulić, "Energoprojekt in Nigeria: Yugoslav Construction Companies in the Developing World," *Southeastern Europe* 41 (2017): 227.

59. George Klein, "Workers' Self-Management and the Politics of Ethnic Nationalism in Yugoslavia," *Nationalities Papers: The Journal of Nationalism and Ethnicity* 5, no. 1 (1977): 1–21, 20n9.

60. Goran Musić, "Two Roads to Self-Managing Socialism," in *Making and Breaking the Yugoslav Working Class: The Story of Two Self-Managed Factories* (Central European University Press, 2021), 17–50, https://doi.org/10.7829/j.ctv1bvndfr.7.

61. Josef Borocz and Akos Rona-Tas, "Small Leap Forward: Emergence of New Economic Elites," *Theory and Society* 24, no. 5 (October 1995): 751–81, 763.

62. Musić, *Making and Breaking*, 40.

63. Marko Grdešić, "Exceptionalism and Its Limits: The Legacy of Self-Management in the Former Yugoslavia," in *Working Through the Past: Labor and Authoritarian Legacies in Comparative Perspective*, ed. Stephen Crowley, Teri Caraway, and Maria Cook (Cornell University Press, 2015), 103–21, 105.

64. Sharon Zukin, "The Problem of Social Class under Socialism," *Theory and Society* 6, no. 3 (1978): 391–427, 403, http://www.jstor.org/stable/656759.

65. Report from the meeting of the workers' council of Energoinvest, Faruk Šarić and Liljana Korjenić, "Vrijeme traži i nove napore, ali je i izazov," *Energoinvest List*, February 6, 1989, 2.

66. For more on social mobility within enterprises, see Ljubica Spaskovska and Anna Calori, "A Nonaligned Business World: The Global Socialist Enterprise between Self-Management and Transnational Capitalism," *Nationalities Papers* 49, no. 3 (2021): 413–27, https://doi-org.ezproxy2.lib.gla.ac.uk/10.1017/nps.2020.27.

67. Edin, interview with author, Sarajevo, February 17, 2016.

68. Asim, interview with author, Sarajevo, May 29, 2016.

69. Till Hilmar, "Economic Change, Skills, and the Shifting Horizons of Social Recognition: East German and Czech Care Workers Remember the Disruptive 1990s," in *Remembering the Neoliberal Turn: Economic Change and Collective Memory in Eastern Europe after 1989*, ed. Veronika Pehe and Joanna Wawrzyniak (Routledge, 2024).

70. Mirsad, interview with author, February 24, 2016.

71. Kenneth Lipartito and David B. Sicilia, eds., "Introduction: Crossing Corporate Boundaries," in *Constructing Corporate America: History, Politics, Culture*, ed. Kenneth Lipartito and David B. Sicilia (Oxford University Press, 2004; online ed, Oxford Academic, September 1, 2007), 17, https://doi-org.ezproxy2.lib.gla.ac.uk/10.1093/acprof: oso/9780199251902.003.0001.

72. Zdravko Leković, quoted in Edvard Kardelj, *Towards Democratic Communication— Mass Communication Research in Yugoslavia* (Yugoslav Center for Theory and Practice of Self-Management, 1984), 107–8.

73. France Vreg, quoted in Edvard Kardelj, *Towards Democratic Communication: Mass Communication Research in Yugoslavia* (Yugoslav Center for Theory and Practice of Self-Management, 1984), 38–39.

74. Zdravko Prlenda, interview with author, Sarajevo, December 10, 2016.

75. For example, in an interview in 1989, the then director of the aluminum plant Birač in Zvornik declared, "Believe me when you visit the world and you say that you are from Energoinvest, then that means something. I am saying that from a personal experience, because I have lived that." "Važno je i zvati se E.," *Energoinvest List*, December 1989, 3.

76. Unkovski-Korica, *Economic Struggle for Power*, 124.

77. Report from the meeting of the workers' council of Energoinvest, Šarić and Korjenić, "Vrijeme traži i nove napore, ali je i izazov," 3.

78. "Titove riječi—riječi budučnosti," *Energoinvest List*, April 26, 1989, 2.

79. I use the word *province* here because at the time Kosovo was a Yugoslav autonomous province. Report from the meeting of the presidency of the League of Communists of Energoinvest, "Dobri rezultati dosadašnje saradnje," *Energoinvest List*, August 10, 1987, 1–2.

80. Faruk Šarić, "Zajedništvo ne smije biti parola," *Energoinvest List*, October 3, 1987, 4.

81. Valerie Bunce, "The Elusive Peace in the Former Yugoslavia," *Cornell International Law Journal* 28, no. 3 (1995): article 10, https://scholarship.law.cornell.edu/cilj/vol28/iss3/10; Dinko Dubravčić, "Economic Causes and Political Context of the Dissolution of a Multinational Federal State: The Case of Yugoslavia," *Communist Economies and Economic Transformation* 5, no. 3 (1993): 259–72, https://doi.org/10.1080/14631379308427758.

82. As an example, for the year 1990: B.M., "Novi posao Energoinvesta u Libiji. Trafostanice za 100 miliona dolara," *Oslobođenje*, June 2, 1990, 3; "Energoinvest u SAD. Kvalitetom

do Tržišta," *Oslobođenje*, June 5, 1990, 6; V. Mrkić, "Jugosloveni u Libiji. Zajednički do najvećeg posla," *Oslobođenje*, June 6, 1990, 4; "Energoinvest kreće za Tajland. Posao vrijedan 670 hiljada dolara," *Oslobođenje*, June 6, 1990, 5; B.M., "Energoinvest u Africi. Osnovan Energozair," *Oslobođenje*, June 21, 1990, 7; "Prvo Jugoslovesko-Kinesko Preduzeće," *Oslobođenje*, October 9, 1990, 5.

83. Patrick Hyder Patterson, "Just Rewards: The Social Contract and Communism's Hard Bargain with the Citizen-Consumer," in *The Socialist Good Life: Desire, Development, and Standards of Living in Eastern Europe*, ed. Cristofer Scarboro, Diana Mincyte, and Zsuzsa Gille (Indiana University Press, 2020), 52–81.

84. Much of the news in Bosnia refers to Energoinvest in similar ways. See, for example, Ibro Čavčić, "Energoinvest se bori s milionskim gubicima, njegovi 'grobari' nagrađeni," Klix.Ba, October 5, 2017, https://www.klix.ba/vijesti/bih/energoinvest-se-bori-s-milionskim -gubicima-njegovi-grobari-nagradjeni/171002013; Dženana Karup-Drusko, "Mustafa Mujezinović Kupuje Dio?!," *Dani*, March 10, 2000, https://www.bhdani.ba/portal/arhiva -67-281/145/t455.htm.

85. Mladen, interview with author, Sarajevo, July 17, 2014.

86. Mate, interview with author, Mostar, December 17, 2016.

87. Branimir, interview with author, phone interview, December 19, 2017.

88. Branimir, Interview with author, phone interview, December 19, 2017.

89. I borrow the expression "geopolitical dignity" from Ljubica Spaskovska, "The 'Children of Crisis': Making Sense of (Post)Socialism and the End of Yugoslavia," *East European Politics and Societies and Cultures* 31, no. 3 (2017): 500–517, 513.

90. An exhaustive account of tourism policies in socialist workplaces is offered by Igor Duda, "Workers into Tourists: Entitlements, Desires, and the Realities of Social Tourism under Yugoslav Socialism," in *Yugoslavia's Sunny Side: A History of Tourism in Socialism (1950s–1980s)*, ed. Hannes Grandits and Karin Taylor (Central European University Press, 2010), 33–68.

91. Nebojša Šerić Šoba, "Bob Rock," Radiosarajevo.Ba, November 23, 2014, https://www .radiosarajevo.ba/metromahala/ja-mislim/Nebojša-seric-soba-bob-rock/172245.

92. Branimir, interview with author, December 19, 2017 (emphasis added).

93. Murat Čilimović, "Ulaganja u budućnost," *Energoinvest List*, February 13, 1989, 5.

94. Robert Donia, *Sarajevo: A Biography* (Hurst, 2006), 313; Faruk Šarić, "Na prvoj liniji do slobode," *Energoinvest List*, May 1993, 4.

95. For a thorough analysis of housing policies in late-socialist Yugoslavia, see Rory Archer, "Social Inequalities and Yugoslavia's Dissolution," in *Debating the End of Yugoslavia*, ed. Florian Bieber, Armina Galijaš, and Rory Archer (Routledge, 2014).

96. Stephen Crowley and David Ost, *Workers after Workers' States: Labor and Politics in Postcommunist Eastern Europe* (Rowman & Littlefield, 2011); Marsha Siefert, ed., *Labor in State-Socialist Europe, 1945–1989: Contributions to a History of Work* (CEU Press, 2020).

97. The historian and sociologist Eszter Bartha demonstrated how the different labor and welfare regimes in Hungary and East Germany created different kinds of expectations of capitalist reforms and globalization among groups of workers in the two countries. See Eszter Bartha, *Alienating Labor: On the Road from Socialism to Capitalism in East Germany and Hungary*, vol. 22 of *International Studies in Social History* (Berghahn, 2013). Looking at previous moments of transformation, Stephen Kotkin illustrated how peasants embraced Stalinism and Bolshevik "modernity" through the workplace. Stephen Kotkin, *Magnetic Mountain: Stalinism as a Civilization* (University of California Press, 1997).

98. Nina Vodopivec, "Yesterday's Heroes: Spinning Webs of Memory in a Postsocialist Textile Factory in Slovenia," in *Negotiating Normality: Everyday Lives in Socialist Institutions*, ed. Daniela Koleva (Transaction, 2012), 43–63, 53.

2. The Cracks in the Promise of Global Socialism

1. Max Trecker, *Red Money for the Global South: East-South Economic Relations in the Cold War* (Routledge, 2020), 156.

2. Max Trecker, "Circle of Debt: How the Crisis of the Global South in the 1980s Affected the Socialist East," *Cold War History* 20, no. 1 (2020): 1–19, 15.

3. "Savezni Sekretarijat za Ekonomske Odnose sa Inostranstvom," 1985, Fond 751, Fasc. 2948, Arhiv Jugoslavije (Federal Secretariat for Foreign Economic Relations, Archive of Yugoslavia); Marijan Svetličić et al., *Ekonomski odnosi Jugoslavije sa zemljama u razvoju* (Istrazivački projekat privredna, politička, kulturna i naučno-tehnička sarandnja Jugoslavije sa zemljama u razvoju, 1971), 51–52.

4. For Panama, see Yugoslav Diplomatic Archive, 1974, 229 PANAMA Dosije 10. For Zambia, see SIV informative on the third meeting of the Yugoslav-Zambian Joint Committee for Economic Cooperation, held in June 1976 in Lusaka, Fond 574, folder 60, Arhiv Jugoslavije.

5. Dobri Dodevski, "Makroprojekt 1989," in *Ekonomisti o Krizi: razgovor ekonomista s mandatorom za SIV Dipl. Ing. Antom Markovićem*, ed. Tomislav Popović (Belgrade: Konzorcijum ekonomskih instituta Jugoslavije, 1989), 154; Petar Požar, ed., *Jugoslavija u Svetskoj Privredi na Pragu XXI Veka. Makroprojekat Novi Međunarodni Ekonomski Poredak* (Informator, 1986), 113.

6. Julianne Ams, et al., *Prevention and Resolution of Sovereign Debt Crises* (International Monetary Fund, 2018), accessed June 28, 2025 https://www.elibrary.imf.org/view/book/97814 84371329/9781484371329.xml.

7. Anna Calori and Ljubica Spaskovska, "Reimagining the World: Decolonization and the Promise of Development," *Contemporary European History* 30 (2021): 613–20, 618. The World Bank itself defined the 1980s as a "lost decade of development" in Latin America and sub-Saharan Africa. See World Bank, *World Development Report 1990* (Oxford University Press, 1990), iii.

8. Susan Woodward, "The Political Economy of Ethno-Nationalism in Yugoslavia," *Socialist Register* 39 (2003): 77. On Yugoslavia's dependency on oil foreign imports, see Ljubica Spaskovska, "'Crude' Alliance: Economic Decolonization and Oil Power in the Non-Aligned World," *Contemporary European History* 30 (2021): 528–43.

9. Susan L. Woodward, *Socialist Unemployment: The Political Economy of Yugoslavia, 1945–1990* (Princeton University Press, 1995), 256–57.

10. Susan L. Woodward, *Balkan Tragedy* (Brookings Institution, 1995), 47.

11. Woodward, *Balkan Tragedy*, 48.

12. Harold Lydall, *Yugoslavia in Crisis* (Clarendon, 1989), 237.

13. Andreja Živković, "From the Market . . . to the Market: The Debt Economy after Yugoslavia," in *Welcome to the Desert of Post-Socialism*, ed. Srećko Horvat and Igor Štiks (Verso, 2015), 48.

14. Woodward, *Socialist Unemployment*, chap. 7.

15. As illustrated in Stephen Collier, *Post-Soviet Social: Neoliberalism, Social Modernity, Biopolitics* (Princeton University Press, 2011), 3; Kean Birch and Vlad Mykhnenko, "Varieties

of Neoliberalism? Restructuring in Large Industrially Dependent Regions across Western and Eastern Europe," *Journal of Economic Geography* 9 (2009): 335–80; Grzegorz Kolodko, *From Shock to Therapy: The Political Economy of Postsocialist Transformation* (Oxford University Press, 2000); Janos Martyas Kovacs and Violetta Zentai, eds., *Capitalism from Outside? Economic Cultures in Eastern Europe after 1989* (CEU Press, 2012).

16. Calori and Spaskovska, "Reimagining the World," 620. On local varieties of neoliberalism, see Tobias Rupprecht, "Global Varieties of Neoliberalism: Ideas on Free Markets and Strong States in Late Twentieth-Century Chile and Russia," *Global Perspectives* 1, no. 1 (2020), https://doi.org/10.1525/gp.2020.13278. Of course, foreign advisers like Jeffrey Sachs contributed to give legitimacy to the neoliberal turn in the region. See Jeffrey Sachs and David Lipton, "How Yugoslavia Can Save Itself," *Washington Post*, December 31, 1989; Jeffrey Sachs, "Crossing the Valley of Tears in East European Reform," *Challenge*, September–October 1991.

17. Gerald W. Creed, *Domesticating Revolution: From Socialist Reform to Ambivalent Transition in a Bulgarian Village* (Pennsylvania State University Press, 1998), 11.

18. Johanna Bockman and Gil Eyal, "Eastern Europe as a Laboratory for Economic Knowledge: The Transnational Roots of Neoliberalism," *American Journal of Sociology* 108, no. 2 (2002): 310–52; Adam Fabry, "The Origins of Neoliberalism in Late 'Socialist' Hungary: The Case of the Financial Research Institute and 'Turnabout and Reform,'" *Capital & Class*, 42, no. 1 (2017): 77–107; Hilary Appel and Mitchell A. Orenstein, "Why Did Neoliberalism Triumph and Endure in the Post-Communist World?," *Comparative Politics*, April 2016, 313–31; Venelin I. Ganev, "The 'Triumph of Neoliberalism' Reconsidered: Critical Remarks on Ideas-Centered Analyses of Political and Economic Change in Post-Communism," *East European Politics and Societies* 19, no. 3 (2005): 343–78.

19. Johanna Bockman, "The Long Road to 1989 Neoclassical Economics, Alternative Socialisms and the Advent of Neoliberalism," *Radical History Review*, no. 112 (2012): 9–42; Dorothee Bohle and Béla Greskovits, "Neoliberalism, Embedded Neoliberalism and Neocorporatism: Towards Transnational Capitalism in Central-Eastern Europe," *West European Politics* 30, no. 3 (2007): 443–66; Cornel Ban, *Ruling Ideas: How Global Neoliberalism Goes Local* (Oxford University Press, 2016).

20. Bockman, *Markets in the Name of Socialism*, 218.

21. Unkovski-Korica, *Economic Struggle for Power*, 42.

22. Harold Lydall, *Yugoslavia in Crisis* (Clarendon, 1989), 80–81. On decentralization in Yugoslavia, see Nicholas R. Lang, "The Dialectics of Decentralization: Economic Reform and Regional Inequality in Yugoslavia," *World Politics* 27, no. 3 (1975): 309–35, https://doi.org/10.2307/2010123; Ellen Turkish Comisso, *Workers' Control under Plan and Market of Yugoslav Self-Management* (Yale University Press, 1979), 211–12.

23. Svjetozar Pejovich, "The Economic Position of the Enterprise in the Yugoslav Economy," *Statsvetenskaplig Tidskrift* 83, no. 5 (1980): 303–11, 303.

24. James C. Conner and Branko Vukmir, "The Legal Anatomy of a Yugoslav 'Enterprise,'" *Business Lawyer* 32, no. 1 (1976): 99–117, 109.

25. Požar, *Jugoslavija u Svetskoj Privredi na Pragu XXI Veka*, 82–83.

26. Bockman, *Markets in the Name of Socialism*, 166.

27. Mihajlo Crnobrnja, interview with author, Belgrade, November 23, 2015, November 25, 2015.

28. Oskar Kovač, "Postoje li uslovi za kompletno tržišno rešenje u privrednom sistemu SFRJ?," In *Privreda u Reformi—Zbornik Radova Za Savetovanje Na Brionima, 4–6 Maj 1989* (Iro Ekonomika i Savez ekonomista Jugoslavije, 1989), 11–37, 24.

29. Vojo Čolović, Magnetofonski Snimak Sjednice Republičkog Društvenog Savjeta za Međunarodne Odnose, March 3, 1989, 73, folder 47 Zapisnici sa sjednice RSMO (1–6), Državni Arhiv Bosne i Hercegovine;Vojnić Dragomir Vojnić, "Socijalizam u Reformi—Jugoslavensko Iskustvo," in *Aktuelni Problemi Privrednih Kretanja i Ekonomske Politike Jugoslavije*, ed. Dragomir Vojnić, 227–46 (Ekonomski Institut Zagreb, Informator, 1989), 237.

30. Požar, *Jugoslavija u Svetskoj Privredi Na Pragu XXI Veka*, 113.

31. Rezime osnovnih mišjlenja, stavova i ocjena iznesenih u raspravi o Aktuelnim Kretanjima u Socijalističkim Zemljama Evrope i Njihovom Uticaju na Savremene Međunarodne Odnose na Sjednici Savjeta od 25 Aprila 1989. Godine, 6–7, Republički Društveni Savjet za Međunarodne Odnose, folder 47 Zapisnici sa sjednice RSMO (1–6), Državni Arhiv Bosne i Hercegovine.

32. Steven L. Burg, "Elite Conflict in Post-Tito Yugoslavia," *Soviet Studies* 38, no. 2 (1986): 170–93, 175.

33. *Službeni List SFRJ* 44, no. 77 (1988): 1942–56.

34. Henry Kamm, "Financial Scandal Shakes Yugoslav Leaders," *New York Times*, September 10, 1987; Paola Butturini, "Big Bank Scandal Stuns Yugoslavia," *Chicago Tribune*, October 29, 1987. See also Nebojša Vladisavljević, "The Breakup of Yugoslavia: The Role of Popular Politics," in *New Perspectives on Yugoslavia: Key Issues and Controversies*, ed. Dejan Djokić and James Ker-Lindsay (Routledge, 2011), 152–53.

35. Manojlo Babić and Hasan Muratović, eds., *Samoupravno Organizovanje u Teoriji i Praksi*, vol. 1 (Institut za organizaciju i ekonomsku, Svjetlost, 1985); Miloš Trifković, ed., *Državna Vlast i Socijalističko Samoupravljanje*, vol. 7 Zbornik Pravnog Fakulteta u Mostaru (Pravni Fakultet Univerziteta "Džemal Bijedić," 1986); Branko Derić, ed., *Produktivnost Rada u Funckiji Efikasnijeg Privredjivanja u Privredi Bosne i Hercegovine* (Ekomski Institut Sarajevo, 1988); Rešad Begtić, "Metodi i Područja Unapređenja Poslovne Saradnje Naših Privrednih Organizacija Sa Stranim Firmama," *Ekonomski Institut Sarajevo*, Makroprojekat Jugoslavija u Svetskoj Privredi, January 1989, 1–66; Rešad Begtić, ed., "Strategija i Organizacija Spoljnotrgovinske Mreže Jugoslavije u Funkciji Efikasnijeg Izvoza," *Ekonomski Institut Sarajevo*, September 1988, 1–56; Hasan Muratović, "Organizovanje Složenih Organizacija Udruženog Rada," *Institut Za Organizaciju i Ekonomiku,Zborniku radova za savjetovanje*, Sarajevo 1986, 35–50; Požar, *Jugoslavija u Svetskoj Privredi Na Pragu XXI Veka*.

36. Vojnić, "Socijalizam u Reformi," Vojnić237.

37. Vojo Čolović, Magnetofonski Snimak Sjednice Republičkog Društvenog Savjeta za Međunarodne Odnose, 73; Vojnić, "Socijalizam u Reformi," Vojnić237.

38. Tomislav Popović, ed., *Jugoslavija u Svetskoj Privredi Na Pragu Xxi Veka, Strategija*, Makroprojekat Novi Medunarodni Ekonomski Poredak (Belgrade: Konzorcijum ekonomskih instituta, Informator, 1986), viii, 74.

39. Ulf Brunnbauer, *Building Ships and Surviving Late Socialism: The Shipyard "Uljanik" in Pula in the 1970s and 1980s*, Series: IOS Mitteilungen 69 (Leibniz-Institut für Ost- und Südosteuropaforschung, 2019) 27–28, https://nbnresolving.org/urn:nbn:de:0168-ssoar-65464-7.

40. Milica Uvalić, *Investment and Property Rights in Yugoslavia: The Long Transition to a Market Economy* (Cambridge University Press, 1992), 10–11; Guido Acquaviva, "The Dissolution of Yugoslavia and the Fate of Its Financial Obligations," *Denver Journal of International Law & Policy* 30, no. 173 (2002).

41. John Tagliabue, "How a Yugoslav Company Built an International Market," *New York Times*, March 28, 1983.

42. "Teze za završni sastanak u upravi za latinsku ameriku i karibe povodom odlaska Vojka Senkera na dužnost Sekretara za ekonomske poslove Amabasade SFRJ u Havani," Belgrade, November 24, 1982, 8–9, Fond 465, Fasc. 6752, Arhiv Jugoslavije.

43. Anna Calori "Cigar Socialism: An Entangled History of Yugoslav-Cuban Relations," *Cold War History*, June 2023, 1–19, https://doi.org/10.1080/14682745.2023.2217759.

44. Platforma za IV Zasedanje Mesovite Jugoslovensko-Meksicke Komisije za Privrednu Saradnju, Mexico, September 26–28, 1984, Fond 465, Fasc. 6758, Arhiv Jugoslavije.

45. Protocol from the seventh meeting of the Yugoslav-Zambian Joint Committee for Economic Cooperation, Zambia, June 1–4, 1983, Fond 130, Fasc. 5559, Arhiv Jugoslavije.

46. V. Mrkić, "Propast 'zdrave' fabrike," *Oslobođenje*, October 10, 1990, 10; Z. J., "Obustava u brojkama," *Oslobođenje*, June 9, 1991, 11.

47. Neca Jovanov, *Sukobi* (Subotica: Nikšić, 1989), 37.

48. I.C., "Kako živiš, druže?," *Energoinvest List*, July 1990, 9.

49. I. Selak, "Uz čestitke i oprez," *Oslobođenje*, February 14, 1990, 9.

50. *Energoinvest List*, May 13, 1991, 6–7.

51. Energoinvest Statute 1990, *Informativni Glasnik Energoinvest s.p.*, December 27, 1990, 3; *Energoinvest List*, February 11, 1991, 3–5; Božidar Matić, interviewed by Ljiljana Korjenić, *Energoinvest List*, March 25, 1991, 3.

52. Nevenko Babčić, "Organizacioni model u funkciji poslovnih ciljeva," *Energoinvest Armature, List Radnika Radne Organizacije*, September 1989, 7.

53. D. Kljajić, "Neka radi ko zna i hoće," *Energoinvest List*, March 12, 1990, 10.

54. The uneven regional development between the richest republics (Slovenia and Croatia) and the poorest regions (Kosovo and Macedonia) is often interpreted as one of the concurring causes of the political and economic friction that led to Yugoslavia's dissolution. See Dijana Pleština, *Regional Development in Communist Yugoslavia: Success, Failure, and Consequences* (Routledge, 1993).

55. *Energoinvest Armature, List Radnika Radne Organizacije*, June 1990, 6.

56. D. Kostić et al., "Kriza je kad nema posla," *Energoinvest List*, April 25, 1990, 11–12.

57. *Sretno, List Radnika Radne Organizacije Energoinvest* (Srebrenica), July 1990, 1, 6.

58. *Službeni List SFRJ* 44, no. 77 (1988): 1942–56.

59. Art. 189, *Laws on Economic Reform in Yugoslavia* (1990), 19.

60. Energoinvest Statute 1990, *Informativni Glasnik Energoinvest s.p.*, December 27, 1990, 1–2.

61. Božidar Matić, interview, Ljiljana Korjenić and Faruk Šarić, *Energoinvest List*, February 6, 1989, 5.

62. Energoinvest Statute, *Informativni Glasnik Energoinvest s.p.*, December 27, 1990, 2.

63. *SRETNO, List Radnika Radne Organizacije Energoinvest* (Srebrenica), April 1989, 7; *Energoinvest Armature, List Radnika Radne Organizacije*, February 1990, 4.

64. *Energoinvest List*, May 13, 1991, 8.

65. *Energoinvest List*, May 13, 1991, 8.

66. Božidar Matić, interview with author, Sarajevo, March 9, 2016.

3. Delivering Change?

1. *Meeting Gorbachev*, written and directed by Werner Herzog and André Singer, produced by Svetlana Palmer and Lucki Stipetic (2018).

2. Oleh Havrylyshyn and Donal McGettigan, "Privatization in Transition Countries: A Sampling of the Literature," IMF Working Paper 99/6 (International Monetary Fund, 1999); Jan Svejnar and Milica Uvalić, "Why Development Patterns Differ: The Czech and Serbian Cases Compared," in *Institutions and Patterns of Economic Development*, ed. Masahiko Aoki, Timur Kuran, and Gerard Roland (Palgrave Macmillan, 2012), 116; Peter Mihályi, "Post-Socialist Transition in a 25-Year Perspective," *Acta Oeconomica* 64, no. 1 (2014): 1–24; Hillel Ticktin, "Why the Transition Failed: Towards a Political Economy of the Post-Soviet Period in Russia," *Critique: Journal of Socialist Theory* 30, no. 1 (2002): 13–41, https://doi.org/10.1080/03017600508413473; Helena Nikolić and Jan Horaček, "Comparison of Privatization in the Republic of Croatia and Selected Former Communist Countries," *Engineering Proceedings* 39, no. 1 (2023): 48, https://doi.org/10.3390/engproc2023039048; Jan Svejnar, "Transition Economies: Performance and Challenges," *Journal of Economic Perspectives* 16, no. 1 (2002): 3–28.

3. As illustrated in Stephen Collier, *Post-Soviet Social: Neoliberalism, Social Modernity, Biopolitics* (Princeton University Press, 2011), 3. See also Kean Birch and Vlad Mykhnenko, "Varieties of Neoliberalism? Restructuring in Large Industrially Dependent Regions across Western and Eastern Europe," *Journal of Economic Geography* 9 (2009): 335–80; Grzegorz Kolodko, *From Shock to Therapy: The Political Economy of Postsocialist Transformation* (Oxford University Press, 2000); Janos Martyas Kovacs and Violetta Zentai, eds., *Capitalism from Outside? Economic Cultures in Eastern Europe after 1989* (CEU Press, 2012).

4. Ulf Brunnbauer, "Making Bulgarians Socialist: The Fatherland Front in Communist Bulgaria, 1944–1989," *East European Politics and Societies* 22, no. 1 (2008): 44–79, 72; Ana Antić, "Raising a True Socialist Individual: Yugoslav Psychoanalysis and the Creation of Democratic Marxist Citizens," *Social History* 44, no. 1 (2019): 86–115.

5. For perhaps the most thorough account of how Stalinism as a civilizing mission resonated among various groups, see Stephen Kotkin, *Magnetic Mountain: Stalinism as a Civilization* (University of California Press, 1997). For the case of Hungary and the GDR, see Eszter Bartha, *Alienating Labor: On the Road from Socialism to Capitalism in East Germany and Hungary* (Berghahn, 2013).

6. Andrea Matošević, *Socijalizam s udarničkim licem: Etnografija radnog pregalaštva* (Institut za etnologiju i folkloristiku, 2015); Rudi Šupek, *Omladina na putu bratstva: Psiho-sociologija radne akcije* (Mladost, 1963).

7. Branko Horvat, *The Yugoslav Economic System: The First Labor-Managed Economy in the Making* (International Arts and Sciences, 1976), 19.

8. Ivan Rajković, "From Freedom to Loaf to Freedom to Work: The Late Socialist Countermovement and Liberalization from Below in Yugoslavia," in *Work, Society and the Ethical Self: Chimeras of Freedom in the Neoliberal Era*, ed. Chris Hann (Berghahn Books, 2021), 158–81, 164. See also Miroslav Stanojević, "Workers' Power in Transition Economies: The Cases of Serbia and Slovenia," *European Journal of Industrial Relations* 9, no. 3 (2003): 283–301, 290.

9. Jovan Djordjević, "O samoupravnom i odgovornom društvu," quoted in Veljko Rus, "Private and Public Ownership in Yugoslavia," *Scandinavian Journal of Management Studies*, May 1986, 187–95, 188.

10. Edvard Kardelj, *Self-Management and the Political System*" (Socialist Thought and Practice, 1980), 26.

11. As in other countries in eastern Europe, such as Poland and Hungary, in Yugoslavia the discipline bloomed in the 1960s and 1970s, as scholars focused on questions of differences and inequalities in the socialist society and the different economic orders existing within

them. For an overview of this, see Svetla Koleva, "Doing Post-Western Sociology in Central and Eastern Europe before and after the Great Change: Some Epistemological Questions," *Journal of Chinese Sociology* 7, no. 20 (2020). In contrast, in countries like Romania sociology was rather marginalized. See Mike Keen and Janusz Mucha, "Sociology in Central and Eastern Europe in the 1990s: A Decade of Reconstruction," *European Societies* 6, no. 2 (2004): 123–47; Ștefan Bosomitu, "Sociology in Communist Romania: An Institutional and Biographical Overview," *Studia UBB Sociologia* 62, no. 1 (2017): 65–84. In Yugoslavia, sociology studies provided the foundation to discuss and review industrial relations and the economic and social mechanisms of self-management. See Josip Obradović, "Workers' Participation: Who Participates?," *Industrial Relations* 14, no. 1 (1975): 32–44, 43; Gary K. Bertsch and Josip Obradović, "Participation and Influence in Yugoslav Self-Management," *Industrial Relations* 18, no. 3 (1979): 322–29, 329; Vladimir Arzenšek, "Individualni Konflikti u Slovenskoj Industriji," *Revija za Sociologiju* 4, no. 1 (1974): 55–75; Vladimir Arzenšek, "Otuđenje i Štrajk," *Revija za Sociologiju* 6, no. 2–3 (1976): 3–16.

12. Ljubo Sirc, *The Yugoslav Economy under Self-Management* (London: Macmillan, 1979), 174.

13. Miloslav Janićijević, et al., eds., *Novi pravci promena društvene strukture Jugoslavije* (Institut društvenih nauka, Centar za sociološka istraživanja, 1990), 169.

14. Stephen Clissold, *Djilas: The Progress of a Revolutionary* (Maurice Temple Smith, 1983), 304–5.

15. Ellen Turkish Comisso, *Workers' Control under Plan and Market of Yugoslav Self-Management* (Yale University Press, 1979), 171–72; Woodward, *Socialist Unemployment*, 315–18.

16. Dobri Dodevski, "Makroprojekt 1989," in *Ekonomisti o krizi: razgovor ekonomista s mandatorom za SIV Dipl. Ing. Antom Markovićem*, ed. Tomislav Popović (Belgrade: Konzorcijum ekonomskih instituta Jugoslavije, 1989), 154; Veljko Rus, "Influence Structure in Yugoslav Enterprises," *Industrial Relations* 1, no. 2 (1970): 148–60.

17. D. Kostić, "Šanse koje treba iskoristiti," *Energoinvest List*, May 11, 1991, 8.

18. "Bez stega i ograničenja," *Sretno—List Radnika Radne Organizacije Energoinvest—Srebrenica*, April 1989, 2.

19. "Changes in the Yugoslav Social System to Meet the Needs of Society," statement by Ante Marković at the joint session of the Federal Chamber and the Chamber of Republics and Provinces of the Assembly of the SFRY on the occasion of the election of the president of the Federal Executive Council on March 16, 1989, in Federal Executive Council Secretariat for Information, *Yugoslav Changes*, 37.

20. Miodrag Stojilović and Momir Brkić, "Poslušnima je zvonilo," *Komunist*, February 3, 1989, 12–13.

21. Manojlo Babić and Hasan Muratović, eds., *Samoupravno Organizovanje u Teoriji i Praksi* (Institut za organizaciju i ekonomsku, Svjetlost, 1985), 1:183; Derić, *Produktivnost Rada*, 163; Laslo Sekelj, "Realno Samoupravljanje, Realni Nacionalizam i Dezintegracija Jugoslavije," *Sociologija* 33, no. 4 (1991): 587–99.

22. Rajković, "From Freedom to Loaf," 171.

23. See Musić, *Making and Breaking the Yugoslav Working Class*. Rory Archer proposes that the antibureaucratic revolution occurred not just in Serbia but in Croatia as well. Archer, "Antibureaucratism as a Yugoslav Phenomenon: The View from Northwest Croatia," *Nationalities Papers* 47, no. 4 (2019): 562–80, 563, https://doi.org/10.1017/nps.2018.40.

24. Nebojša Vladisavljević, "The Breakup of Yugoslavia: The Role of Popular Politics," in *New Perspectives on Yugoslavia: Key Issues and Controversies*, ed. Dejan Djokić and James Ker-Lindsay (Routledge, 2011), 143–60, 152–53.

25. Woodward, *Socialist Unemployment*, 30.

26. Rory Archer and Goran Musić, "When Workers' Self-Management Met Neoliberalism: Positive Perceptions of Market Reforms among Blue-Collar Workers in Late Yugoslav Socialism," in *Labor in State Socialist Europe, 1945–1989: Contributions to a Global History of Work*, ed. Marsha Siefert (Central European University Press, 2020), 395–418; Ulrike Schult, "Social Fragmentation of Industrial Workforces: Yugoslav Motor Vehicle Industry during Self-Managed Socialism," *Südost-Forschungen* 73 (2014): 351–73.

27. D. Kljajić, "Probleme moramo i rješavati," *Energoinvest List*, September 28, 1987, 6.

28. D. Kljajić, "Neka radi ko zna i hoće," *Energoinvest List*, March 12, 1990, 10.

29. D. Kljajić, "Svijest se ne mijenja preko noći," *Energoinvest List*, September 28, 1987, 7.

30. *Yugoslav Survey: A Record of Facts and Information* 31, no. 3 (1990): 53.

31. *Yugoslav Survey*, 57.

32. Giuseppe Tomasi di Lampedusa, *Il Gattopardo* (Feltrinelli, 1958).

33. Aleksander Bajt, "Social Ownership—Collective and Individual," in *Self-Governing Socialism: A Reader*, ed. Branko Horvat, Mihailo Marković, and Rudi Supek (Taylor and Francis, 1975), 2:151–63, 158.

34. Horvat, *Yugoslav Economic System*, 168.

35. Dušan Drezga, *Radnici Govore o Samoupravljanju* (Globus, 1982), 44.

36. On the circulation of these ideas, see Bockman, *Markets in the Name of Socialism*, 173, 186, 212–13. See also David Ellerman, *Management and Employee Buy-Outs as a Technique of Privatization* (Central and Eastern European Privatization Network, 1993), 15. On Yugoslav models in Latin America, see Johanna Bockman. "Democratic Socialism in Chile and Peru: Revisiting the 'Chicago Boys' as the Origin of Neoliberalism," *Comparative Studies in Society and History* 61, no. 3 (2019): 654–79, 657–59. See also Branko Horvat, "Industrial Partnership: Utopia or Necessity?," in *Scott Bader Commonwealth Monograph* (Tavistock Institute of Human Relations, 1986), 1.

37. Joseph Raphael Blasi and Douglas Lynn Kruse, *The New Owners: The Mass Emergence of Employee Ownership in Public Companies and What It Means to American Business* (Harper Collins, 1991), 12.

38. Trevor Buck and Mike Wright, "Soft Budget and Employee Buy-Outs," *Ekonomska Analiza* 4 (1990): 384.

39. Ante Ćićin-Sain, quoted in Miloš Marković, "Čije je vlasništvo. Okrugli sto ekonomista," *Ekonomska Politika*, December 12, 1988, 26.

40. Branko Horvat, "Farewell to the Illyrian Firm," *Economic Analysis and Workers' Management* 20, no. 1 (1986): 23–29.

41. Frane Černe, quoted in Marković, "Čije je vlasništvo," 27; Daniel Cvjetičanin, Diana Dragutinović, and Nina Petrović, "O tržištu kapitala u Jugoslaviji," in *Prestrukturiranje, Razvojni Ciklus i Privatizacija: Zbornik Radova Jugoslovenskih Ekonomista Za Savetovanje, 8–10 Maj 1990, Brioni*, ed. Nebojša Šavić (Savez Ekonomista Jugoslavije, 1990), 185.

42. Živko Pregl, "Foreword: Program of Reforms in Yugoslavia," in *Yugoslavia in Turmoil: After Self-Management?*, ed. Jože Dekleva and James Simmie (Pinter, 1991), xi–xvi, xiv.

43. Quoted in Saul Estrin, "Competition and Corporate Governance in Transition," *Journal of Economic Perspectives* 16, no. 1 (2002): 101–24, 107.

44. Fabry, "Origins of Neoliberalism," 2.

45. Jože Mencinger, interview with author, Ljubljana, December 11, 2015.

46. Ante Marković, "Introduction to Reforms," in *The Laws on Economic Reform in Yugoslavia*, ed. Federal Executive Council Secretariat for Information (Belgrade: Jugoslovenski

Pregled, 1990), ix. See also Šavić, "Prestrukturiranje, razvojni ciklus i privatizacija," 1; Dragomir Vojnić, "Neki problemi ekonomske i razvojne politike za 1989 i 1990 godinu," in *Ekonomisti o krizi: Razgovor ekonomista s mandatorom za SIV Dipl. Ing. Antom Markovićem. Makroprojekt 'Jugoslavija u svjetskoj privredi,'* ed. Tomislav Popović (Konzorcijum Ekonomskih Instituta Jugoslavije, 1989), 51–59, 55.

47. Ante Marković, "The Outlines of the Program," address at the session of the Presidency of the Federal Conference of the Socialist Alliance of Working People of Yugoslavia on January 28, 1989, in Federal Executive Council Secretariat for Information, *Yugoslav Changes*, 21.

48. *Službeni List SFRJ*, no. 84 (1989): 2043.

49. Art 1, *The Laws on Economic Reform in Yugoslavia* (Jugoslovenski Pregled, 1990), 5.

50. Pregl, "Foreword," xiii.

51. France Černe, quoted in Marković, "Čije je vlasništvo," 20–30, 27.

52. Žarko Papić, "Nova Koncepcija Razvoja," in Šavić, *Prestrukturiranje, Razvojni Ciklus i Privatizacija*, 23–32, 25; Bogomir Kovač, "Program Prestrukturiranja Jugoslovenske Priverde Izmedju Iluzija I Realnosti," in *Prestrukturiranje, Razvojni Ciklus I Privatizacija*, ed. Nejboša Šavić, 42–51; *Jugoslovenskih Ekonomista za Savetovanje* (Savez Ekonomista Jugoslavije, 1990), 44. See also Branko Milanović, "Privatization in Post-Communist Societies," *Communist Economies and Economic Transformation* 3, no. 1 (1992): 5–39, 21; Josip Županov, "Is Enterprise Management Becoming Professionalized?," *International Studies of Management & Organization* 3, no. 3 (1973): 42–83.

53. F. Zimić, "Koliko je daleko Evropa?," *Ekonomska Politika*, February 1, 1988, 14.

54. Živko Pregl, "Konkurencija i motivacija," *Komunist*, February 24, 1989, 4.

55. "Nema svojine bez sopstvenika," *Komunist*, January 19, 1990, 18.

56. Milica Uvalić, *Investment and Property Rights in Yugoslavia: The Long Transition to a Market Economy* (Cambridge University Press, 1992), 192.

57. *Energoinvest List*, February 11, 1991, 3–5.

58. "Podrška Promjenama," *Oslobođenje*, September 24, 1988, 3.

59. Miroslav Stanojević, "Conditions for a Neoliberal Turn: The Cases of Hungary and Slovenia," *European Journal of Industrial Relations* 20, no. 2 (2014): 97–112, https://doi.org/10.1177/0959680113515609.

60. In October 1990, for example, Marković's vice president and Slovenian economist met with entrepreneurs, including Energoinvest's finance director, Žarko Primorac, to discuss reforms. "Hod do mukama etatizma," *Oslobođenje*, October 13, 1990, 3.

61. T.C., "Direktori uz Vladu," *Oslobođenje*, September 19, 1990, 1.

62. Žarko Papić, interview with author, Sarajevo, May 18, 2016, and June 22, 2016.

63. Neven Anđelić, *Bosnia-Herzegovina: The End of a Legacy* (Frank Cass, 2003), 182.

64. Reported in "Borbin barometer: Ante vodi za tri koplija," *Oslobođenje*, May 22, 1990, 11, quoted in Alfredo Sasso, "The Defeat of the Democratic Yugoslavism in Bosnia-Herzegovina: The Alliance of Reformist Forces of Yugoslavia (SRSJ)," in *Empires and Nations from the Eighteenth to the Twentieth Century*, ed. Antonello Biagini and Giovanni Motta (Cambridge Scholars, 2014), 2:563–75, 566.

65. VIII Sjednica Republičkog Društvenog Savjeta za Privredni Razvoj i Ekonomsku Politiku, Sarajevo, November 10, 1988, Republički Društveni Savjet za Privredni Razvoj i Ekonomsku Politiku, folder 51, Državni Arhiv Bosne i Hercegovine.

66. Žarko Primorac, interview with author, Zagreb, March 16, 2016.

67. Stevan Santo, interview with author, Subotica, June 24, 2016.

4. Our World Came Tumbling Down

1. Mladen, former engineer in Energoinvest's informatics branch in Sarajevo, interview with author, Sarajevo, July 7, 2014.

2. Andrew Gilbert, "The Past in Parenthesis: (Non)Post-Socialism in Post-War Bosnia-Herzegovina," *Anthropology Today* 22, no. 4 (2006): 14–18.

3. Chiara Milan, *Social Mobilization beyond Ethnicity: Civic Activism and Grassroots Movements in Bosnia and Herzegovina* (Routledge, 2020), 22. See also Stef Jansen, "Remembering with a Difference: Clashing Memories of Bosnian Conflict in Everyday Life," in *The New Bosnian Mosaic: Identities, Memories, and Moral Claims in a Post-War Society*, ed. Xavier Bougarel, Elissa Helms, and Gert Duijzings (Ashgate, 2007), 193–210, 193; Rogers Brubaker, "Ethnicity without Groups," *European Journal of Sociology* 43, no. 2 (2015): 163–89, https://doi.org/10.1017/S0003975602001066.

4. Fedja Burić, "Dwelling on the Ruins of Socialist Yugoslavia," in *Post-Communist Nostalgia*, ed. Marija Nikolaeva Todorova and Zsuzsa Gille (Berghahn Books, 2010), 227, https://doi.org/10.1515/9781845458348.

5. Popis Stanovništva 1981, *Opštine u SFR Jugoslaviji, Osnovni Podaci o Stanovništvu, Domaćinstvima i Stanovima* (Savezni Zavod za Statistiku, 1987); *Statistički Godišnjak SFR Jugoslavije 1991* (Belgrade: Savezni Zavod za Statistiku, 1991). For an analysis of broken-down data for Bosnia and Herzegovina, see Anna Calori, "Salt and Socialism: A Deconstruction of Tuzla's Political Identity in the Context of the Bosnian Conflict" (Ethnopolitics Papers, no. 35, 2015). For further analysis of census data collection in the Yugoslav case, see Leonard Kukić, "The Last Yugoslavs: Ethnic Diversity and National Identity," *Explorations in Economic History* 88 (2023), https://doi.org/10.1016/j.eeh.2022.101504.

6. Ljubica Spaskovska, *The Last Yugoslav Generation: The Rethinking of Youth Politics and Cultures in Late Socialism* (Manchester University Press, 2017), 92.

7. Branimir, interview with author, phone interview, December 19, 2017.

8. Jasmin Ramović, "Looking into the Past to See the Future? Lessons Learned from Self-Management for Economies in Post-Conflict Societies of the Former Yugoslavia," *Civil Wars* 20, no. 2 (2018): 171–92, 186, https://doi.org/10.1080/13698249.2018.1497859.

9. Dževad, interview with author, Sarajevo, December 16, 2016.

10. Božidar Matić, interview with author, Sarajevo, March 9, 2016.

11. Workers of TDS, collective interview with author, Sarajevo, February 17, 2016.

12. Larisa Kurtović, "What Is a Nationalist? Some Thoughts on the Question from Bosnia-Herzegovina," *Anthropology of East Europe Review* 29, no. 2 (2011): 242–53, 246; Kristin M. Bakke and Michael Ward, "Social Distance in Bosnia-Herzegovina and the North Caucasus Region of Russia: Inter- and Intra-Ethnic Attitudes and Identities," *Nations and Nationalism* 15, no. 2 (2009): 227–53.

13. Munevera, interview with author, Sarajevo, March 26, 2016.

14. Mitja Velikonja, "The Past with a Future: The Emancipatory Potential of Yugonostalgia," in *Transcending Fratricide: Political Mythologies, Reconciliations, and the Uncertain Future in the Former Yugoslavia*, ed. Srđa Pavlović and Marko Živković (Nomos, 2013), 109–28. See also Tanja Petrović, "The Past That Binds Us: Yugonostalgia as the Politics of Future," in Pavlović and Živković, *Transcending Fratricide*, 129–47.

15. Ognjen Kojanić, "Nostalgia as a Practice of the Self in Post-Socialist Serbia," *Canadian Slavonic Papers/Revue canadienne des slavistes* 57, nos. 3–4 (2015): 195–212, 206.

16. Andrew Gilbert, "Beyond Nostalgia: Other Historical Emotions," *History and Anthropology* 30, no. 3 (2019): 293–312, 302, https://doi.org/10.1080/02757206.2019.1579089.

17. *Yugoslav Survey: A Record of Facts and Information* (Jugoslavenski pregled, 1990), 58.

18. Goran Opačić, Ivana Vidaković, and Branko Vujadinović, eds., *Living in Post-War Communities* (IAN, 2005), 19.

19. For a definition and discussion of Yugoslavism, see Dejan Jović, "Yugoslavism and Yugoslav Communism: From Tito to Kardelj," in *Yugoslavism*, ed. Dejan Djokić (Hurst, 2003), 157–81, 166.

20. "Niko nas neće zavaditi," *Energoinvest List*, April 25, 1990, 1–12.

21. Jake Lowinger, "Economic Reform and the 'Double Movement' in Yugoslavia: An Analysis of Labor Unrest and Ethnonationalism in the 1980s" (PhD diss., Johns Hopkins University, 2009), 135.

22. Goran Musić, "'They Came as Workers and Returned as Serbs': The Role of Rakovica's Blue-Collar in Serbian Social Mobilizations of the Late 1980s," in *Social Inequalities and Discontent in Yugoslavia*, ed. Igor Duda, Paul Stubbs, and Rory Archer (Ashgate, 2016), 132–54, 134–35.

23. Ost, *Defeat of Solidarity*, 35.

24. R.I., "Panem et Circenses," *Energoinvest Armature List Radnika Radne Organizacije*, April 1990, 3.

25. Lowinger, "Economic Reform and the 'Double Movement,'" 135.

26. Anđelić, *Bosnia-Herzegovina: End of a Legacy*, 176.

27. Zavod za statistiku Bosne i Hercegovine, Bilten 234, Sarajevo, 1991.

28. "Blokade vode u kolaps," *Birač—List Radnika Preduzeća*, March 25, 1992, 1.

29. Cvjetko Cvjetinović, "Otvoreno Pismo," *Birač—List Radnika Preduzeća*, February 12, 1992, 5; "Paralele," *Birač—List Radnika Preduzeća*, March 25, 1992, 4. The author of this article remained anonymous but specified that he thought it was "absolutely irrelevant whether he was a Serb, Croat, Muslim, or maybe Bulgarian." "Kuće Pored Linije," *Birač—List Radnika Preduzeća*, March 25, 1992, 7.

30. "Veće za Pamćenje," *Birač—List Radnika Preduzeća*, March 25, 1992, 3.

31. Jasna Dragović-Soso, "Why Did Yugoslavia Disintegrate? An Overview of Contending Explanations," in *State Collapse in South-Eastern Europe: New Perspectives on Yugoslavia's Disintegration*, ed. Jasna Dragović-Soso and Lenard J. Cohen (Purdue University Press, 2007), 1–39; Dejan Jović, *Yugoslavia: A State That Withered Away* (Purdue University Press, 2009); Tomislav Dulić and Roland Kostić, "Yugoslavs in Arms: Guerrilla Tradition, Total Defense and the Ethnic Security Dilemma," *Europe-Asia Studies* 62, no. 7 (2010): 1051–72; Paul Roe, "Which Security Dilemma? Mitigating Ethnic Conflict: The Case of Croatia," *Security Studies* 13, no. 4 (2004): 280–313; Sabrina P. Ramet, "Explaining the Yugoslav Meltdown, 'For a Charm of Powerful Trouble, Like a Hell-Broth Boil and Bubble': Theories about the Roots of the Yugoslav Troubles," *Nationalities Papers* 32, no. 4 (2004): 731–63.

32. Federico Giulio Sicurella has written a compelling analysis of the role of intellectual elites throughout the history of postsocialist Yugoslavia, describing these elites as unprepared to cope with regime pluralization at the turn of the 1990s. Federico Giulio Sicurella, *Speaking for the Nation: Intellectuals and Nation-Building in the Post-Yugoslav Space* (John Benjamins, 2020).

33. Alfredo Sasso. "The Political Dimension of Ante Marković's Reform Project: 'We Must Develop Democracy and a Third Yugoslavia,'" *Contemporary Southeastern Europe* 7, no. 1 (2020): 25–48, 45.

34. Chip V. P. Gagnon, *The Myth of Ethnic War: Serbia and Croatia in the 1990s* (Cornell University Press, 1999), 85.

35. Gagnon, *Myth of Ethnic War*, 132–33.

36. Damir Mirkovic, "The Historical Link between the Ustasha Genocide and the Croato-Serb Civil War: 1991–1995," *Journal of Genocide Research* 2, no. 3 (2000): 363–73, 370.

37. Sabrina P. Ramet, *The Three Yugoslavias: State-Building and Legitimation, 1918–2005* (Indiana University Press, 2006), 378–79.

38. Nina Caspersen, *Contested Nationalism: Serb Elite Rivalry in Croatia and Bosnia in the 1990s* (Berghahn Books, 2010), 101.

39. Noel Malcolm, *Bosnia: A Short History* (NYU Press, 1994), 217–21.

40. Petrović, *Utopia of the Uniform*, 41.

41. Glenn E. Curtis, ed., *Yugoslavia: A Country Study* (Federal Research Division, Library of Congress, 1992), 237.

42. Faruk Šarić, "Armija rata za narod i mira," *Energoinvest List*, July 4, 1988, 1.

43. Bryan S. Turner, "The Erosion of Citizenship," *British Journal of Sociology* 52, no. 2 (2001): 189–209, 195. See also David A. Kideckel, *Getting By in Postsocialist Romania: Labor, the Body, & Working-Class Culture* (Indiana University Press, 2008); Rachel Funari and Bernard Mees, "Socialist Emulation in China: Worker Heroes Yesterday and Today," *Labor History* 54, no. 3 (2013): 240–55, https://doi.org/10.1080/0023656X.2013.804269; Lisa Mundey, "Citizen-Soldiers or Warriors," *Semiotics* 130 (2008): 130–39; Ronald R. Krebs, "The Citizen-Soldier Tradition in the United States: Has Its Demise Been Greatly Exaggerated?," *Armed Forces & Society* 36, no. 1 (2009): 153–74, https://doi-org.ezproxy1.lib.gla.ac.uk/10.1177/0095327 X09337370.

44. Martin Baumeister and Benjamin Ziemann, "Introduction: Peace Movements in Southern Europe during the 1970s and 1980s," *Journal of Contemporary History* 56, no. 3 (2021): 563–78, https://doi-org.ezproxy1.lib.gla.ac.uk/10.1177/00220094211014940; Steve Brigham, "The American-Soviet Walks: Large-Scale Citizen Diplomacy at Glasnost's Outset," *Peace & Change* 35, no. 4 (2010): 594–625.

45. Irina Gordeeva, "Solidarity in Search of Human Agency: 'Détente from Below' and Independent Peace Activists in the Soviet Union," *Labor History Review* 86 (2021): 339–68, https://doi.org/10.3828/lhr.2021.15; Robert English, "Eastern Europe's Doves," *Foreign Policy*, no. 56 (1984): 44–60, https://doi.org/10.2307/1148473.

46. Benjamin Ziemann, "A Quantum of Solace? European Peace Movements during the Cold War and Their Elective Affinities," *Archiv für Sozialgeschichte*, no. 49 (2009): 351–89. Mary Kaldor, "The 1989 Revolutions and the Peace Movement," openDemocracy, November 12, 2019, https://www.opendemocracy.net/en/can-europe-make-it/1989-revolutions-and -peace-movement/.

47. Curtis, *Yugoslavia*, 101.

48. For a more detailed account of antiwar movements, see Ljubica Spaskovska, "Landscapes of Resistance, Hope and Loss: Yugoslav Supra-Nationalism and Anti-Nationalism," in *Resisting the Evil, (Post)Yugoslav Anti-War Contention*, ed. Bojan Bilić and Vesna Janković, Southeast European Integration Perspectives (Nomos, 2012), 7:37–62, 48; Dora Komnenović, "(Out)Living the War: Anti-War Activism in Croatia in the Early 1990s and Beyond," *Journal on Ethnopolitics and Minority Issues in Europe* 13, no. 4 (2014): 111–28.

49. Ana Dević, "Anti-War Initiatives and the Un-Making of Civic Identities in the Former Yugoslav Republics," *Journal of Historical Sociology* 10 (1997): 127–56, 135, https://doi.org /10.1111/1467-6443.00034.

50. Sulejman Hrle, "Sindikat po mjeri interesa radnika. Referat na kongresu," Prvi posleratni kongres Sindikata Bosne i Hercegovine, September 25, 1997, Vijeće Saveza Sindkata Bosne i Hercegovine, 197:61, Državni Arhiv Bosne i Hercegovine, Sarajevo.

51. Spaskovska, "Landscapes of Resistance," 58.

52. Ioannis Armakolas, "The 'Paradox' of Tuzla City: Explaining Non-Nationalist Local Politics during the Bosnian War," *Europe-Asia Studies* 63, no. 2 (2011): 229–61.

53. Arben, interview with author, Tuzla, July 17, 2012.

54. Asim, interview with author, Sarajevo, May 29, 2016.

55. Mladen, interview with author, Sarajevo, July 17, 2014.

56. Branimir, interview with author, phone interview, December 19, 2017.

57. Bosnia at the time was characterized by an ethnically mixed population of 43.5 percent "Bosnian Muslims," 31.2 percent "Serbs," 17.3 percent "Croats," and 5.5 percent "Yugoslavs." Data from the last Yugoslav census of 1991, Zavod za statistiku Bosne i Hercegovine, Bilten 234, Sarajevo, 1991, 44.

58. Carl Schierup, "From Fraternity to Fratricide: Nationalism, Globalism and the Fall of Yugoslavia," in *State Building in the Balkans: Dilemmas on the Eve of the 21st Century*, ed. Stefano Bianchini and George Schöpflin (Longo, 1998), 216.

59. Jože Pirjevec, *Le guerre jugoslave, 1991–1999* [The Yugoslav Wars] (Giulio Einaudi Editore, 2001), 134.

60. Malcolm, *Bosnia*, 230.

61. Ramet, *Three Yugoslavias*, 414.

62. For a thorough account of the organization of the Bosnian War and of its internal defenses, see Marko Attila Hoare, "Civilian-Military Relations in Bosnia-Herzegovina, 1992–1995," in *The War in Croatia and Bosnia-Herzegovina, 1991–1995*, ed. Branka Magaš and Ivo Zanić (Oxon: Frank Cass, 2005), 178–99, 179; Nedžad Ajnadžić, "Sociološka Analiza Poginule Boračke Populacije u Jedinicama Odbrambenih Struktura u i Oko Grada Sarajeva," in *Opsada i Odbrana Sarajeva 1992–1995*, ed. Smahil Čekić, Omer Ibrahimagić, and Nijaz Đuraković (Sarajevo: Institut za istraživanje zločina protiv čovječnosti i međunarodnog prava Univerziteta u Sarajevu, 2008), 122. According to Mirko Pejanović, there were roughly 2.5 percent Serbs and 2.6 percent Croats in the army. Mirko Pejanović, "Uloga Sarajeva u Odbrani Multietničnosti i Državnosti BiH," in Čekić, Ibrahimagić, and Đuraković, *Opsada i Odbrana Sarajeva*, 59.

63. Ismet, Unija Veterana, interview with author, Sarajevo, December 13, 2016.

64. Faruk Šarić, "Na prvoj liniji do slobode," *Energoinvest List*, April–May 1993, 4. It is estimated that over forty thousand citizens were living in this area.

65. Robert J. Donia, *Sarajevo: A Biography* (Hurst, 2006), 313.

66. Jovan Divjak, "The First Phase, 1992–1993: Struggle for Survival and Genesis of the Army of Bosnia-Herzegovina," In Magaš and Zanić, *War in Croatia and Bosnia-Herzegovina*, 131.

67. "Danas ratnici, sutra radnici," *Energoinvest List*, September–October 1992, 3.

68. Dževad, interview with author, Sarajevo, December 16, 2016.

69. Čekić, Ibrahimagić, and Đuraković, *Opsada i Odbrana Sarajeva*, 364–65; F. Šarić, "Ne Posustajemo!," *Energoinvest List*, November 1992–March 1993, 1; H. Arifagić, "Biće nova Lukavica," *Oslobođenje*, November 17, 1994, 5. See also "Pojedinačan popis broja ratnih žrtava u svim općinama BiH", February 27 2013. Available at: http://www.prometej.ba/clanak /drustvo-i-znanost/pojedinacan-popis-broja-ratnih-zrtava-u-svim-opcinama-bih-997.

70. Divjak, "First Phase," 173.

71. Šarić, "Na prvoj liniji do slobode," 4. Subsequently, the ARBiH-controlled Dobrinja would become strategically essential, as the infamous Sarajevo Tunnel (Tunel Spasa) connected this area to the area outside the besieged city (Butmir). See Donia, *Sarajevo*, 26. Hadžić and other residents of the borough tried to organize a brigade between May and September 1992, as Dobrinja was becoming more and more isolated. He estimates that at the beginning of the siege between three thousand and five thousand people left in exodus from Dobrinja to the center of the city. He was later made commander of this brigade, which was part of the ARBiH, and was defending roughly twenty thousand people (according to him). He also indicates that he had roughly two thousand men; 60 percent of his soldiers were Bosnjaks, while roughly 13 percent were Serbs and 6 percent Croats. Case Number IT-98-29-T, the Prosecutor versus Stanislav Galić, no. 12140 (July 23, 2002).

72. "U posjeti delegacija sindikata BiH," *Energoinvest List*, April–May 1993, 2.

73. Peter Andreas, *Blue Helmets and Black Markets: The Business of Survival in the Siege of Sarajevo* (Cornell University Press, 2008), 35.

74. See the interview with Božidar Begović, vice president of the sector for machine and process equipment. Božidar Begović, "Radi se i planira," interview, *Energoinvest List*, April–May 1993, 3.

75. This is also a common scholarly interpretation of the conflict, one that views the war as a Serbian aggression resulting from Greater Serbia's expansionist goals. See Sabrina P. Ramet, *Thinking about Yugoslavia: Scholarly Debates about the Yugoslav Breakup and the Wars in Bosnia and Kosovo* (Cambridge University Press, 2005).

76. Faruk Šarić, "Pišem radnicima Srbije i Crne Gore," *Energoinvest List*, April–May 1993, 1.

77. Faruk Šarić, "Ne posustajemo!," *Energoinvest List*, November 1992–March 1993, 1. In the national newspaper, an article noted, "Energoinvest has already produced extensively with the goal of strengthening the economy as a form of struggle for the liberation and renovation of the country." N.N., "Podrška vladinom konceptu," *Oslobođenje*, December 10, 1994, 6.

78. "Svijet i dalje nudi poslove," *Energoinvest List*, April–May 1993, 4.

79. Božidar Matić, interview by Dušica Kljajić, in "Od najivećeg izvoznika do rizičkog partnera," *Energoinvest List*, December 1991, 3.

80. Mary Kaldor and Vesna Bojičić-Dželilović, "The 'Abnormal' Economy of Bosnia-Herzegovina," in *Scramble for the Balkans: Nationalism, Globalism and the Political Economy of Reconstruction*, ed. Carl-Ulrik Schierup (St. Martin's, 1999), 92–117, 94.

81. Stup, Dobrinja, and Lukavica were directly on the front line and were at different times under the control of the Serb forces or of the Bosnian national army (Dobrinja and Stup); Lukavica, since the start of the war, belonged to the Serb claimed territories and is now part of Republika Srpska. Andreas, *Blue Helmets and Black Markets*, 51–55.

82. "Srpski (neuspjeli) plagijat," *Energoinvest List*, November–December 1994, 3.

83. "I ostali i opstali," *Energoinvest List*, January–March 1995, 1.

84. Bosnia and Herzegovina filed a case against Serbia at the International Court of Justice based precisely on the understanding of Serbia and Montenegro as aggressor states (accused but then acquitted of genocide).

85. SDA was the nationalist party, at the time led by president Alija Izetbegović.

86. Bukvić appointment speech, quoted in R. T., "Moglo je i bolje i savjesnije," *Energoinvest List*, June–August 1994, 1.

87. Mirko Pejanović and Marina Bowder, *Through Bosnian Eyes: The Political Memoirs of a Bosnian Serb* (Purdue University Press, 2004), 151, https://doi.org/10.2307/j.ctt6wq4d4.

88. Radio Free Europe, *Balkan Report* 2, no. 4 (January 28, 1998), https://www.rferl.org/a/1341328.html.

89. H. Arifagić, "Biće nova Lukavica," *Oslobođenje*, November 17, 1994, 5.

90. Miro Klepić, interview with author, Lukavica, March 29, 2016.

91. Mirsad Kapetanović, interview with author, Sarajevo, May 12, 2016.

92. CIA Document C05 962553, DCI Interagency Balkan Task Force, November 20, 1995.

93. One estimate put the rate of unemployment in Tuzla in 1996 at 90 percent. Kitty McKinsey, "Widespread Poverty Makes Life Difficult In Bosnia," Radio Free Europe, January 9, 1996, https://www.rferl.org/a/1079919.html.

94. "SSSBiH Will Continue to Seek Bosnia's Property in Croatia FENA," N1 Sarajevo, June 6, 2018, https://n1info.ba/english/news/a264941-sssbih-will-continue-to-seek-bosniaand39s-property-in-croatia/.

95. "Javnu prodaju nekretnina i pokretnina stečajnog dužnika," *Energoinvest Termoaparati*, January 26, 2017, http://www.tat.ba/novosti2.html.

96. Amer Kapetanović, "Lijepe fabrike lijepo gore," *Dani*, July 28, 2000, archived at "Lijepe fabrike lijepo gore (Arhiva: DANI, 165)," *Uvod u Bosnu i Hercegovinu / Introduction to Bosnia and Herzegovina* (blog), April 29, 2019, https://uvodubih.blogspot.com/2019/04/lijepe-fabrike-lijepo-gore-arhiva-dani.html.

97. "Čudo Bosanskog otpora," *Energoinvest List*, February–March 1996, 4.

98. Dževad, interview with author, Sarajevo, December 16, 2016.

99. Ivana Maček, *Sarajevo under Siege: Anthropology in Wartime* (University of Pennsylvania Press, 2009), 9.

5. Layers of Deservingness

1. Gerard Toal and Carl T. Dahlman, *Bosnia Remade: Ethnic Cleansing and Its Reversal* (Oxford University Press, 2011), 295; Malcolm, *Bosnia: A Short History*, 249.

2. Resolution 836 (1993), adopted by the Security Council at its 3228th meeting, on June 4, 1993, https://digitallibrary.un.org/record/166973?ln=es&v=pdf.

3. Milošević had supported the plan; he was interested in ending the conflict given the severe crisis facing the Serbian economy and, by extension, the People's Army itself. See Melanie Greenberg and Margaret McGuinness, "From Lisbon to Dayton: International Mediation and the Bosnia Crisis," in *Words over War: Mediation and Arbitration to Prevent Deadly Conflict*, ed. M. C. Greenberg, J. H. Barton, and M. E. McGuinness (Rowman & Littlefield, 2000), 35–75, 56.

4. Stefano Bianchini, *La questione Jugoslava* (Giunti Editore, 1999), 170.

5. I am aware that there exist many ways of identifying ethnonational or religious groups. I used the ones mentioned above, as they are the ones my interviewees use. While Serbs (Srbi) and Croats (Hrvati) use these terms, the definition for Bosnjaks (Bosnjaci) or Muslims (Muslimani) is interchangeable and often used alternatively. I tend to stick as close as possible to the terminology interviewees themselves use.

6. Additionally, the autonomous district of Brčko in northeastern Bosnia, self-governed and characterized by an ethnically mixed population, was established in 1999.

7. Florian Bieber, "Institutionalizing Ethnicity in the Western Balkans: Managing Change in Deeply Divided Societies," working paper 19 (European Center for Minority Issues, 2004).

8. Kimberley A. Coles, "Ambivalent Builders: Europeanization, the Production of Differ-ence, and Internationals in Bosnia-Herzegovina," *PoLAR: Political and Legal Anthropology Review* 25 (2002): 1–18, 3.

9. Carrie Manning, "Elections and Political Change in Post-War Bosnia and Herzegov-ina," *Democratization* 11, no. 2 (2004): 60–86, 64.

10. Eldar Sarajlić, "Conceptualizing Citizenship Regime(s) in Post-Dayton Bosnia and Herzegovina," *Citizenship Studies* 16, no. 3–4 (2012): 367–82, 372. See also Igor Štiks, "Nation-ality and Citizenship in the Former Yugoslavia: From Disintegration to European Integra-tion," *Southeast European and Black Sea Studies* 6, no. 4 (2006): 483–500, 489.

11. Denisa Kostovicova and Vesna Bojičić-Dželilović, "Ethnicity Pays: The Political Economy of Post-Conflict Nationalism in Bosnia-Herzegovina," in *After Civil War: Division, Reconstruction, and Reconciliation in Contemporary Europe*, ed. Bill Kissane (Pennsylvania State University Press, 2014), 187–213, 206.

12. Korf, "Ethnicized Entitlements?," 25. See also James Muzondidya and Sabelo Ndlovu-Gatsheni, "Echoing Silences: Ethnicity in Post-Colonial Zimbabwe, 1980–2007," *African Journal on Conflict Resolution* 7, no. 2 (2007): 275–97; Alan Emery, "Privatization, Neoliberal Development, and the Struggle for Workers' Rights in Post-Apartheid South Africa," *Social Justice* 33, no. 3 (2006): 6–19; Bruce J. Berman, "Ethnicity, Patronage and the African State: The Politics of Uncivil Nationalism," *African Affairs* 97 (1998): 305–41.

13. Rajesh Venugopal, "Privatization, Private-Sector Development and Horizontal In-equalities in Post-Conflict Countries," in *Horizontal Inequalities and Post-Conflict Devel-opment: Conflict, Inequality and Ethnicity*, ed. Arnim Langer, Frances Stewart, and Rajesh Venugopal (Palgrave Macmillan, 2012), 114, https://doi-org.ezproxy2.lib.gla.ac.uk/10.1057/9780230348622_5.

14. Amy L. Chua, "The Privatization-Nationalization Cycle: The Link between Markets and Ethnicity in Developing Countries," *Columbia Law Review* 95, no. 2 (March 1995): 223–303.

15. Gershon Shafir, *Immigrants and Nationalists: Ethnic Conflict and Accommodation in Catalonia, the Basque Country, Latvia, and Estonia* (State University of New York Press, 1995), 192.

16. Till Hilmar, "The Temporal Logic of Deservingness: Inequality Beliefs in Two Postso-cialist Societies," *Socius* 5 (January 1, 2019): 1–16, https://doi.org/10.1177/2378023119864231.

17. Institute for War and Peace Reporting, "Bosnia's Book of the Dead," June 26, 2007, https://iwpr.net/global-voices/bosnias-book-dead.

18. Daria Sito-Sucic, "Sarajevo's War Damage Totaled $18.5 Billion: Study," Reuters, August 9, 2007, https://www.reuters.com/article/us-sarajevo-war-damage-idUSL12880608 20061212/.

19. CIA Document C05 962553, DCI Interagency Balkan Task Force, November 20, 1995.

20. Florence Kondylis, "Conflict Displacement and Labor Market Outcomes in Post-War Bosnia and Herzegovina," *Journal of Development Economics* 93, no. 2 (2010): 235–48, https://doi.org/10.1016/j.jdeveco.2009.10.004.

21. *Službeni Glasnik BiH*, November 1992, 529.

22. Direct Request (CEACR), adopted 2007, published 97th ILC session (2008), *Labor Inspection Convention, 1947 (No. 81)—Bosnia and Herzegovina* (ratification: 1993), http://www.ilo.org/dyn/normlex/en/f?p=NORMLEXPUB:13100:0::NO::P13100_COMMENT _ID:2278709.

23. Paula M. Pickering, *Peacebuilding in the Balkans: The View from the Ground Floor* (Cornell University Press, 2007), 99–100; Daniela Lai, "Transitional Justice and Its

Discontents: Socioeconomic Justice in Bosnia and Herzegovina and the Limits of International Intervention," *Journal of Intervention and Statebuilding* 10, no. 3 (2016): 361–81.

24. Human Rights Watch, "War Crimes in Bosnia-Hercegovina: U.N. Cease-Fire Won't Help Banja Luka," press release, 6, no. 8, June 8, 1994, 8.

25. Teofik Jusufagić v. The Republika Srpska, case no. CH/00/3862 (Human Rights Commission within Constitutional Court of Bosnia and Herzegovina, November 1, 2004), 2. The court here noted the accusations of ethnic discrimination but found that the applicant had not been able to provide substantial evidence in support of his claim.

26. Fikreta Bjekić v. The Republika Srpska, case no. CH/99/2356, May 13, 2000; Ljiljana Radović v. The Federation of Bosnia and Herzegovina, case no. CH/98/959 (Human Rights Commission within Constitutional Court of Bosnia and Herzegovina, May 7, 2004), 3; Hamid Čoban v. The Federation of Bosnia and Herzegovina, case no. CH/99/2898 (Human Rights Commission within Constitutional Court of Bosnia and Herzegovina, May 5, 2004), 2; Jasminka Sarač v. The Federation of Bosnia and Herzegovina, case no. CH/99/2743 (Human Rights Commission within Constitutional Court of Bosnia and Herzegovina, June 3, 2003), 3; Appeal of Silvana Tomić v. the judgment of the Supreme Court of the Federation of Bosnia and Herzegovina ("the Supreme Court"), no. 070–0-Rev-06-000170 of January 24, 2007, no. AP-1093/07 (Constitutional Court of Bosnia and Herzegovina, September 25, 2009), 4.

27. UN Committee on the Elimination of Racial Discrimination, Reports Submitted by State Parties under Article 9 of the Convention, information provided by the government of Bosnia and Herzegovina on the implementation of the concluding observations of the Committee on the Elimination of Racial Discrimination, June 18, 2009, 2–3.

28. Amnesty International, *Bosnia and Herzegovina. Behind Closed Gates: Ethnic Discrimination in Employment* report, January 26, 2006, 13. See also Gordana Sandić-Hadžihasanović, "Vlastima RS Stiglo Upozorenje Iz Strazbura," Radio Slobodna Evropa, June 11, 2007, https://www.slobodnaevropa.org/a/706309.html.

29. Oliwia Berdak, "Reintegrating Veterans in Bosnia and Herzegovina and Croatia: Citizenship and Gender Effects," *Women's Studies International Forum* 49 (2015): 48–56, 51.

30. For unemployment as a socially and politically unacceptable malaise in socialist Yugoslavia, see Woodward, *Socialist Unemployment*, 347.

31. BH Press, "Dogovor o zapošljavanju RVI," *Oslobođenje*, March 23, 1995, 3. See also MINA, "Posao za vojne invalide," *Oslobođenje*, October 18, 1995, 6.

32. Sulejman Hrle, open letter to workers, "Saopštenje za javnost prvomajski proglas," April 30, 1997, folder 142, Documents Collection of the Council of Independent Unions, Državni Arhiv Bosne i Hercegovine, Sarajevo.

33. Sulejman Hrle, head of the general union, at the "Sjednica Ustavotvorne Skupštine Federacije Bosne i Hercegovine," June 3, 1996, Ustavotvorna Skupštine Federacije Bosne i Hercegovine, no. 2354, folder 56, Arhiv Federacije Bosne i Hercegovine, 52/1.

34. Sulejman Hrle, "Zapisnik Sa Prve Konstituirajuće Sjednice Glavnog Odbora Saveza Samostalnih Sindikata Bosne i Hercegovine" (speech, founding meeting of the Council of Independent Unions of Bosnia and Herzegovina, November 26, 1997), folder 142, Documents Collection of the Council of Independent Unions, Državni Arhiv Bosne i Hercegovine, Sarajevo, 3.

35. Sulejman Hrle, speech at an assembly of the Council of the Independent Unions, September 29, 1997, folder 142, Documents Collection of the Council of Independent Unions, Državni Arhiv Bosne i Hercegovine, Sarajevo, 6.

36. Vesna Bojičić-Dželilović, "Peace on Whose Terms? War Veterans' Associations in Bosnia and Herzegovina," in *Challenges to Peacebuilding: Managing Spoilers during Conflict Resolution*, ed. Edward Newman and Oliver Richmond (United Nations University Press, 2006), 14.

37. Kendra Gregson, *Veterans' Programs in Bosnia-Herzegovina* (World Bank, 2000), 11.

38. Xavier Bougarel, "The Shadow of Heroes: Former Combatants in Post-War Bosnia-Herzegovina," *International Social Science Journal* 189 (2006): 479–90, 483.

39. This meant that companies that already had a substantial liquidity deficit and lacked appropriate resources were to provide for more than BAM 116 million (roughly EUR 60 million) for the waiting-list status of more than fifty thousand employees—of which 65 percent were in the industrial sector. Fikret Čaušević, "Bosanska Ekonomska Enigma: O Tranziciji od 1996. do 2013. Godine," *Međunarodni forum Bosnia*, no. 63–64 (2013): 13

40. Edhem Bičakcić, recorded in the "Magnetofonski Snimak 5. Sjednice Doma Naroda Parlamenta Federacije Bosne i Hercegovine," January 12–13, 1996, 19/3; Ustavotvorna Skupština Federacije Bosne i Hercegovine, no. 2389, folder 91, Arhiv Federacije Bosne i Hercegovine; "Zakon o radu republike srpske," *Službeni Glasnik Republike Srpske* 3/97, 10/98.

41. Article 143, *Službene novine Federacije BiH*, number 43/99; *Službeni Glasnik Republike Srpske*, number 16/96. See also Gregson, *Veterans' Programs*, 2.

42. S.T., "Povratak poslu," *Oslobođenje*, November 24, 1995, 7.

43. M. R. Babić, "Demobilizacija pa posao," *Oslobođenje*, December 18, 1995, 8. On workers' demobilization and return to work, see also Edhem Badžak, "Ratnici Se Vraćaju Poslu," *Oslobođenje*, December 14, 1995, 13.

44. N. Lozančić (HDZ), "Nastavak 5 sjednice doma naroda parlamenta federacije Bosne i Hercegovine," (speech, Federal Parliament, May 19, 1998), Sednice doma naroda parlamenta federacije Bosne i Hercegovine, no. 2389, folder 91, Arhiv Federacije Bosne i Hercegovine, 4/1.

45. Mate, interview with author, Mostar, December 17, 2016.

46. Dževad, interview with author, Sarajevo, December 16, 2016.

47. Željko, interview with author, phone interview, December 18, 2017.

48. Goran Dokić, "States of Victimhood and Irreparable Losses: Serbian Veterans of the Post-Yugoslav Wars," *Glasnik Etnografskog Instituta SANU* 44, no. 1 (2017): 97–110, 104.

49. Addis, interview with author, Tuzla, July 26, 2012.

50. *Službeni List Republike Bosne i Hercegovine*, 7/93, 33/94.

51. Ibrahim Polimac, "Politikantstvo zaustavlja zakone," *Oslobođenje*, December 23, 1994, 3.

52. *Službeni Glasnik Republike Srpske* 4/93, 29/94, 31/94; Ervin Mujkić, "Državna imovina u Bosni i Hercegovini—Geneza Problema," in *Državna imovina*, ed. Edin Šarčević (Fondacija Centar za javno pravo, 2012), 23–65, 33.

53. Bockman, *Markets in the Name of Socialism*, 207.

54. One Bosnian mark is around two euros. Čaušević and Zupčević, "Case Study: Bosnia and Herzegovina," 45.

55. Kostovicova and Bojičić-Dželilović, "Ethnicity Pays," 206.

56. *OHR Bulletin* 15, August 20, 1996, OHR Archive.

57. Decision imposing the Framework Law on Privatization of Enterprises and Banks in BiH, Sarajevo, July 22, 1998, OHR archive.

58. For the ethnic homogenization of citizenship, see Igor Štiks, "Being Citizen the Bosnian Way: Transformations of Citizenship and Political Identities in Bosnia-Herzegovina," in

From Peace to Shared Political Identities: Exploring Pathways in Contemporary Bosnia-Herzegovina, ed. Sylvie Ramel and Francis Cheneval (Institut de Sociologie de l'Université libre de Bruxelles, 2011), 245–67.

59. Storey, "Economics and Ethnic Conflict," 57.

60. As David Ellerman argues, however, both the "no-cash" and the "rapidity" arguments were fallacious. David Ellerman, "Lessons from Eastern Europe's Voucher Privatization," *Challenge* 44, no. 4 (2001): 14–37, 16. On the disappointing results of Czech voucher privatization, see Katia Hristova, "Czech Voucher Privatization: A Case of Decision Making under Uncertainty," *University Avenue Undergraduate Journal of Economics* 7, no. 1, Article 5 (2002): 1–24

61. "Pitanja i odgovori," *Privatizacija. Stručni Časopis Agencije Za Privatizaciju u Federaciji Bosne i Hercegovine*, January 1999, 109.

62. Andrijić is an economist and former dean of the Economics Faculty; he was the first president of the Privatization Agency of the FBiH. Stiepo Andrijić, interview with author, Sarajevo, September 20, 2014.

63. Aleksa Milojević, interview with author, Bijeljina, July 4, 2014.

64. Similar points were raised by advisers of the privatization agencies in both the FBiH and Republika Srpska. Dželal Ibraković, "Privatizacija—Najznačajniji Faktor Promjena," *Privatizacija. Stručni Časopis Agencije Za Privatizaciju u Federaciji Bosne i Hercegovine*, July 2000, 61–62; "10. Sjednica Predstavničkog Doma Parlamentarne Skupštine Bosne i Hercegovine," July 14, 1998, 6/2, Online Archive of the Parliament of Bosnia and Herzegovina, https://www.parlament.ba/session/SessionDetails?id=2420 &ConvernerId=1.

65. Ismet, Sindikat Metalaca Bosne i Hercegovine, interview with author, Sarajevo, July 8, 2016.

66. Karim Medjad argues that the only way to privatize in Yugoslavia would have been to take care of workers' attachment to their workplaces. Karim Medjad, "The Fate of the Yugoslav Model: A Case against Legal Conformity," *American Journal of Comparative Law* 52, no. 1 (2004): 287–319, 315.

67. Danko Ružičić, interview by the author, in Goran Musić, *Svjedoci Jednog Vremena: U Sindikatima BiH 1990–2015* (Friedrich Ebert Stiftung, 2015), 56.

68. Katherine Verdery, "Fuzzy Property: Rights, Power, and Identity in Transylvania's Decollectivization," in *National Research Council*, ed. Joan M. Nelson, Charles Tilly, and Lee Walker (National Academies Press, 1998), 102–17, 103.

69. Verdery, "Fuzzy Property," 116.

70. Kate Bayliss, "Post-Conflict Privatization: A Review of Development in Serbia and Bosnia-Herzegovina," ESAU Working Paper 12 (Overseas Development Institute, London, 2005), 43–44.

71. Bajro, Savez Samostalnih Sindikata, interview with author, Sarajevo, July 8, 2016.

72. Generalni Servis ONASA, "Od ukupne vrijednosti podijeljenih certifikata iskorišteno 1 posto," December 6, 1999.

73. Timothy Donais, "The Politics of Privatization in Post-Dayton Bosnia," *Southeast European Politics* 3, no. 1 (2002): 3–19, 9.

74. Numerous studies later confirmed that in Bosnia the "sales of enterprises to managers and employees have been successful where the sale has been through a tender process rather than using vouchers or certificates." Bayliss, "Post-Conflict Privatization," 34.

75. Generalni Servis ONASA, "Od ukupne vrijednosti podijeljenih certifikata iskorišteno 1 posto."

76. Generalni Servis ONASA, "Od ukupne vrijednosti podijeljenih certifikata iskorišteno 1 posto."

77. Quotations from, respectively, Osman, interview with author, Sarajevo, February 17, 2016; Muamer, interview with author, Tuzla, May 9, 2016; Asim, interview with author, Sarajevo, May 29, 2016.

78. Sadudin Musabegović and Emir Nuhanović, "Građani i privatizacija," in *Uticaj Transformacije Vlasništva Na Nezaposlenost i Zapošljavanje*, ed. Murat Prašo, Mišo Carević, Mesud Sabitović, and Izudin Kešetović (Sedam, 2000), 230–40, 233.

79. Musabegović and Nuhanović, "Građani i privatizacija," 236–38.

80. Stiepo Andrijić, "Tvorba stručne i pravne osnovice," *Privatizacija: Stručni Časopis Agencije Za Privatizaciju u Federaciji Bosne i Hercegovine*, January 1998, 7.

81. David Chandler, *Peace without Politics? Ten Years of International State-Building in Bosnia* (Routledge, 2006), 145. Approximately two thousand non-Croat small shareholders were excluded from property rights. See International Crisis Group, *Bosnia's Precarious Economy: Still Not Open for Business*, Europe Report no. 115 (Brussels: International Crisis Group, August 7, 2001), 25; Tina Jelin Dizdar, "Hiljade Radnika Zaboravljeno Zbog Nacionalne Nepodobnosti," *Diskriminacija*, July 8, 2012, http://diskriminacija.ba/hiljade-radnika -zaboravljeno-zbog-nacionalne-nepodobnosti; Tina Jelin Dizdar, "Nastavak Diskriminacije Radnika u Mostarskom Aluminiju," *Diskriminacija*, November 20, 2013, http://www .diskriminacija.ba/aluminijum-ad-nastavak-diskriminacije-radnika, "Privatizacija Mostarskog Aluminija," Centar za istraživačko novinarstvo (CIN), April 30, 2007, https://www.cin .ba/privatizacija-mostarskog-aluminija/.

82. Adnan Demić, "Prof. Milan Jovičić: Koordinaciju Srpskog Naroda Čine Dodikovci," *Oslobođenje*, September 17, 2017, https://www.Oslobođenje.ba/dosjei/intervjui/prof-milan -jovicic-koordinaciju-srpskog-naroda-cine-dodikovci; R. D., "Milan Jovičić: Ja Sam Srbin, Prije Svega Bosanac, Ali Za Dodika Sam Rezervni Srbin," Klix.Ba, August 13, 2017. https:// www.klix.ba/vijesti/bih/milan-jovicic-ja-sam-srbin-prije-svega-bosanac-ali-za-dodika -sam-rezervni-srbin/170723020.

83. Following Rory Archer and Igor Duda, I view ethnicity as contingent, crosscutting and intersecting with other concepts of identity. Rory Archer, Igor Duda, and Paul Stubbs, eds., *Social Inequalities and Discontent in Yugoslav Socialism* (Routledge, 2016).

84. Maček, *Sarajevo under Siege*, 132.

85. John O'Loughlin, "Inter-Ethnic Friendships in Post-War Bosnia-Herzegovina: Sociodemographic and Place Influences," *Ethnicities* 10, no. 1 (2010): 26–53, 31, https://doi .org/10.1177/1468796809354153.

86. Munevera, interview with author, Sarajevo, March 26, 2016.

87. Muamer, interview with author, Tuzla, May 9, 2016.

88. Marko, interview with author, TTU Tuzla, July 15, 2016.

89. Veronica Forrest-Thomson, "The Hyphen," in *Collected Poems and Translations* (Shearsman Books, 2008), 88.

90. As Zsuzsa Gille, among others, has highlighted. See Zsuzsa Gille, "Is There a Global Post-Socialist Condition?," *Global Society* 24, no. 1 (2010): 9–30, 27–28.

91. For an interesting analysis of veterans as the "body" of the nation, see Salih Can Aciksoz, "Sacrificial Limbs of Sovereignty: Disabled Veterans, Masculinity, and Nationalist Politics in Turkey," *Medical Anthropology Quarterly* 26, no. 1 (2012): 4–25.

6. Expecting the Global

1. Fritz Bartel, *The Triumph of Broken Promises: The End of the Cold War and the Rise of Neoliberalism* (Harvard University Press, 2022).

2. Rupprecht, "Global Varieties of Neoliberalism," 1.

3. Sara Lorenzini, *Global Development: A Cold War History* (Princeton University Press, 2019), 160.

4. Nebojša Stojčić and Zoran Aralica, "(De)Industrialization and Lessons for Industrial Policy in Central and Eastern Europe," *Post-Communist Economies* 30, no. 6 (2018): 713–34, https://doi.org/10.1080/14631377.2018.1443251; Francesca Gambarotto, Marco Rangone, and Stefano Solari, "Financialization and Deindustrialization in the Southern European Periphery," *Athens Journal of Mediterranean Studies* 5, no. 3 (2019): 151–72.

5. As, among others, Veronika Pehe and Joanna Wawrzyniak suggest in *Remembering the Neoliberal Turn: Economic Change and Collective Memory in Eastern Europe after 1989* (Routledge, 2024).

6. Mario Castillo and Antonio Martins Neto, "Premature Deindustrialization in Latin America," *ECLAC—Production Development Series*, no. 205 (United Nations ECLAC) June 2016, 1–27.

7. Seth Schindler et al., "Deindustrialization in Cities of the Global South," *Area Development and Policy* 5, no. 3 (2020): 283–304, https://doi.org/10.1080/23792949.2020.1725393; Andy Pike, "Coping with Deindustrialization in the Global North and South," *International Journal of Urban Sciences* 26, no. 1 (2022): 1–22, https://doi.org/10.1080/12265934.2020.1730225; Lachlan MacKinnon and Stephen High, "Deindustrialization," in *The Routledge Handbook to the Political Economy and Governance of the Americas*, ed. Olaf Kaltmeier, Anne Tittor, Daniel Hawkins, and Eleonora Rohland (Taylor & Francis Group, 2020), 59; Kerstin Barndt, "Fordist Nostalgia: History and Experience at the Henry Ford," *Rethinking History* 11, no. 3 (2007): 379–410, https://doi.org/10.1080/13642520701353330; George Steinmetz, "Colonial Melancholy and Fordist Nostalgia: The Ruinscapes of Namibia and Detroit," in *Ruins of Modernity*, ed. Julia Hell, Andreas Schönle, Julia Adams, and George Steinmetz (Duke University Press, 2009), 294–320; Mariah Cannon and Silvia Emili, "'Empresas Recuperadas': Argentina's Recovered Factory Movement," case summary 4 (Institute for Development Studies, Brighton, 2019); Immanuel Ness and Dario Azzellini, *Ours to Master and to Own: Workers' Control from the Commune to the Present* (Haymarket Books, 2011).

8. Corinna R. Unger, *International Development: A Postwar History* (Bloomsbury, 2018), 146.

9. Paul Adler, "Creating 'The NGO International': The Rise of Advocacy for Alternative Development, 1974–1994," in *The Development Century*, ed., Stephen J. Macekura and Erez Manela (Cambridge University Press, 2018), 305–25.

10. Janos Kornai, "The Soft Budget Constraint," *International Review for Social Sciences* 39, no. 1 (1986): 3–30.

11. Zoltan J. Acs, et al., "The Internationalization of Small and Medium-Sized Enterprises: A Policy Perspective," *Small Business Economics* 9 (1997): 7–20, 17. The study of SMEs has often been approached in a functionalist and often policy-driven fashion, without unearthing the theoretical assumptions behind the choice of favoring small over larger businesses in the context of market transformation. See Robert Blackburn and Anne Kovalainen, "Researching Small Firms and Entrepreneurship: Past, Present and Future," *International Journal of Management Reviews* 11, no. 2 (2008): 127–48.

12. Gilbert Rist, *The History of Development: From Western Origins to Global Faith* (Zed Books, 1997), 254; UNCTAD, *Small and Medium-Sized Transnational Corporations: Role, Impact and Policy Implications* (United Nations, 1993).

13. OECD, "Promoting SMEs for Development," in *Promoting Entrepreneurship and Innovative SMEs in a Global Economy: Towards a More Responsible and Inclusive Globalization* (OECD, 2004), 11. See also Hansjörg Herr and Zeynep M. Nettekoven, *The Role of Small and Medium-Sized Enterprises in Development: Can It Be Learned from the German Experience?* (Friedrich Ebert Stiftung, 2017), http://library.fes.de/pdf-files/iez/14056.pdf; Will Bartlett, Milford Bateman, and Maja Vehovec, ed., *Small Enterprise Development in South-East Europe: Policies for Sustainable Growth* (Springer, 2002).

14. UNCTAD, *Improving the Competitiveness of SMEs in Developing Countries: The Role of Finance to Enhance Enterprise Development* (United Nations Conference on Trade and Development, 2001).

15. *Enterprise Policy Performance Assessment and Herzegovina* (OECD, EBRD, Stability Pact for South Eastern Europe, 2005), 7–8; IMF, "Bosnia and Herzegovina: Poverty Reduction Strategy Paper—Mid-Term," IMF Country Report, April 2004, 62–63. On entrepreneurship in central and eastern Europe, see Ivan Tchalakov and Nikula Jouko, *Innovations and Entrepreneurs in Socialist and Post-Socialist Societies* (Cambridge Scholars, 2013), 3.

16. *OECD Advisory Group on Privatization Plenary Session, Competition and Privatization NOTE* (OECD, 1998), 1. https://www.oecd.org/daf/ca/corporategovernanceofstate-ownedenterprises/1929692.pdf; Carlos Corti and Myrna Alexander, "Argentina's Privatization Program," CFS Discussion Paper Series 103 (World Bank, 1993), http://documents.worldbank.org/curated/en/698941468767394378/Argentinas-privatization-program.

17. Ira W. Lieberman, Stilpon Nestor, and Raj M. Desai, eds., *Between State and Market: Mass Privatization in Transition Economies* (World Bank, OECD, 1997), vii.

18. Joseph E. Stiglitz, "Quis Custodiet Ipsos Custodes? Corporate Governance Failures in the Transition," Governance, Equity and Global Markets, Proceedings from the Annual Bank Conference on Development Economics in Europe, June 1999, Pierre-Alain Muet and J. E. Stiglitz, eds. (Conseil d'Analyse Economique, 2000), 51–84. (Originally presented as keynote address at the Annual Bank Conference on Development Economics in Europe, Paris, June 23, 1999); Grzegorz W. Kolodko, "Transition to a Market Economy and Sustained Growth: Implications for the Post-Washington Consensus," *Communist and Post-Communist Studies* 32, no. 3 (1999): 233–61; David Stark and László Bruszt, *Postsocialist Pathways: Transforming Politics and Property in East Central Europe* (Cambridge University Press, 1998).

19. Michael Pugh, "The Political Economy of Peacebuilding: A Critical Theory Perspective," *International Journal of Peace Studies* 10, no. 2 (2005): 23–42, 25; *Bosnia's Precarious Economy: Still Not Open for Business*, ICG Balkans Report (International Crisis Group, 2001), 18.

20. Aleksandar Mesarović, "Bring the Right One In: International Organizations and Privatization Strategies in Slovenia, Croatia, and Serbia," *LIMESplus* 15, no. 1 (2018): 79–101.

21. *OHR Bulletin* 15, August 20, 1996, OHR Archive.

22. USAID, *Bosnian Reconstruction Program* (USAID Bosnia and Herzegovina, 1998), 4.

23. "Bosnia and Herzegovina Post-Conflict Reconstruction and the Transition to a Market Economy," OED Evaluation of World Bank Support (World Bank, 2004), 11.

24. *20 Years of USAID Economic Growth Assistance in Europe and Eurasia* (USAID, 2013), 36–37; Stuart Shields, "The European Bank for Reconstruction and Development and the

Lessons from Eastern Central Europe for Middle East/North African Transition," *Spectrum Journal of Global Studies* 7, no. 2 (2015): 45–67, 55; World Bank's Poverty Reduction and Economic Management (PREM) Network, *Economic Growth in the 1990s: Learning from a Decade of Reform* (World Bank, 2005), 169; "PIC Declaration: Annex; The Peace Implementation Agenda Reinforcing Peace in Bosnia And Herzegovina—the Way Ahead," December 16, 1998, Madrid, OHR Archive, http://www.ohr.int/?p=54101.

25. *OHR Economic Newsletter,* May 25, 2002.

26. *OHR Economic Newsletter,* October 2000.

27. "Pregled realiziranih tendera u velikoj privatizaciji u saradnji sa Međunarodnom savjetodavnom grupom za privatizaciju (IAGP), prilog 4," *Privatization Agency of the Federation of Bosnia and Herzegovina,* accessed July 1, 2025, at http://apf.gov.ba/info/izvj/privatizacija99 _2006/prilozi/4%20realizirani%20iagp.pdf.

28. International Monetary Fund, European Department, *Bosnia and Herzegovina: Request for Extended Arrangement under the Extended Fund Facility—Press Release; Staff Report; and Statement by the Executive Director for Bosnia and Herzegovina* (International Monetary Fund, 2016), 48.

29. OECD, "Promoting SMEs for Development," in *Promoting Entrepreneurship and Innovative SMEs in a Global Economy: Towards a More Responsible and Inclusive Globalization* (OECD, 2004), 11. The deputy high representative Donald Hays argued in a speech that bankruptcy should not be seen as a taboo. Donald Hays. "Bankruptcy is not a taboo," March 23, 2004, Sarajevo, OHR archive, http://www.ohr.int/?p=46355.

30. Carl Bildt, *Peace Journey: The Struggle for Peace in Bosnia* (Weidenfeld and Nicolson, 1998), 248.

31. Sabina Arslanagić, "Entrepreneurs Get Task of Making Bosnia More Business-Friendly," AFP Sarajevo, April 7, 2003, OHR archive, http://www.ohr.int/?p=47844.

32. Lord Paddy Ashdown, interview with author, London, January 23, 2018.

33. John Nellis, *The World Bank, Privatization and Enterprise Reform in Transition Economies: A Retrospective Analysis* (Operations Evaluation Department, World Bank, 2002), 6.

34. Danijela Majstorović, "Decoloniality as Peripherality in Bosnia and Herzegovina," in *Decolonial Theory and Practice in Southeast Europe,* ed. Katarina Kušić, et al. (dVersia, special issue 03.2019), 139.

35. IMF, "Poverty Reduction Strategy," 22. The "motto of growth" was in SMEs, as the deputy high representative declared in an interview. Ralph Johnson, "Prvi Zamjenik Visokog Predstavnika u BiH," *Privatizacija. Stručni Časopis Agencije Za Privatizaciju u Federaciji Bosne i Hercegovine,* no. 10/11 (July 2000): 5.

36. Bildt, *Peace Journey,* 248.

37. Donald Hays, principal deputy high representative, speech at the USAID-sponsored SME Donor Roundtable, Sarajevo, April 7, 2004, OHR Archive, http://www.ohr.int/?p=46231.

38. "Bosnia and Herzegovina: Poverty Reduction Strategy Paper—Mid-Term," IMF Country Report (IMF, April 2004), 69.

39. Dragoljub Stojanov, *Economics in Peacemaking: Lessons from Bosnia and Herzegovina* (Portland Trust, 2009), 14.

40. USAID, *Bosnian Reconstruction Program,* 2.

41. In the period of intense privatization between the late 1990s and mid-2000s, there was a decrease in overall exports and a redirection of foreign trade to neighboring countries. See Milica Uvalić, "Trade Liberalisation in Southeast Europe—Recent Trends and Some Policy Implications" (UNECE Spring Seminar, "Financing for Development in the ECE Region:

Promoting Growth in Low-income Transition Economies," 2005), 8. See also World Bank national accounts data and OECD National Accounts data files, available at https://data .worldbank.org/indicator/NE.EXP.GNFS.ZS?locations=BA.

42. Burić, "Dwelling on the Ruins," 227.

43. Katerina Kušić and the contributors of *Decolonial Theory and Practice in Southeast Europe* reflect on the complex role of southeastern Europe both as a cocreator of the project of European modernity and the capitalist world system and as a subject of its power structures. Katerina Kušić, et al., *Decolonial Theory*, 51.

44. Jeffrey Sachs and David Lipton, "Poland's Economic Reform," *Foreign Affairs* 69, no. 3 (Summer 1990): 47–66.

45. In contrast with the roughly forty thousand employees it had before the war. General Servis ONASA, "B.Matić: Novac međunarodnih organizacija nije našao put do Energoinvesta," April 8, 1997.

46. Sejjfudin Zahirović and Sead Omerhodžić, "Javni upis dionica," *Privatizacija. Stručni Časopis Agencije Za Privatizaciju u Federaciji Bosne i Hercegovine*, January 2000, 13.

47. "Visok ugled u zemlji i svijetu," *Energoinvest List*, March 2000, 2.

48. Darko Omeragić "Džemail Vlahovljak i Edhem Bičakčić za SB o zlatnim I poratnim godinama energoinvesta," *Slobodna Bosna*, September 3, 2022, https://www.slobodna-bosna .ba/vijest/265548/dzemail_vlahovljak_i_edhem_bichakchic_za_sb_o_zlatnim_i_poratnim _godinama_energoinvesta_kako_je_ono_sto_je_stvorio_emerik_blum_tokom_rata _razoreno_i_sumnjivo_opuhano_a_onda_rasparchano u daytonu.html.

49. "Usvojen izmijenjeni program," *Energoinvest List*, August–September 2001, 1. For example, Energopetrol was sold to the Croatian-Hungarian consortium INA-MOL; TAT did not find a suitable buyer and has been declared bankrupt; TDS and DVI were bought by the Turkish investment group Attila Group. *PRODAJA POKRETNE I NEPOKRETNE IMOVINE (ZEMLJIŠTE, OBJEKTI, OPREMA, MAŠINE) STEČAJNOG DUŽNIKA: Imovina u stečaju/ likvidaciji/plenidbi*, Oslobođenje, October 28, 2017, accessed July 1, 2025, https://ba.ekapija .com/tender/1922962/prodaja-pokretne-i-nepokretne-imovine-zemljiste-objekti-oprema -masine-stecajnog-duznika-e; "Privatizacija u Federaciji Bosne i Hercegovine 1999–2006," Agencija za Privatizaciju u Federaciji Bosne i Hercegovine, June 2007, 15, http://www.apf .com.ba/info/izvj/privatizacija99_2006/prilozi/99-06.pdf.

50. Most of it was domestic investment. See Registar vrijednosnih papiri Federacije Bosne i Herzegovine, June 14, 2009, Arhiv Prvih Deset Dionicara, http://www.rvp.ba/Section3 /Top10Arh.aspx; http://www.rvp.ba/Section2/Top10.aspx. Companies that had not gone bankrupt, such as Energoinvest-TAT (steam generators), TDS (metal structures), and DVI (transmission lines and engineering), had most of their shares bought by investment funds. Fortuna Fond in Bihac, CROBIH fond in Mostar, and Prof Plus Fond in Sarajevo, to name a few, owned between 20 and 40 percent of shares. Over 40 percent of Energoinvest VMC (metal structures) was owned by Enver Malagić, a constructor close to the then prime minister Edhem Bičakčić. "Od prijeratnog obućara do tajkuna," *Slobodna Bosna—Nezavisni Informativni Portal*, October 22, 2012, https://www.slobodna-bosna.ba/vijest/2901/od_prijeratnog_obucara_do_tajkuna.html.

51. "Ekspoze premijera Federacije Bosne i Hercegovine Dr. Izudina Kapetanovića na ustavotvornoj Skupštini Federacije BiH," June 3, 1996, Ustavotvorna Skupština Federacije Bosne i Hercegovine, no. 2354, folder 56, Arhiv Federacije Bosne i Hercegovine, 11.

52. *Službeni Glasnik Republike Srpske* 24/98; *Službeni Glasnik FBiH* 27/97.

53. Generalni Servis ONASA, "Prijedog zakona o općem bilansu preduzeća Republiku Srpsku tretira kao inostranstvo?," August 11, 1997.

54. Svetlana Cenić, "Birač—Hronika Jedne Privatizacije," *Buka*, October 21, 2013, http://www.6yka.com/novost/%204404/birac-hronika-jedne-privatizacije.

55. TAT, producing thermal devices, for example, was sold for BAM 10 million though its initial value was over 40 million. TDS and Elektrooprema, producing transmission lines, had a similar fate. Perhaps the worst example is of the Tuzla TTU (Energoinvest until 1992), which had its initial capital of BAM 11 million and was sold for BAM 1 (roughly EUR 0.50). The buyer's agreement of investing BAM 5 million in its restructuring never occurred, and the company is now completely bankrupt. "Privatizacija u Tuzlanskom Kantonu 1999—2007," Tuzla Canton Agency for Privatization, December 2007, 42; "Privatizacija u Federaciji," APFB, accessed October 15, 2021, 15, http://www.apf.com.ba/info/izvj/privatizacija99_2006/prilozi/99-06.pdf.

56. Fikret Talić, interview with author, Sarajevo, September 22, 2014.

57. Faruk Šarić, "Eutanazija i privatizacija," *Energoinvest List*, April–May 2003, 2.

58. "Project Appraisal Document on a Proposed Credit in the Amount of SDR 15.6 Million (US$ 19.8 Million Equivalent) to Bosnia and Herzegovina for a Privatization Technical Assistance," World Bank Private and Financial Sectors Development Unit South East Europe Country Unit Europe and Central Asia Region, May 31, 2001, tables 2, 5; "Implementation Completion and Results Report on a Credit in the Amount of SDR 15.60 Million (US$19.80 Million Equivalent) to Bosnia and Herzegovina for a Privatization Technical Assistance Credit," IDA-35310, World Bank Private and Financial Sector Development Unit South East Europe Country Unit Europe and Central Asia Region, March 21, 2007, 8.

59. Mićo Čarević, "Zapošljavanje u Kontekstu tzv 'tranzicije,'" in *Uticaj Transformacije Vlasništva Na Nezaposlenost i Zapošljavanje*, ed. Murat Prašo, Mišo Čarević, Mesud Sabitović, and Izudin Kešetović (Sedam, 2000), 50–56, 55.

60. Sabrija Pojskić, "Položaj Radnika u Procesu Privatizacije," in Prašo, et al., *Uticaj Transformacije Vlasništva Na Nezaposlenost i Zapošljavanje*, 166–72, 168.

61. "Cetiri bh. koraka do prokletstva," *Oslobođenje*, January 1, 2004, 7.

62. Anto Domazet, interview with author, Sarajevo, April 5, 2016.

63. "Diktirana budućnost," *Energoinvest list*, October 2000, 2.

64. "Plod znanja i bosanskog inata," *Energoinvest List*, September 1996, 2 (emphasis added). These kinds of views were frequently remarked on in the journal. See H. Arifagić, "Zajednički nastup sa tvornicom u Lukavici," *Oslobođenje*, December 23, 2005, 16.

65. Amer Kapetanović, "Zaokret za deset milijardi," *Dani*, September 15, 2000.

66. Faruk Šarić, "Strateški partner," *Energoinvest List*, December 2000, 2.

67. Mihad Hajro, assistant director, interview, *Energoinvest List*, June 2006, 7.

68. As noted for the context of other eastern European countries in transition by Josef Borocz and Ákos Róna-Tas, "Small Leap Forward: Emergence of New Economic Elites," *Theory and Society* 24, no. 5 (October 1995): 751–81, 777.

69. Džemajl Vlahovljak, interview with author, Sarajevo, March 4, 2016.

70. "Energoinvestova mladost u razgovoru sa direktorom Energoinvesta," *Energoinvest List*, July 2008, 3.

71. Dževad, interview with author, Sarajevo, December 16, 2016.

72. Mladen, interview with author, Sarajevo, July 17, 2014.

73. Organised Crime and Corruption Reporting Project, "Energoinvest Sold Debts in Secret for a Fraction of Value," November 16, 2011, https://www.occrp.org/en/daily/1236-energoinvest-sold-debts-in-secret-for-a-fraction-of-value.

74. Dževad Ganić, interview with author, Sarajevo, June 9, 2016.

75. "Jedna od najtežih a najbolja poslovodna godina," *Energoinvest List*, November–December 2003, 1.

76. Senka Kurt, "Libya Revolution: Bosnian Companies Count the Cost," Balkan Insight, August 24, 2011, https://balkaninsight.com/2011/08/24/libya-revolution-bosnian-companies-count-the-cost/.

77. Anesa Rustemović, "Nastavak uspješnog poslovanja," *Energoinvest List*, June 2010, 3.

78. Džemajl Vlahovljak, interview with author, Sarajevo, March 4, 2016.

79. "Novi posao u Tanzaniji," *Energoinvest List*, November 2017, 1–2. The wars in Libya and Iraq, two of the most important partners for Energoinvest, had led the company to pursue deals in other countries like Tanzania and Algeria. N. N., "Energoinvest u problemima: Plaće kasne dva mjeseca, uprava traži rješenje," *KlixBiznis*, May 7, 2015. Available at https://www.klix.ba/biznis/privreda/energoinvest-u-problemima-place-kasne-dva-mjeseca-uprava-trazi-rjesenje/150507012. Accessed July 1, 2025.

7. Bound by Promises

1. David Byrne, "Industrial Culture in a Post-Industrial World: The Case of the North East of England," *City* 6, no. 3 (2002): 279–89, 287, https://doi.org/10.1080/1360481022000037733.

2. Devika Sharma and Frederik Tygstrup, *Structures of Feeling: Affectivity and the Study of Culture* (De Gruyter, 2015), 1.

3. Jakob Finci, interview with author, Sarajevo, March 8 2016. On an interview for the company's newspaper, Finci remarked that people said a simple sentence with great pride: "I work for Energoinvest", and that meant that people would recognize each other to be part of the same family". "Naša Anketa. Energoinvest je simbol uspjeha," interviewed by Esad Smajlović, *Energoinvest list*, March 2001, 2.

4. Musić, *Making and Breaking*, 80–81.

5. Zdravko Prlenda, interview with author, Sarajevo, December 10, 2016.

6. Dževad, interview with author, Sarajevo, December 16, 2016.

7. Tim Strangleman, "Work Identity in Crisis? Rethinking the Problem of Attachment and Loss at Work," *Sociology* 46, no. 3 (2012): 411–25, 419, https://doi.org/10.1177/0038038511422585.

8. Most of the production would be exported to the Soviet Union, Cuba, and other nonaligned countries. "Proizvodnja aluminija veća od planiranje," *Energoinvest List*, January 12, 1987, 3–5.

9. Workers of TDS, collective interview with author, Sarajevo, February 17, 2016.

10. Asim, interview with author, Sarajevo, April 6, 2016.

11. Amila, interview with author, Sarajevo, July 2, 2014.

12. Elizabeth C. Dunn, *Privatizing Poland: Baby Food, Big Business, and the Remaking of Labor* (London: Cornell University Press, 2004), 130; Sanja Potkonjak and Nevena Škrbić Alempijević, "Rethinking the City in the Industrial Aftermath: Socio-Industrial Memory and Environmental Fallouts," *Narodna Umjetnost* 60, no. 3 (2023): 15.

13. Munevera, interview with author, Sarajevo, March 26, 2016.

14. Fred Davis, *Yearning for Yesterday: A Sociology of Nostalgia* (Free Press, 1979).

15. Maya Nadkarni, *Remains of Socialism: Memory and the Futures of the Past in Postsocialist Hungary* (Cornell University Press, 2020), 96, http://www.jstor.org/stable/10.7591/j.ctvq2w1j5.

16. For broader discussions of the phenomenon of working-class memory and nostalgia in former state-socialist eastern European countries, see Svetlana Boym, "From the Russian Soul to Post-Communist Nostalgia," *Representations* 59 (1995): 133–66. See also Sanja Potkonjak and Tea Škokić, "'In the World of Iron and Steel': On the Ethnography of Work, Unemployment and Hope," *Narodni Umjetnosti* 50, no. 1 (2013): 74–95; Nina Vodopivec, "Social Memory of Textile Workers in Slovenia," *Slovene Studies* 30, no. 1 (2008): 63–78.

17. Petrović, "The Past That Binds Us," 136.

18. Tanja Petrović, "'When We Were Europe': Socialist Workers in Serbia and Their Nostalgic Narratives," in *Remembering Communism: Genres of Representation*, ed. Maria Todorova (Social Science Research Council, 2010), 127–54, 148.

19. Alice Mah, *Industrial Ruination, Community and Place: Landscapes and Legacies of Urban Decline* (Toronto University Press, 2012), 12.

20. Maria O'Donovan, "Nostalgia and Heritage in the Carousel City: Deindustrialization, Critical Memory, and the Future," *Journal of Community Archaeology & Heritage* 6, no. 4 (2019): 272–82, 278, https://doi.org/10.1080/20518196.2019.1653517.

21. Hannah Skoda, "Nostalgia and Pre-Modernity," *History and Theory* 62, no. 2 (June 2023): 251–71, 271.

22. Yanqiu Rachel Zhou, "Nostalgia in Times of Uncertainty: (Re)Articulations of the Past, Present, and Future of Globalization," in *Globalization: Past, Present, Future*, ed. Manfred B. Steger, Roland Benedikter, Harald Pechlaner, and Ingrid Kofler (University of California Press, 2023), 43–58.

23. For a generational approach to the late-socialist period in Yugoslavia, see Spaskovska, *Last Yugoslav Generation*.

24. Sasso, "Political Dimension," 46.

25. Šaban, Sindikat Solidarnosti Tuzla, interview with author, Tuzla, April 29, 2016.

26. Dževad, interview with author, Sarajevo, December 16, 2016.

27. Munevera, interview with author, Sarajevo, March 26, 2016.

28. Asim, interview with author, Sarajevo, May 29, 2016.

29. Mustafa, interview with author, Sarajevo, June 23, 2016.

30. Dževad, interview with author, Sarajevo, December 16, 2016.

31. Asim, interview with author, Sarajevo, May 29, 2016, April 6, 2016.

32. Sulejman Hrle, at the "Sjednica Ustavotvorne Skupštine Federacije Bosne i Hercegovine," August 27, 1996, Ustavotvorna Skupštine Federacije Bosne i Hercegovine, no. 2354, folder 56, Arhiv Federacije Bosne i Hercegovine, 24/3.

33. Milica Uvalić, *Investment and Property Rights in Yugoslavia: The Long Transition to a Market Economy* (Cambridge University Press, 1992), 185.

34. I. Polimac, "Politikantstvo zaustavlja zakone," *Oslobođenje*, December 23, 1994, 3.

35. Šaban and Marko, Sindikat Solidarnosti Tuzla, interview with author, Tuzla, April 29, 2016.

36. "Pitanja i odgovori," *Privatizacija. Stručni Časopis Agencije Za Privatizaciju u Federaciji Bosne i Hercegovine*, January 1999, 100.

37. Again here the overlapping worker-fighter is evident in a worker's account. Asim, interview with author, Sarajevo, May 29, 2016.

38. Omer, interview with author, Gradačac, June 30, 2016.

39. Dunn, *Privatizing Poland*, 159.

40. *Službeni Glasnik BiH*, broj 14/98; *Službene novine FBiH*, broj 8/99.

41. F. Borić, "Privatizacija privatiziranog preduzeća?!," *Dani*, December 15, 2006, 10. In response to this article, Amila Omersofitć published a reply in the same newspaper, claiming that there was no record of the shares ever being bought by workers "because Karadžic's forces during the war had destroyed the factory and taken away all the documentation." Amila Omersoftić, "Fokus: Privatizacija Privatiziranog Preduzeća," *Dani*, December 22, 2006, 4, 77.

42. Belma Bećirbašić, "Plaća od jedne marke," *Dani*, August 26, 2005, 38–39.

43. Asim, interview with author, Sarajevo, May 29, 2016.

44. *The Association for the Protection of Unemployed Shareholders of Agrokomerc v. The Federation of Bosnia and Herzegovina*, no. CH/00/5134, CH/00/5136, CH/00/5138, and CH/01/7668 (Human Rights Chamber for Bosnia and Herzegovina, March 8, 2002), paragraphs 67, 69.

45. SRNA, "Radnici nastavljaju štrajk," *Nezavisne Novine*, August 11, 2009, 2.

46. Branimir, interview with author, phone interview, December 19, 2017. Branimir, who identifies as a Yugoslav Serb, is one of the few former workers who still spends time with his colleagues from the FBiH. According to him, this is because they have an interest in common: they are all seeking to establish their rights as shareholders.

47. Srna, "Ponovo protest ispred kapije RAOP-a," *Nezavisne Novine*, March 14, 2016, https://www.nezavisne.com/ekonomija/privreda/Ponovo-protest-ispred-kapije-RAOP-a/359359.

48. Appeal of Ms. Milica Mirković-Kalinić v. the judgment of the Cantonal Court in Sarajevo ("the Cantonal Court") no. Gz-1733/04 of September 17, 2004, and judgment of Municipal Court in Sarajevo ("the Municipal Court") no. Pr-377/02 of March 5, 2004, no. AP 1070/06 (Constitutional Court of Bosnia and Herzegovina, March 30, 2007), 5; Appeal of *Ms. Mara Memić et al. v. Supreme Court of the Federation of Bosnia and Herzegovina*, no. 070–0-Rev-07-001747 of April 17, 2008, no. AP 2581/08 (Constitutional Court of Bosnia and Herzegovina, June 29, 2011), 4. See also Duraković et al., cases no. CH/98/377 et al. (Constitutional Court of Bosnia and Herzegovina, November 7, 2003), 11.

49. Minka, interview with author, Dita Tuzla, May 4, 2016.

50. Larisa Kurtović, "When All That Is Solid Does Not Melt into Air: Labor, Politics and Materiality in a Bosnian Detergent Factory," *PoLAR: Political and Legal Anthropology Review* 43, no. 2 (2020): 228–46, 238.

51. Damir Arsenijević, Jasmina Husanović, and Vanessa Vasić-Janeković, "Protesting for Production: The Dita Factory Occupation and the Struggle for Justice in Bosnia and Herzegovina," in *The Cultural Life of Capitalism in Yugoslavia*, ed. Dijana Jelaca, Maša Kolanović, and Danijela Lugarić (Springer International, 2017), 225–42, 226.

52. "Doboj: radnici pretvorili potraživanja u akcije i pokrenuli proizvodnju," Generalni Servis ONASA, August 18, 2006.

53. N. N., "Proizvodnja za korejsko tržište," *Oslobođenje*, August 16, 2010, 19.

54. Sanja Čakarević, "Strajkom traže plate i doprinose," *Nezavisne Novine*, June 16, 2009, https://www.nezavisne.com/novosti/gradovi/Strajkom-traze-plate-i-doprinose/42342.

55. B. Turković, "Otkazi svim radnicima osim menadžmenta?," *Dnevni Avaz*, March 17, 2010, 9.

56. Kurtović, "When All That Is Solid," 242.

57. "Energoinvest D.D.—najbolje rješenje," *Energoinvest List*, September–October 2003, 4.

58. "Zapisnik sa četvrtog sastanka radne grupe za privatizaciju," Ekonomski Fakultet Sarajevo: Koordinacioni odbor za ekonomski razvoj i EU integracije Radna grupa za privatizaciju, October 20, 2003, 5.

59. Alexandre Escudier, "Temporalization and Political Modernity: A Tentative Systematization of the Work of Reinhart Koselleck," in *Political Concepts and Time: New Approaches to Conceptual History*, ed. Javier Fernández Sebastián (Cantabria University Press, 2011), 131–77.

60. Anna Friberg, "History Politics and (Re)Forming the Future: Visions of Democracy and the Category of the Utopian," *Redescriptions: Political Thought, Conceptual History and Feminist Theory* 23, no. 1 (2020): 36–53.

61. Strangleman, "Deindustrialization," 478.

62. Susan Bayly, "Vietnamese Narratives of Tradition, Exchange and Friendship in the Worlds of the Global Socialist Ecumene," in *Enduring Socialism: Explorations of Revolution and Transformation, Restoration and Continuation*, ed. Harry G. West and Parvathi Raman (Berghahn Books, 2010), 125–47, http://www.jstor.org/stable/j.ctt9qcqbs.9.

63. Miro Klepić, interview with author, Lukavica, March 29, 2016.

64. Lisa Taylor, "Landscapes of Loss: Responses to Altered Landscape in an Ex-Industrial Textile Community," *Sociological Research Online* 25, no. 1 (2020): 46–65, https://doi-org.ezproxy2.lib.gla.ac.uk/10.1177/1360780419846508.

Conclusions

1. Helmuth Berking, "'Ethnicity Is Everywhere': On Globalization and the Transformation of Cultural Identity," *Current Sociology* 51, nos. 3/4 (2003): 248–64.

2. Tom Chodor, *Neoliberal Hegemony and the Pink Tide in Latin America* (London: Palgrave Macmillan, 2015), 178; Gabriel Fernandes Pimenta & Pedro Casas V. M. Arantes, *Rethinking Integration in Latin America: The "Pink Tide" and the Post-Neoliberal Regionalism* (FLACSO-ISA Joint International Conference Buenos Aires, Argentina, July 23–25, 2014), 17.

BIBLIOGRAPHY

Archives

Archive of the Federation of Bosnia and Herzegovina
(Arhiv Federacije Bosne i Hercegovine)

Dom Naroda Parlamentarne Skupštine Federacije Bosne i Hercegovine (Fond 2353, 1996;
2363, 1997; 2373, 1998; 2392, 1999–2000)
Fond Branko Mikulić (1984–1988)
Predstavnički Dom Parlamentarne Skupštine Republike Bosne i Hercegovine (Fond 2362,
1997; 2384, 1998; 2393, 1999–2000)
Ustavotvorna Skupština Federacije Bosne i Hercegovine (Fond 2350, 1994; 2352, 1996)

Archive of Yugoslavia (Arhiv Jugoslavije)

Institut za Međunarodnu Politiku i Privredu (Fond 740)
Interesna Zajednica za Ekonomske Odnose sa Inostranstvo (Fond 750)
Savezni Komitet za Ekonomsku Saradnju sa Zemljama u Razvoju (Fond 574)
Savezni Sekretarijat za Spoljnu Trgovinu (Fond 751)
Savezni Zavod za Međunarodnu Naučnu, Prosvetno-kulturnu i Tehničku Saradnju'
(Fond 465)
Savezno Izvršno Veće (SIV) (Fond 130)

Online Archive OHR

Available at http://www.ohr.int/?page_id=1204.

Online Arhiv Parlamentarna Skupština BiH

Available at https://www.parlament.ba/session/Read?ConvernerId=1.

State Archive of Bosnia and Herzegovina
(Državni Arhiv Bosne i Hercegovine)

Republički Društveni Savjet za Privredni Razvoj i Ekonomsku Politiku (1989–1990)
Republički Sekretarijat za Međunarodnu Saradnju (1989)
Republički Zavod za Međunarodnu, Naučno-tehničku i Kulturnu Saradnju (1989–1992)
Savez Sindikata, Savez Samostalnih Sindikata Bosne i Hercegovine (1988–1999)
Skupštine Socijalističke Republike Bosne i Hercegovine (1989–1991)
Zastupnički Dom Parlamentarne Skupštine Republike Bosne i Hercegovine (1997–2000)
Službene Novine Federacije Bosne i Hercegovine (1994–1997)
Službeni Glasnik Republike Srpske (1993–1998)

Službeni List Republike Bosne i Hercegovine (1992–1997)
Službeni List Socijalističke Republike Bosne i Hercegovine (1989–1990)
Službeni List Socijalističke Republike Federativne Jugoslavije (1988–1990)

Newspapers and Magazines

BH Dani (1992–2014)
General Servis ONASA
Glas Srpski
Naši Dani (1987–1992)
Nezavisne Novine
Oslobođenje (1988–2014)

Specialist Magazines

Direktor: Mesečni časopis za teoriju, praksu i informisanje o organizovanju, upravljanju i rukovođenju u udruženom radu (1989–1991)
Ekonomika (1987–1991)
Ekonomist (1987–1991)
Ekonomska Analiza (1986–1991)
Ekonomska Politika (1987–1991)
Ekonomski Glasnik Bosne i Hercegovine (1987–1991)
Komunist: Organ Saveza Komunista Jugoslavije (1989–1991)
Naše Teme: Stručni časopis Ekonomskog Instituta Zagreb (1986–1991)
Privatizacija: Stručni časopis Agencije za privatizaciju Federacije Bosne i Hercegovine (1998–2000)
Radni Odnosi i Samoupravljanje (1989–1991)

Company Journals

Energoinvest Aluminij Mostar: List radnih ljudi Radne Organizacije Aluminij Mostar (1988–1991)
Energoinvest Armature: List radnika Radne Organizacije (1988–1991)
Energoinvest Birač Zvornik: List radnica tvornice glinice Birač Zvornik (1984–1992)
Energoinvest Energopetrol: List radnika Radne Organizacije Energopetrol Sarajevo (1988–1991)
Energoinvest List: List Radnika SOUR-a (1986–2018)
Energoinvest Livac: List Energoinvestove OOUR Livnica Čelika Tuzla (1985)
Energoinvest Sretno Srebrenica: List radnika Radne Organizacije Srebrenica (1989–1991)

Secondary Sources

Abrams, Lynn. *Oral History Theory*. New York: Routledge, 2010.
Aciksoz, Salih Can. "Sacrificial Limbs of Sovereignty: Disabled Veterans, Masculinity, and Nationalist Politics in Turkey." *Medical Anthropology Quarterly* 26, no. 1 (2012): 4–25.
Acquaviva, Guido. "The Dissolution of Yugoslavia and the Fate of Its Financial Obligations." *Denver Journal of International Law & Policy* 30, no. 173 (2002): 173–216.
Acs, Zoltan J. "The Internationalization of Small and Medium-Sized Enterprises: A Policy Perspective." *Small Business Economics* 9 (1997): 7–20.

Adler, Paul. "Creating 'The NGO International': The Rise of Advocacy for Alternative Development, 1974–1994." In *The Development Century: A Global History*, edited by Stephen J. Macekura and Erez Manela. Global and International History. Cambridge University Press, 2018.

Ageev, Alexander I., Mikhail V. Gratchev, and Robert D. Hisrich. "Entrepreneurship in the Soviet Union and Post-Socialist Russia." *Small Business Economics* 7, no. 5 (1995): 365–76.

Ahearne, James. "Neoliberal Economic Policies and Post-Conflict Peace-Building: A Help or Hindrance to Durable Peace?" *Polis Journal* 2 (2009): 1–44.

Ams, Julianne, Tamon Asonuma, Wolfgang Bergthaler, Chanda M. DeLong, Nouria El Mehdi, Mark J. Flanagan, Sean Hagan, Yan Liu, Charlotte J. Lundgren, Martin Mühleisen, Alex Pienkowski, Gustavo Pinto, and Eric Robert. *Prevention and Resolution of Sovereign Debt Crises* (International Monetary Fund, 2018).

Anđelić, Neven. *Bosnia-Herzegovina: The End of a Legacy*. Frank Cass, 2003.

Andreas, Peter. *Blue Helmets and Black Markets: The Business of Survival in the Siege of Sarajevo*. Cornell University Press, 2008.

Angé, Olivia, David Berliner, and Jonathan Bach, eds. *Anthropology and Nostalgia*. Berghahn, 2015.

Antić, Ana. "Raising a True Socialist Individual: Yugoslav Psychoanalysis and the Creation of Democratic Marxist Citizens." *Social History* 44, no. 1 (2019): 86–115.

Appel, Hilary, and Mitchell A. Orenstein. "Why Did Neoliberalism Triumph and Endure in the Post-Communist World?" *Comparative Politics*, April 2016, 313–31.

Arandarenko, Mihail. "Waiting for the Workers: Explaining Labor Quiescence in Serbia." In *Workers after Workers' States*, edited by Stephen Crowley and David Ost. Rowman & Littlefield, 2001.

Archer, Rory. "Social Inequalities and Yugoslavia's Dissolution." In *Debating the End of Yugoslavia*, edited by Florian Bieber, Armina Galijaš, and Rory Archer. Routledge, 2014.

Archer, Rory. "'Antibureaucratism' as a Yugoslav Phenomenon: The View from Northwest Croatia." *Nationalities Papers* 47, no. 4 (2019). https://doi.org/10.1017/nps.2018.40.

Archer, Rory, Igor Duda, and Paul Stubbs. *Social Inequalities and Discontent in Yugoslav Socialism*. Routledge, 2016.

Archer, Rory, and Goran Musić. "Approaching the Socialist Factory and Its Workforce: Considerations from Fieldwork in (Former) Yugoslavia." *Labor History* 58, no. 1 (2016): 44–66.

Archer, Rory, and Goran Musić. "When Workers' Self-Management Met Neoliberalism: Positive Perceptions of Market Reforms among Blue-Collar Workers in Late Yugoslav Socialism." In *Labor in State Socialist Europe, 1945–1989: Contributions to a Global History of Work*, edited by Marsha Siefert. Central European University Press, 2020.

Armakolas, Ioannis. "The 'Paradox' of Tuzla City: Explaining Non-Nationalist Local Politics during the Bosnian War." *Europe-Asia Studies* 63, no. 2 (2011): 229–61.

Arsenijević, Damir, Jasmina Husanović, and Vanessa Vasić-Janeković. "Protesting for Production: The Dita Factory Occupation and the Struggle for Justice in Bosnia and Herzegovina." In *The Cultural Life of Capitalism in Yugoslavia*, edited by Dijana Jelaca, Maša Kolanović, and Danijela Lugarić. Springer International, 2017.

Atanasoski, N., and E. McElroy. "Postsocialism and the Afterlives of Revolution: Impossible Spaces of Dissent." In *Reframing Critical, Literary, and Cultural Theories*, edited by N. Pireddu. Palgrave Macmillan, 2018.

Azzellini, Dario. *The Class Strikes Back*. Brill, 2018.

Bajt, Aleksander. "Social Ownership—Collective and Individual." In *Self-Governing Socialism: A Reader*, edited by Branko Horvat, Mihailo Marković, and Rudi Supek. Taylor and Francis, 1975.

Baker, Catherine. *Race and the Yugoslav Region*. Manchester University Press, 2018.

Baker, Catherine, et al. *Off White: Central and Eastern Europe and the Global History of Race*. Manchester University Press, 2024.

Bakke, Kristin M., and Michael Ward. "Social Distance in Bosnia-Herzegovina and the North Caucasus Region of Russia: Inter- and Intra-Ethnic Attitudes and Identities." *Nations and Nationalism* 15, no. 2 (2009): 227–53.

Ban, Cornel, and Johanna Bockman. "Ruling Ideas: How Global Neoliberalism Goes Local." *Radical History Review*, no. 112 (2016): 9–42.

Barndt, Kerstin, and George Steinmetz. "Fordist Nostalgia: History and Experience at the Henry Ford." In *Ruins of Modernity*, edited by Julia Hell, Andreas Schönle, Julia Adams, and George Steinmetz. Duke University Press, 2009.

Bartel, Fritz. *The Triumph of Broken Promises. The End of the Cold War and the Rise of Neoliberalism*. Harvard University Press, 2022.

Bartha, Eszter. Alienating Labor: On the Road from Socialism to Capitalism in East Germany and Hungary. Vol. 22 of *International Studies in Social History*. Berghahn, 2013.

Bartmanski, Dominik. "Successful Icons of Failed Time: Rethinking Post-Communist Nostalgia." *Acta Sociologica* 54, no. 3 (2011): 213–31.

Baumeister, Martin, and B. Benjamin Ziemann. "Introduction: Peace Movements in Southern Europe during the 1970s and 1980s." *Journal of Contemporary History* 56, no. 3 (2021): 563–78.

Bayliss, Kate. "Post-Conflict Privatization: A Review of Development in Serbia and Bosnia-Herzegovina." ESAU Working Paper 12, Overseas Development Institute, London, 2005.

Bayly, Susan. "Vietnamese Narratives of Tradition, Exchange and Friendship in the Worlds of the Global Socialist Ecumene." In *Enduring Socialism: Explorations of Revolution and Transformation, Restoration and Continuation*, edited by Harry G. West and Parvathi Raman. New ed. Berghahn Books, 2010.

Berdak, Oliwia. "Reintegrating Veterans in Bosnia and Herzegovina and Croatia: Citizenship and Gender Effects." *Women's Studies International Forum* 49 (2015): 48–56.

Berking, Helmuth. "'Ethnicity Is Everywhere': On Globalization and the Transformation of Cultural Identity." *Current Sociology* 51, nos. 3/4, monograph 1/2 (2003): 248–264.

Berman, Bruce J. "Ethnicity, Patronage and the African State: The Politics of Uncivil Nationalism." *African Affairs* 97 (1998): 305–41.

Bernard, Sara. *Deutsch Marks in the Head, Shovel in the Hands and Yugoslavia in the Heart: The Gastarbeiter Return to Yugoslavia (1965–1991)*. Harrassowitz, 2019.

Bianchini, Stefano. *La questione Jugoslava*. Milan: Giunti Editore, 1999.

Bieber, Florian. "Institutionalizing Ethnicity in the Western Balkans: Managing Change in Deeply Divided Societies." Working paper 19, European Center for Minority Issues, 2004.

Bieber, Florian. *Post-War Bosnia: Ethnicity, Inequality and Public Sector Governance*. Palgrave Macmillan, 2006.

Bildt, Carl. *Peace Journey: The Struggle for Peace in Bosnia*. Weidenfeld and Nicolson, 1998.

Birch, Kean, and Vlad Mykhnenko. "Varieties of Neoliberalism? Restructuring in Large Industrially Dependent Regions across Western and Eastern Europe." *Journal of Economic Geography* 9, no. 3 (May 2009): 355–80.

Blackburn, Robert, and Anne Kovalainen. "Researching Small Firms and Entrepreneurship: Past, Present and Future." *International Journal of Management Reviews* 11, no. 2 (2008): 127–48.

Blasi, Joseph Raphael, and Douglas Lynn Kruse. *The New Owners: The Mass Emergence of Employee Ownership in Public Companies and What It Means to American Business.* Harper Collins, 1991.

Blokker, Paul. "Post-Communist Modernization, Transition Studies, and Diversity in Europe." *European Journal of Social Theory* 8, no. 4 (2005): 503–25.

Bockman, Johanna. *Markets in the Name of Socialism: The Left-Wing Origins of Neoliberalism.* Stanford University Press, 2011.

Bockman, Johanna. "Socialist Globalization against Capitalist Neocolonialism: The Economic Ideas behind the New International Economic Order." *Humanity: An International Journal of Human Rights, Humanitarianism, and Development* 6, no. 1 (2015): 109–28.

Bockman, Johanna. "Democratic Socialism in Chile and Peru: Revisiting the 'Chicago Boys' as the Origin of Neoliberalism." *Comparative Studies in Society and History* 61, no. 3 (2019): 654–79. https://doi-org.ezproxy2.lib.gla.ac.uk/10.1017/S0010417519000239.

Bockman, Johanna, and Gil Eyal. "Eastern Europe as a Laboratory for Economic Knowledge: The Transnational Roots of Neoliberalism." *American Journal of Sociology* 108, no. 2 (2002): 310–52.

Bohle, Dorothee, and Béla Greskovits. "Neoliberalism, Embedded Neoliberalism and Neocorporatism: Towards Transnational Capitalism in Central-Eastern Europe." *West European Politics* 30, no. 3 (2007): 443–66.

Bojičić-Dželilović, Vesna. "Peace on Whose Terms? War Veterans' Associations in Bosnia and Herzegovina." In *Challenges to Peacebuilding: Managing Spoilers during Conflict Resolution*, edited by Edward Newman and Oliver Richmond. United Nations University Press, 2006.

Bonfiglioli, Chiara. "Post-Socialist Deindustrialization and Its Gendered Structure of Feeling: The Devaluation of Women's Work in the Croatian Garment Industry." *Labor History* 61, no. 1 (2020): 36–47. https://doi.org/10.1080/0023656X.2019.1681643.

Bonfiglioli, Chiara. *Women and Industry in the Balkans: The Rise and Fall of the Yugoslav Textile Sector.* I. B. Tauris, 2019.

Borocz, Josef, and Akos Rona-Tas. "Small Leap Forward: Emergence of New Economic Elites." *Theory and Society* 24, no. 5 (October 1995): 751–81.

Bosomitu, Ştefan. "Sociology in Communist Romania: An Institutional and Biographical Overview." *Studia UBB Sociologia* 62, no. 1 (2017): 65–84.

Bougarel, Xavier. "The Shadow of Heroes: Former Combatants in Post-War Bosnia-Herzegovina." *International Social Science Journal* 189 (2006): 479–90.

Bougarel, Xavier. "Death and the Nationalist: Martyrdom, War Memory, and Veteran Identity among Bosnian Muslims." In *The New Bosnian Mosaic: Identities, Memories and Moral Claims in a Post-War Society*, edited by Xavier Bougarel, Elissa Helms, and Ger Duijzings. Ashgate, 2007.

Boym, Svetlana. "From the Russian Soul to Post-Communist Nostalgia." *Representations*, no. 49 (1995): 133–66. https://doi.org/10.2307/2928753.

Boym, Svetlana. *The Future of Nostalgia*. Basic Books, 2001.

Brigham, Steve. "The American-Soviet Walks: Large-Scale Citizen Diplomacy at Glasnost's Outset." *Peace & Change* 35, no. 4 (2010): 594–625.

Brubaker, Rogers. "National Minorities, Nationalizing States, and External National Homelands in the New Europe." *Daedalus* 124, no. 2 (1995): 107–32.

Brubaker, Rogers. "Ethnicity without Groups." *European Journal of Sociology* 43, no. 2 (2015): 163–89.

Brunnbauer, Ulf. "Making Bulgarians Socialist: The Fatherland Front in Communist Bulgaria, 1944—1989." *East European Politics and Societies* 22, no. 1 (2008): 44–79.

Brunnbauer, Ulf. *Building Ships and Surviving Late Socialism: The Shipyard "Uljanik" in Pula in the 1970s and 1980s*, Series: IOS Mitteilungen 69. Leibniz-Institut für Ost- und Südosteuropaforschung, 2019.

Burawoy, Michael, and Katherine Verdery, eds. *Uncertain Transition: Ethnographies of Change in the Postsocialist World*. Rowman & Littlefield, 2000.

Burg, Stephen L., and Paul S. Shoup. *The War in Bosnia-Herzegovina: Ethnic Conflict and International Intervention*. M. E. Sharpe, 2000.

Burić, Fedja. "Dwelling on the Ruins of Socialist Yugoslavia." In *Post-Communist Nostalgia*, edited by Marija Nikolaeva Todorova and Zsuzsa Gille. Berghahn Books, 2010.

Byrne, David. "Industrial Culture in a Post-Industrial World: The Case of the North East of England." *City* 6, no. 3 (2002): 279–89.

Byrne, Jeffrey James. "Beyond Continents, Colours, and the Cold War: Yugoslavia, Algeria, and the Struggle for Non-Alignment." *International History Review* 37, no. 5 (2015): 912–32.

Byrne, Jeffrey James. *Mecca of Revolution: Algeria, Decolonization, and the Third World Order*. Oxford University Press, 2016.

Calori, Anna. "Salt and Socialism: A Deconstruction of Tuzla's Political Identity in the Context of the Bosnian Conflict." *Ethnopolitics Papers*, no. 35, 2015.

Calori, Anna. "Losing the Global: (Re)Building a Bosnian Enterprise across Transition." *Business History* 65, no. 7 (2020): 1226–41. https://doi.org/10.1080/00076791.2020.1819242.

Calori, Anna. "Cigar Socialism: An Entangled History of Yugoslav-Cuban Relations." *Cold War History*, June 2023, 1–19.

Calori, Anna, Anne Hartmetz, Bence Kocsev, Jan Zofka, and James Mark, eds. *Globalization Projects East and South: Spaces of Economic Interaction during the Cold War*. DeGruyter, 2019.

Calori, Anna, and Ljubica Spaskovska. "Reimagining the World: Decolonisation and the Promise of Development." *Contemporary European History* 30, no. 4 (2021): 613–20.

Cannon, Mariah, and Silvia Emili. "'Empresas Recuperadas': Argentina's Recovered Factory Movement." Case summary 4, Institute for Development Studies, Brighton, 2019.

Caspersen, Nina. *Contested Nationalism: Serb Elite Rivalry in Croatia and Bosnia in the 1990s*. Berghahn Books, 2001.

Castillo, Mario, and Antonio Martins Neto. "Premature Deindustrialization in Latin America," *ECLAC—Production Development Series*, no. 205. United Nations ECLAC, June 2016.

Čaušević, Fikret. "Bosanska Ekonomska Enigma: O Tranziciji od 1996. do 2013. Godine," *Međunarodni forum Bosnia* no. 63–64 (2013).

Čaušević, Fikret, and Merima Zupčević. "Case Study: Bosnia and Herzegovina." In *Final Report Peace and Development Democratization, Poverty Reduction and Risk Mitigation in Fragile and Post-Conflict States*, edited by Philip Oxhorn. McGill University and the World Bank, 2009.

Chandler, David. *Peace without Politics? Ten Years of International State-Building in Bosnia.* Routledge, 2006.

Chen, Feng. "Between the State and Labor: The Conflict of Chinese Trade Unions' Double Identity in Market Reform." *The China Quarterly* no. 176 (2003): 1006–28.

Chen, Feng. "Privatization and Its Discontents in Chinese Factories." *The China Quarterly,* no. 185 (2006): 42–60.

Chodor, Tom, Fernandes Pimenta, and Pedro Casas V. M. Arantes. *Neoliberal Hegemony and the Pink Tide in Latin America.* Palgrave Macmillan, 2015.

Chua, Amy L. "The Privatization-Nationalization Cycle: The Link between Markets and Ethnicity in Developing Countries." *Columbia Law Review* 95, no. 2 (March 1995): 223–303.

Clissold, Stephen. *Djilas: The Progress of a Revolutionary.* Maurice Temple Smith, 1983.

Cohen, Lenard. *Broken Bonds: Yugoslavia's Disintegration and Balkan Politics in Transition.* Westview, 1995.

Coles, Kimberley A. "Ambivalent Builders: Europeanization, the Production of Difference, and Internationals in Bosnia-Herzegovina." *PoLAR: Political and Legal Anthropology Review* 25 (2002): 1–18.

Collier, Stephen J. "Neoliberalism as Big Leviathan, or . . . ? A Response to Wacquant and Hilgers." *Social Anthropology/Anthropologie Sociale* 20, no. 2 (2012): 186–95.

Comisso, Ellen Turkish. *Workers' Control under Plan and Market of Yugoslav Self-Management.* Yale University Press, 1979.

Conner, James C., and Branko Vukmir. "The Legal Anatomy of a Yugoslav 'Enterprise.'" *Business Lawyer* 32, no. 1 (1976): 99–117.

Corea, Gamani. "Unctad and the New International Economic Order." *International Affairs* 53, no. 2 (1977): 177–87.

Cortada, James W. *Inside IBM: Lessons of a Corporate Culture in Action.* Columbia University Press, 2023.

Corti, Carlos, and Myrna Alexander. "Argentina's Privatization Program." CFS Discussion Paper Series 103, World Bank, Washington, DC, 1993. http://documents.worldbank.org/curated/en/698941468767394378/Argentinas-privatization-program.

Creed, Gerald W. *Domesticating Revolution: From Socialist Reform to Ambivalent Transition in a Bulgarian Village.* UPennsylvania State University Press, 1998.

Crowley, Stephen, and David Ost. *Workers after Workers' States: Labor and Politics in Postcommunist Eastern Europe.* Rowman & Littlefield, 2001.

Curtis, Glenn E., ed. *Yugoslavia: A Country Study* Federal Research Division, Library of Congress, 1992.

Dahler-Larsen, Peter. "Corporate Culture and Morality: Durkheim-Inspired Reflections on the Limits of Corporate Culture." *Journal of Management Studies* 31, no. 1 (January 1994): 1–18.

Davis, Fred. *Yearning for Yesterday: A Sociology of Nostalgia.* Free Press, 1979.

Deal, Terrence E., and Allan A. Kennedy. *Corporate Cultures: The Rites and Rituals of Corporate Life.* Addison-Wesley, 1982.

Debouzy, Marianne. "In Search of Working-Class Memory: Some Questions and a Tentative Assessment." In *Between Memory and History,* edited by Marie-Noëlle Bourguet, Lucette Valensi, and Nathan Wachtel. Harwood Academic, 1990.

Dellheim, Charles. "Business in Time: The Historian and Corporate Culture." *Public Historian* 8, no. 2 (1986): 9–22.

Dello Buono, Richard A. "Latin America and the Collapsing Ideological Supports of Neoliberalism." *Critical Sociology* 37, no. 1 (2011): 9–25.

Dević, Ana. "Anti-War Initiatives and the Un-Making of Civic Identities in the Former Yugoslav Republics." *Journal of Historical Sociology* 10 (1997): 127–56. https://doi.org/10.1111/1467-6443.00034.

Dietrich, Christopher R. W. *Oil Revolution: Anticolonial Elites, Sovereign Rights, and the Economic Culture of Decolonization.* Cambridge University Press, 2017.

Dillon, Niamh. "From Market Trader to Global Player: Oral History and Corporate Culture in Tesco, Britain's Largest Supermarket." *Oral History* 43, no. 1 (2015): 52–62.

Dinkel, Jurgen. *The Non-Aligned Movement: Genesis, Organization and Politics (1927–1992).* Brill, 2019.

Divjak, Jovan. "The First Phase, 1992–1993: Struggle for Survival and Genesis of the Army of Bosnia-Herzegovina." In *The War in Croatia and Bosnia-Herzegovina, 1991–1995,* edited by Branka Magaš and Ivo Zanić. Frank Cass, 2005.

Dokić, Goran. "States of Victimhood and Irreparable Losses: Serbian Veterans of the Post-Yugoslav Wars." *Glasnik Etnografskog Instituta SANU* 44, no. 1 (2017): 97–110.

Donais, Timothy. "The Politics of Privatization in Post-Dayton Bosnia." *Southeast European Politics* 3, no. 1 (2002): 3–19.

Donia, Robert J. *Sarajevo: A Biography.* Hurst, 2006.

Dragostinova, Theodora. *The Cold War from the Margins: A Small Socialist State on the Global Cultural Scene.* Cornell University Press, 2021.

Dragović-Soso, Jasna. "Why Did Yugoslavia Disintegrate? An Overview of Contending Explanations." In *State Collapse in South-Eastern Europe: New Perspectives on Yugoslavia's Disintegration,* edited by Jasna Dragović-Soso and Lenard J. Cohen. Purdue University Press, 2007.

Dubravčić, Dinko. "Economic Causes and Political Context of the Dissolution of a Multinational Federal State: The Case of Yugoslavia." *Communist Economies and Economic Transformation* 5, no. 3 (1993): 259–72.

Duda, Igor. "Workers into Tourists: Entitlements, Desires, and the Realities of Social Tourism under Yugoslav Socialism." In *Yugoslavia's Sunny Side: A History of Tourism in Socialism (1950s–1980s),* edited by Hannes Grandits and Karin Taylor. Central European University Press, 2010.

Dulić, Tomislav, and Roland Kostić. "Yugoslavs in Arms: Guerrilla Tradition, Total Defence and the Ethnic Security Dilemma." *Europe-Asia Studies* 62, no. 7 (2010): 1051–72.

Dunn, Elizabeth C. *Privatizing Poland: Baby Food, Big Business, and the Remaking of Labor.* Cornell University Press, 2004.

Džinić, Firdus, et al., eds. *Towards Democratic Communication: Mass Communication Research in Yugoslavia.* Yugoslav Center for Theory and Practice of Self-Management, 1984.

Ekbladh, David. *The Great American Mission: Modernization and the Construction of an American World Order.* Princeton University Press, 2011.

Ellerman, David. *Management and Employee Buy-Outs as a Technique of Privatization.* Ljubljana: Central and Eastern European Privatization Network, 1993.

Ellerman, David. "Lessons from Eastern Europe's Voucher Privatization." *Challenge* 44, no. 4 (2001): 14–37.

Emery, Alan. "Privatization, Neoliberal Development, and the Struggle for Workers' Rights in Post-Apartheid South Africa." *Social Justice* 33, no. 3 (2006): 6–19.

English, Robert. "Eastern Europe's Doves." *Foreign Policy,* no. 56 (1984): 44–60.

Escudier, Alexandre. "'Temporalization' and Political Modernity: A Tentative Systematization of the Work of Reinhart Koselleck." In *Political Concepts and Time: New Approaches to Conceptual History*, edited by Javier Fernández Sebastián. Cantabria University Press, 2011.

Estrin, Saul. "Competition and Corporate Governance in Transition." *Journal of Economic Perspectives* 16, no. 1 (2002): 101–24.

Fabry, Adam (2017). "The Origins of Neoliberalism in Late 'Socialist' Hungary: The Case of the Financial Research Institute and 'Turnabout and Reform.'" *Capital & Class* 42, no. 1 (2017): 77–107.

Ferguson, James. "The Uses of Neoliberalism." *Antipode* 41, no. 1 (2009): 166–84.

Filipović, Izudin. *Emerik Blum: Monografija*. Šahinpašić, 2002.

Flaherty, Diane. "Economic Reform and Foreign Trade in Yugoslavia." *Cambridge Journal of Economics* 6, no. 2 (1982): 105–43.

Flew, Terry. "Six Theories of Neoliberalism." *Book Eleven* 122, no. 1 (2014): 49–71.

Funari, Rachel, and Bernard Mees. "Socialist Emulation in China: Worker Heroes Yesterday and Today." *Labor History* 54, no. 3 (2013): 240–55.

Gagnon, Chip. *The Myth of Ethnic War: Serbia and Croatia in the 1990s*. Cornell University Press, 2004.

Gambarotto, Francesca, Marco Rangone, and Stefano Solari. "Financialization and Deindustrialization in the Southern European Periphery." *Athens Journal of Mediterranean Studies* 5, no. 3 (2019): 151–72.

Getachew, Adom. *Worldmaking after Empire: The Rise and Fall of Self-Determination*. Princeton University Press, 2019.

Ghodsee, Kristen Rogheh, and Mitchell A. Orenstein. *Taking Stock of Shock: Social Consequences of the 1989 Revolutions*. Oxford University Press, 2021.

Gilbert, Andrew "The Past in Parenthesis: (Non)Post-Socialism in Post-War Bosnia-Herzegovina." *Anthropology Today* 22, no. 4 (2006): 14–18.

Gilbert, Andrew. "Beyond Nostalgia: Other Historical Emotions." *History and Anthropology* 30, no. 3 (2019): 293–312. https://doi.org/10.1080/02757206.2019.1579089.

Gille, Zsuzsa. "Is There a Global Post-Socialist Condition?" *Global Society* 24, no. 1 (2010): 9–30.

Godelier, Eric. "The Corporate Nationality: A Question of Culture and Community?" *Journal of Modern European History* 18, no. 1 (2020): 28–47. https://doi.org/10.1177/1611894419895228.

Gordeeva, Irina. "Solidarity in Search of Human Agency: 'Détente from Below' and Independent Peace Activists in the Soviet Union." *Labor History Review* 86 (2021): 339–68. https://doi.org/10.3828/lhr.2021.15.

Grandits, Hannes, and Karin Taylor, eds. *Yugoslavia's Sunny Side: A History of Tourism in Socialism (1950s–1980s)*. Central European University Press, 2010.

Grdešić, Marko. "Mapping the Paths of the Yugoslav Model: Labor Strength and Weakness in Slovenia, Croatia and Serbia." *European Journal of Industrial Relations* 14, no. 2 (2008): 133–51.

Grdešić, Marko. "Exceptionalism and Its Limits: The Legacy of Self-Management in the Former Yugoslavia." In *Working Through the Past: Labor and Authoritarian Legacies in Comparative Perspective*, edited by Stephen Crowley, Teri Caraway, and Maria Cook. Cornell University Press, 2015.

Greenberg, Melanie, and Margaret E. McGuinness. "From Lisbon to Dayton: International Mediation and the Bosnia Crisis." In *Words over War: Mediation and Arbitration to*

Prevent Deadly Conflict, edited by M. C. Greenberg, J. H. Barton, and M. E. McGuinness. Rowman & Littlefield, 2000.

Gregson, Kendra. *Veterans' Programs in Bosnia-Herzegovina*. Sarajevo: World Bank, 2000.

Guiso, Luigi, Paola Sapienza, and Luigi Zingales. "The Value of Corporate Culture." *Journal of Financial Economics* 117, no. 1 (2015): 60–76. https://doi.org/10.1016/j.jfineco.2014.05.010.

Hann, Chris. "Beyond Otherness: With Reference to Hungarian Villagers, Academic Colleagues, Gypsies, Eastern Europe, Socialism, and Anthropology at Large." Working paper 132, Halle (Saale): Max Planck Institute for Social Anthropology, 2011.

Hann, Chris. "Backwardness Revisited: Time, Space, and Civilization in Rural Eastern Europe." *Comparative Studies in Society and History* 57, no. 4 (2015): 881–911.

Hansjörg, Herr, and Zeynep M. Nettekoven. *The Role of Small and Medium-Sized Enterprises in Development Can Be Learned from the German Experience?* Friedrich Ebert Stiftung, 2017. http://library.fes.de/pdf-files/iez/14056.pdf.

Harvey, Rachel. "The Persistence of the Particular in the Global." In *Framing the Global: Entry Points for Research*, edited by Hilary Kahn. Indiana University Press, 2014.

Havrylyshyn, Oleh, and Donal McGettigan. "Privatization in Transition Countries: A Sampling of the Literature." IMF Working Paper 99/6, International Monetary Fund, 1999.

Hilmar, Till. "The Temporal Logic of Deservingness: Inequality Beliefs in Two Postsocialist Societies." *Socius* 5 (January 1, 2019): 1–16.

Hoare, Marko A. "The War of Yugoslav Succession." In *Central and Southeast European Politics since 1989*, edited by Sabrina P. Ramet. Cambridge University Press, 2010.

Horvat, Branko. *The Yugoslav Economic System: The First Labor-Managed Economy in the Making*. International Arts and Sciences Press, 1976.

Horvat, Branko. "Farewell to the Illyrian Firm." *Economic Analysis and Workers' Management* 20, no. 1 (1986): 23–29.

Horvat, Branko. "Nationalization, Privatization or Socialization: The Emergence of the Social Corporation." *Economic Analysis and Workers' Management* 1, no. 25 (1991): 1–10.

Horvat, Srećko, and Igor Štiks, eds. *Welcome to the Desert of Post-Socialism: Radical Politics after Yugoslavia*. Verso, 2015.

Hristova, Katia. "Czech Voucher Privatization: A Case of Decision Making under Uncertainty." *University Avenue Undergraduate Journal of Economics* 7, no. 1 (2002): 1–24.

Human Rights Watch. "War Crimes in Bosnia-Hercegovina: U.N. Cease-Fire Won't Help Banja Luka." *Human Rights Watch Report* 6, no. 8 (1994).

Iandolo, Alessandro. "De-Stalinizing Growth: Decolonization and the Development of Development Economics in the Soviet Union." In *The Development Century*, edited by Stephen Macekura and Erez Manela. Cambridge University Press, 2018.

Iglesias, Oriol, Nicholas Ind, and Majken Schultz. "History Matters: The Role of History in Corporate Brand Strategy." *Business Horizons* 63, no. 1 (2020): 51–60.

IMF. "Bosnia and Herzegovina: Poverty Reduction Strategy Paper—Mid-Term." IMF Country Report. IMF, April 2004.

Jakovina, Tvrtko. *Treća Strana Hladnog Rata*. Zagreb: Fraktura, 2016.

Janićijević, Milosav, Silvano Bolčić, Silvano, Lidija Topić, Milena Davidović, and Nada Novaković, eds. *Novi Pravci Promena Društvene Strukture Jugoslavije*. Institut Društvenih Nauka, Centar za Sociološka Istraživanja, 1990.

Jansen, Stef. "Remembering with a Difference: Clashing Memories of Bosnian Conflict in Everyday Life." In *The New Bosnian Mosaic: Identities, Memories, and Moral Claims in a Post-War Society*, edited by Xavier Bougarel, Elissa Helms, and Gert Duijzings. Ashgate, 2007.

Jansen, Stef, Čarna Brković, and Vanja Čelebičić, eds. *Negotiating Social Relations in Bosnia and Herzegovina: Semiperipheral Entanglements*. Routledge, 2017.

Jović, Dejan. "Yugoslavism and Yugoslav Communism: From Tito to Kardelj." In *Yugoslavism*, edited by Dejan Djokić. Hurst, 2003.

Jović, Dejan. "Communist Yugoslavia and Its 'Others.'" In *Ideologies and National Identities: The Case of Twentieth-Century Southeastern Europe*, edited by John Lampe and Mark Mazower. Central European University Press, 2006.

Jović, Dejan. *Yugoslavia: A State That Withered Away*. West Purdue University Press, 2009.

Kahn, Hilary, ed. *Framing the Global: Entry Points for Research.*Indiana University Press, 2014.

Kaldor, Mary. "The 1989 Revolutions and the Peace Movement." OpenDemocracy, November 12, 2019. https://www.opendemocracy.net/en/can-europe-make-it/1989-revolutions -and-peace-movement/.

Kaldor, Mary, and Vesna Bojičić-Dželilović. "The 'Abnormal' Economy of Bosnia-Herzegovina." In *Scramble for the Balkans: Nationalism, Globalism and the Political Economy of Reconstruction*, edited by Carl-Ulrik Schierup. St. Martin's, 1999.

Kamm, Henry. "Financial Scandal Shakes Yugoslav Leaders." *New York Times*, September 10, 1987.

Kardelj, Edvard. *Self-Management and the Political System*. Socialist Thought and Practice, 1980.

Keen, Mike, and Janusz Mucha. "Sociology in Central and Eastern Europe in the 1990s: A Decade of Reconstruction." *European Societies* 6, no. 2 (2004): 123–47.

Kideckel, David A. *The Unmaking of an East-Central European Working Class. In Postsocialism: Ideals, Ideologies and Practices in Eurasia*, edited by Chris Hann. Routledge, 2002.

Kideckel, David A. *Getting By in Postsocialist Romania: Labor, the Body, & Working-Class Culture*. Indiana University Press, 2008.

Kirn, Gal. "A Critique of Transition Studies on Post-Socialism, or How to Rethink and Reorient 1989? The Case of (Post)Socialist (Post)Yugoslavia." In *Beyond Neoliberalism, Social Analysis after 1989*, edited by Marian Burchardt and Gal Kirn. Palgrave Macmillan, 2017.

Klein, George. "Workers' Self-Management and the Politics of Ethnic Nationalism in Yugoslavia." *Nationalities Papers: The Journal of Nationalism and Ethnicity* 5, no. 1 (1977): 1–21.

Kojanić, Ognjen. "Nostalgia as a Practice of the Self in Post-Socialist Serbia." *Canadian Slavonic Papers/Revue canadienne des slavistes* 57, nos. 3–4 (2015): 195–212.

Koleva, Svetla. "Doing Post-Western Sociology in Central and Eastern Europe before and after the Great Change: Some Epistemological Questions." *Journal of Chinese Sociology* 7, no. 20 (2020): 1–15.

Kolodko, Grzegorz. *From Shock to Therapy: The Political Economy of Postsocialist Transformation*. Oxford University Press, 2000.

Komnenović, Dora. "(Out)Living the War: Anti-War Activism in Croatia in the Early 1990s and Beyond." *Journal on Ethnopolitics and Minority Issues in Europe* 13, no. 4 (2014): 111–28.

Kondylis, Florence. "Conflict Displacement and Labor Market Outcomes in Post-War Bosnia and Herzegovina." *Journal of Development Economics* 93, no. 2 (2010): 235–48.

Kono, Toyohiro, and Stewart R. Clegg. *Transformations of Corporate Culture: Experiences of Japanese Enterprises*. De Gruyter, 2017.

Korf, Benedikt. "Ethnicised Entitlements? Property Rights and Civil War in Sri Lanka." ZEF—Discussion Paper on Development Policy 75, Bonn, 2003.

Kornai, Janoš. "The Soft Budget Constraint." *International Review for Social Sciences* 39, no. 1 (1986): 3–30.

Koselleck, Reinhart. *Futures Past: On the Semantics of Historical Time*. MIT Press, 1985.

Kostovicova, Denisa, and Vesna Bojčić-Dželilović. "Europeanizing the Balkans: Rethinking the Post-Communist and Post-Conflict Transition." *Ethnopolitics* 5, no. 3 (2006): 223–41.

Kostovicova, Denisa, and Vesna Bojičić-Dželilović. "Ethnicity Pays: The Political Economy of Post-Conflict Nationalism in Bosnia-Herzegovina." In *After Civil War: Division, Reconstruction, and Reconciliation in Contemporary Europe*, edited by Bill Kissane. National and Ethnic Conflict in the 21st Century. University of Pennsylvania Press, 2014.

Kotkin, Stephen. *Steeltown, USSR: Soviet Society in the Gorbachev Era*. University of California Press, 1992.

Kotkin, Stephen. *Magnetic Mountain: Stalinism as a Civilization*.University of California Press, 1997.

Kovač, Oskar. "Postoje li uslovi za kompletno tržišno rešenje u privrednom sistemu SFRJ?" In *Privreda u Reformi—Zbornik Radova Za Savetovanje Na Brionima*, edited by Tomislav Bandin, et al. Iro Ekonomika i Savez ekonomista Jugoslavije, 1989.

Kovacs, Janos Martyas, and Violetta Zentai. *Capitalism from Outside? Economic Cultures in Eastern Europe after 1989*. CEU Press, 2012.

Krebs, Ronald R. "The Citizen-Soldier Tradition in the United States: Has Its Demise Been Greatly Exaggerated?" *Armed Forces & Society* 36, no. 1 (2009): 153–74. https://doi .org/10.1177/0095327X09337370.

Kuczi, Tibor, and György Lengyel. "The Spread of Entrepreneurship in Eastern Europe." In *Transformations in Hungary: Contributions to Economics*, edited by P. Meusburger and H. Jöns. Physica, 2001.

Kukić, Leonard. "The Last Yugoslavs: Ethnic Diversity and National Identity." *Explorations in Economic History* 88 (2023): 1–42.

Kurtović, Larisa. "What Is a Nationalist? Some Thoughts on the Question from Bosnia-Herzegovina." *Anthropology of East Europe Review* 29, no. 2 (2011): 242–53.

Kurtović, Larisa. "'Who Sows Hunger, Reaps Rage': On Protest, Indignation and Redistributive Justice in Post-Dayton Bosnia-Herzegovina." *Southeast European and Black Sea Studies* 15, no. 4 (2015): 639–59.

Kurtović, Larisa. "When All That Is Solid Does Not Melt into Air: Labor, Politics and Materiality in a Bosnian Detergent Factory." *PoLAR: Political and Legal Anthropology Review* 43, no. 2 (2020): 228–46.

Kušić, Katerina, Polina Manolova, and Philipp Lottholz, eds. *Decolonial Theory and Practice in Southeast Europe*. dVersia, 2019.

Lai, Daniela. "Transitional Justice and Its Discontents: Socioeconomic Justice in Bosnia and Herzegovina and the Limits of International Intervention." *Journal of Intervention and Statebuilding* 10, no. 3 (2016): 361–81.

Lal, Priya. *African Socialism in Postcolonial Tanzania: Between the Village and the World.* Cambridge University Press, 2015.

Lang, Nicholas R. "The Dialectics of Decentralization: Economic Reform and Regional Inequality in Yugoslavia." *World Politics* 27, no. 3 (1975): 309–35. https://doi.org/10.2307/2010123.

Laszlo, Ervin, Jorge Lozoya, and A. K. Bhattacharya. *The Obstacles to the New International Economic Order.* Pergamon, 1980.

Lawson, George. "Introduction: The 'What,' 'When' and 'Where' of the Global 1989." In *The Global 1989: Continuity and Change in World Politics*, edited by George Lawson, Chris Armbruster, and Michael Cox. Cambridge University Press, 2010.

Lazić, Milorad. "Comrades in Arms: Yugoslav Military Aid to Liberation Movements of Angola and Mozambique, 1961–1976." In *Southern African Liberation Movements and the Global Cold War 'East': Transnational Activism 1960–1990*, edited by Lena Dallywater, Chris Saunders, and Helder Adegar Fonseca. De Gruyter, 2019.

Lazić, Milorad. "Arsenal of the Global South: Yugoslavia's Military Aid to Nonaligned Countries and Liberation Movements." *Nationalities Papers* 49, no. 3 (2021): 428–45. https://doi.org/10.1017/nps.2020.6.

Lazić, Mladen, and Slobodan Cvejić. "Working Class in Post-Socialist Transformation: Serbia and Croatia Compared." *Corvinus Journal of Sociology and Social Policy*, no. 1 (2010): 3–29.

Lee, Christopher J. *Making a World after Empire: The Bandung Moment and Its Political Afterlives.* Ohio University Press, 2010.

Lieberman, Ira W., Stilpon S. Nestor, and Raj M. Desai, eds. *Between State and Market: Mass Privatization in Transition Economies.* World Bank, OECD, 1997.

Linkon, Sherry Lee. *The Half-Life of Deindustrialization: Working-Class Writing about Economic Restructuring.* University of Michigan Press, 2018.

Lipartito, Kenneth. "Connecting the Cultural and the Material in Business History." *Enterprise & Society* 14, no. 4 (2013): 686–704.

Lipartito, Kenneth, and David B. Sicilia, eds. *Constructing Corporate America: History, Politics, Culture.* Oxford University Press, 2004.

Lipton, David, and Jeffrey Sachs. "Creating a Market Economy in Eastern Europe: The Case of Poland." *Brookings Papers on Economic Activity* 1 (1990): 75–147.

Lorenzini, Sara. *Global Development: A Cold War History.* Princeton University Press, 2019.

Lowinger, Jake. "Economic Reform and the 'Double Movement' in Yugoslavia: An Analysis of Labor Unrest and Ethnonationalism in the 1980s." PhD diss., Johns Hopkins University, 2009.

Lubinski, Christina, R. Daniel Wadhwani, William B. Gartner, and Renee Rottner. "Humanistic Approaches to Change: Entrepreneurship and Transformation." *Business History* 66, no. 2 (2023): 347–63. https://doi.org/10.1080/00076791.2023.2213193.

Lydall, Harold. *Yugoslavia in Crisis.* Business & Economics. Clarendon, 1989.

Maček, Ivana. *Sarajevo under Siege: Anthropology in Wartime.* University of Pennsylvania Press, 2009.

MacKinnon, Lachlan, and Stephen High. "Deindustrialization." In *The Routledge Handbook to the Political Economy and Governance of the Americas*, edited by Olaf Kaltmeier, Anne Tittor, Daniel Hawkins, and Eleonora Rohland. Taylor & Francis Group, 2020: 57–68.

Magaš, Branka, and Ivo Žanić, eds. *The War in Croatia and Bosnia-Herzegovina*. Frank Cass, 1991.

Mah, Alice. *Industrial Ruination, Community and Place: Landscapes and Legacies of Urban Decline*. Toronto University Press, 2012.

Majstorović, Danijela. "Decoloniality as Peripherality in Bosnia and Herzegovina." In *Decolonial Theory and Practice in Southeast Europe*, edited by K. Kušić, P. Manolova, and P. Lottholz. dVersia, 2019.

Malcolm, Noel. *Bosnia, a Short History*. NYU Press, 1994.

Mandel, Ruth, Caroline Humphrey, and Elizabeth C. Dunn, eds. *Markets and Moralities: Ethnographies of Postsocialism*. Berg, 2002.

Manning, Carrie. "Elections and Political Change in Post-War Bosnia and Herzegovina." *Democratization* 11, no. 2 (2004): 60–86.

Mark, James, Bogdan Iacob James, Tobias Rupprecht, and Ljubica Spaskovska. *1989: A Global History of Eastern Europe*. Cambridge University Press, 2019.

Mark, James, Artemy M. Kalinovsky, and Steffi Marung, eds. *Alternative Globalizations: Eastern Europe and the Postcolonial World*. Indiana University Press, 2020.

Mark, James, and Tobias Rupprecht. "Europe's '1989' in Global Context." In *The Cambridge History of Communism*, edited by Juliane Fürst, Silvio Pons, and Mark Selden. Cambridge University Press, 2017.

Marković, Goran. "Workers' Councils in Yugoslavia: Successes and Failures." *Socialism and Democracy* 25, no. 3 (2011): 107–29.

Matošević, Andrea. "Socijalizam s udarničkim licem: etnografija radnog pregalaštva." Institut za etnologiju i folkloristiku, 2015.

McKinsey, Kitty. "Widespread Poverty Makes Life Difficult in Bosnia." Radio Free Europe, January 9, 1996.

Medjad, Karim. "The Fate of the Yugoslav Model: A Case against Legal Conformity." *American Journal of Comparative Law* 52, no. 1 (2004): 287–319.

Meier, Viktor. *Yugoslavia: A History of Its Demise*. Routledge, 1999.

Mesarović, Aleksandar. "Bring the Right One In: International Organizations and Privatization Strategies in Slovenia, Croatia and Serbia." *LIMESplus* 15, no. 1 (2018): 79–101.

Michel, Christian. "It Is Not a Question of Rigidly Planning Trade: UNCTAD and the Regulation of the International Trade in the 1970s." In *Planning in Cold War Europe: Competition, Cooperation, Circulations (1950s–1970s)*, edited by Christian Michel, Sandrine Kott, and Ondřej Matějka. DeGruyter, 2018.

Mihályi, Peter. "Post-Socialist Transition in a 25-Year Perspective." *Acta Oeconomica* 64 (2014): 1–24.

Milan, Chiara. *Social Mobilization beyond Ethnicity: Civic Activism and Grassroots Movements in Bosnia and Herzegovina*. Routledge, 2020.

Milanović, Branko. "Privatization in Post-Communist Societies." *Communist Economies and Economic Transformation* 3, no. 1 (1992): 5–39.

Miller, Robert F. "The Pitfalls of Economic Reform in Yugoslavia." *Australian Journal of International Affairs* 45, no. 2 (1991): 213–22.

Mirković, Damir. "The Historical Link between the Ustasha Genocide and the Croato-Serb Civil War: 1991–1995." *Journal of Genocide Research* 2, no. 3 (2000): 363–73.

Mulaj, Isa. "Redefining Property Rights with Specific Reference to Social Ownership in the Successor States of the Former Yugoslavia: Did It Matter for Economic Efficiency?" *CEU Political Science Journal*, no. 3 (2007): 225–79.

Mundey, Lisa. "Citizen-Soldiers or Warriors." *Semiotics* (2008): 130–39.

Murthy, Changavalli Siva Rama. "Non-Aligned Movement Countries as Drivers of Change in International Organizations." *Comparativ: Zeitschrift für Globalgeschichte und vergleichende Gesellschaftsforschung* 23 (2013): 118–36.

Musić, Goran. *Svjedoci Jednog Vremena. U Sindikatima BiH 1990–2015*. Friedrich Ebert Stiftung, 2015.

Musić, Goran. "'They Came as Workers and Returned as Serbs': The Role of Rakovica's Blue-Collar in Serbian Social Mobilizations of the Late 1980s." In *Social Inequalities and Discontent in Yugoslavia*, edited by Igor Duda, Paul Stubbs, and Rory Archer. Ashgate, 2016.

Musić, Goran. *Making and Breaking the Yugoslav Working Class: The Story of Two Self-Managed Factories*. Central European University Press, 2021.

Musić, Goran. "Two Roads to Self-Managing Socialism." In *Making and Breaking the Yugoslav Working Class: The Story of Two Self-Managed Factories*. Central European University Press, 2021.

Muzondidya, James, and Sabelo Ndlovu-Gatsheni. "Echoing Silences: Ethnicity in Post-Colonial Zimbabwe, 1980–2007." *African Journal on Conflict Resolution* 7, no. 2 (2007): 275–97.

Nadkarni, Maya. *Remains of Socialism: Memory and the Futures of the Past in Postsocialist Hungary*. Cornell University Press, 2020.

Nadkarni, Maya, and Olga Shevchenko. "The Politics of Nostalgia in the Aftermath of Socialism's Collapse." In *Anthropology and Nostalgia*, edited by Olivia Angé, David Berliner, and Jonathan Bach. Berghahn, 2015.

Nellis, John. "The World Bank, Privatization and Enterprise Reform in Transition Economies: A Retrospective Analysis." Operations Evaluation Department, the World Bank, 2002.

Ness, Immanuel, and Dario Azzellini. *Ours to Master and to Own: Workers' Control from the Commune to the Present*. Haymarket Books, 2011.

Nikolić, Helena, and Jan Horaček. "Comparison of Privatization in the Republic of Croatia and Selected Former Communist Countries." *Engineering Proceedings* 39, no. 1 (2023): 48.

Obradović, Josip, and Gary K. Bertsch. "Workers' Participation: Who Participates?" *Industrial Relations* 14, no. 1 (1975): 32–44.

O'Donovan, Maria. "Nostalgia and Heritage in the Carousel City: Deindustrialization, Critical Memory, and the Future." *Journal of Community Archaeology & Heritage* 6, no. 4 (2019): 272–82.

OECD. *Enterprise Policy Performance Assessment and Herzegovina*. OECD, EBRD, Stability Pact for South Eastern Europe, 2005.

OECD. *OECD Advisory Group on Privatization Plenary Session, Competition and Privatization NOTE*. Helsinki: OECD, 1998. https://www.oecd.org/daf/ca/corporategovernanceofstate-ownedenterprises/1929692.pdf.

OECD. "Promoting SMEs for Development." In *Promoting Entrepreneurship and Innovative SMEs in a Global Economy: Towards a More Responsible and Inclusive Globalization*. Istanbul: OECD, 2004.

O'Loughlin, John. "Inter-Ethnic Friendships in Post-War Bosnia-Herzegovina: Sociodemographic and Place Influences." *Ethnicities* 10, no. 1 (2010): 26–53.

Ost, David. *The Defeat of Solidarity: Anger and Politics in Postcommunist Europe*. Cornell University Press, 2005.

Oteiza, Enrique, and Francisco Sercovich. "Collective Self-Reliance." *Social Science Journal* 28, no. 4 (1976): 664–71.

Patterson, Patrick Hyder. *Bought and Sold: Living and Losing the Good Life in Socialist Yugoslavia*. Cornell University Press, 2012.

Patterson, Patrick Hyder. "Just Rewards: The Social Contract and Communism's Hard Bargain with the Citizen-Consumer." In *The Socialist Good Life: Desire, Development, and Standards of Living in Eastern Europe*, edited by Cristofer Scarboro, Diana Mincyte, and Zsuzsa Gille. Indiana University Press, 2020.

Pehe, Veronika, and Joanna Wawrzyniak. *Remembering the Neoliberal Turn: Economic Change and Collective Memory in Eastern Europe after 1989*. Routledge, 2024.

Pejanović, Mirko, and Marina Bowder. *Through Bosnian Eyes: The Political Memoirs of a Bosnian Serb*. Purdue University Press, 2004.

Pejovich, Svjetozar. "The Economic Position of the Enterprise in the Yugoslav Economy." *Statsvetenskaplig Tidskrift* 83, no. 5 (1980): 303–11.

Petrović, Tanja. "'When We Were Europe': Socialist Workers in Serbia and Their Nostalgic Narratives." In *Remembering Communism: Genres of Representation*, edited by Maria Todorova. Social Science Research Council, 2010.

Petrović, Tanja. "The Past That Binds Us: Yugonostalgia as the Politics of Future." In *Transcending Fratricide: Political Mythologies, Reconciliations, and the Uncertain Future in the Former Yugoslavia*, edited by Srđa Pavlović and Marko Živković. Nomos, 2013.

Petrović, Tanja. *Utopia of the Uniform: Affective Afterlives of the Yugoslav People's Army*. Duke University Press, 2024.

Petrovići, Norbert. "Framing Criticism and Knowledge Production in Semi-Peripheries: Post-Socialism Unpacked." *Intersections* 1, no. 2 (2015): 801–2.

Pickering, Paula M. *Peacebuilding in the Balkans: The View from the Ground Floor*. Cornell University Press, 2007.

Pike, Andy. "Coping with Deindustrialization in the Global North and South." *International Journal of Urban Sciences* 26, no. 1 (2022): 1–22.

Pirjevec, Joze. *Le guerre jugoslave, 1991–1999*. Turin: Giulio Einaudi Editore, 2001.

Popović, Tomislav (eds.) *Ekonomisti o krizi: razgovor ekonomista s mandatorom za SIV Dipl. Ing. Antom Markovićem*. Konzorcijum ekonomskih instituta Jugoslavije, 1989.

Portelli, Alessandro. *The Death of Luigi Trastulli and Other Stories: Form and Meaning in Oral History*. State University of New York Press, 1991.

Potkonjak, Sanja, and Tea Škokić. "'In the World of Iron and Steel': On the Ethnography of Work, Unemployment and Hope." *Narodni Umjetnosti* 50, no. 1 (2013): 74–95.

Potkonjak, Sanja, and Nevena Škrbić Alempijević. "Rethinking the City in the Industrial Aftermath: Socio-Industrial Memory and Environmental Fallouts." *Narodna Umjetnosti* 60, no. 3 (2023): 9–24.

Pozniak, Kinga. *Nowa Huta: Generations of Change in a Model Socialist Town*. University of Pittsburgh Press, 2014.

Pugh, Michael. "The Political Economy of Peacebuilding: A Critical Theory Perspective." *International Journal of Peace Studies* 10, no. 2 (2005): 23–42.

Pugh, Michael, Neil Cooper, with Jonathan Goodhand. *War Economies in a Regional Context: Challenges of Transformation*. Lynne Rienner, 2004.

Pula, Besnik. *Globalization under and after Socialism: The Evolution of Transnational Capital in Central and Eastern Europe*. Stanford University Press, 2018.

Qu, Sandy Q., and John Dumay. "The Qualitative Research Interview." *Ethnography in Organizations* 8, no. 3 (2011): 238–64.

Rabinbach, Anson. "The End of the Utopias of Labor: Metaphors of the Machine in the Post-Fordist Era." *Thesis Eleven*, no. 73 (1998): 29–44.

Radonjić, Nemanja. "A Nonaligned Continent: Africa in the Global Imaginary of Socialist Yugoslavia." In *Socialist Yugoslavia and the Non-Aligned Movement: Social, Cultural, Political, and Economic Imaginaries*, edited by Paul Stubbs, 302–31. McGill-Queen's University Press, 2023.

Rainnie, Al, Adrian Smith, and Adam Swain, eds. *Work Employment and Transition: Restructuring Livelihoods in Post Communism*. Routledge, 2002.

Rajak, Dinah. "Corporate Memory: Historical Revisionism, Legitimation and the Invention of Tradition in a Multinational Mining Company." *Political and Legal Anthropology Review* 37, no. 2 (2014): 259–80.

Rajak, Svetozar. "No Bargaining Chips, No Spheres of Interest: The Yugoslav Origins of Cold War Non-Alignment." *Journal of Cold War Studies* 16, no. 1 (2014): 146–79.

Rajković, Ivan. "From Freedom to Loaf to Freedom to Work: The Late Socialist Countermovement and Liberalization from Below in Yugoslavia." In *Work, Society and the Ethical Self: Chimeras of Freedom in the Neoliberal Era*, edited by Chris Hann. Berghahn Books, 2021.

Ramet, Sabrina P. "Explaining the Yugoslav Meltdown, 'for a Charm of Pow'rful Trouble, like a Hell-Broth Boil and Bubble': Theories about the Roots of the Yugoslav Troubles." *Nationalities Papers* 32, no. 4 (2004): 731–63.

Ramet, Sabrina P. *Thinking about Yugoslavia: Scholarly Debates about the Yugoslav Breakup and the Wars in Bosnia and Kosovo*. Cambridge University Press, 2005.

Ramet, Sabrina P. *The Three Yugoslavias: State-Building and Legitimation, 1918–2005*. Indiana University Press, 2006.

Ramet, Sabrina P. *The Three Yugoslavias: State-Building and Legitimation, 1918–2005*. Indiana University Press, 2006.

Ramet, Sabrina P. "Trajectories of Post-Communist Transformation: Myths and Rival Theories about Change in Central and Southeastern Europe." *Perceptions* 18, no. 2 (2013): 57–89.

Ramović, Jasmin. "Looking into the Past to See the Future? Lessons Learned from Self-Management for Economies in Post-Conflict Societies of the Former Yugoslavia." *Civil Wars* 20, no. 2 (2018): 186. https://doi.org/10.1080/13698249.2018.1497859.

Read, Jason. "A Genealogy of Homo-Economicus: Neoliberalism and the Production of Subjectivity." *Foucault Studies*, no. 6 (2009): 25–36.

Rist, Gilbert. *The History of Development: From Western Origins to Global Faith*. Zed Books, 1997.

Roe, Paul. "Which Security Dilemma? Mitigating Ethnic Conflict: The Case of Croatia." *Security Studies* 13, no. 4 (2004): 280–313.

Roskam, Cole. "Non-Aligned Architecture: China's Designs on and in Ghana and Guinea, 1955–92." *Architectural History*, no. 58 (2015): 261–91.

Rowlinson, Michael, and John Hassard. "The Invention of Corporate Culture: A History of the Histories of Cadbury." *Human Relations* 46, no. 3 (1993): 299–326.

Rubinstein, Alvin Z. *Yugoslavia and the Nonaligned World*. Princeton University Press, 1970.

Rupprecht, Tobias. "Global Varieties of Neoliberalism: Ideas on Free Markets and Strong States in Late Twentieth-Century Chile and Russia." *Global Perspectives* 1, no. 1 (2020): 1–13.

Ryant, Carl. "Oral History and Business History." *Journal of American History* 75, no. 2 (1988): 560–66.

Sachs, Jeffrey. "Crossing the Valley of Tears in East European Reform." *Challenge*, September–October 1991: 26–31, 34.

Sachs, Jeffrey, and David Lipton. "Poland's Economic Reform." *Foreign Affairs* 69, no. 3 (1990): 47–66.

Sanchez-Sibony, Oscar. *Red Globalization: The Political Economy of the Soviet Cold War from Stalin to Khrushchev*. Cambridge University Press, 2014.

Sarajlić, Eldar. "Conceptualizing Citizenship Regime(s) in Post-Dayton Bosnia and Herzegovina." *Citizenship Studies* 16, no. 3–4 (2012): 367–82.

Sasso, Alfredo. "The Defeat of the Democratic Yugoslavism in Bosnia-Herzegovina: The Alliance of Reformist Forces of Yugoslavia (SRSJ)." In *Empires and Nations from the Eighteenth to the Twentieth Century*, edited by Antonello Biagini and Giovanni Motta. Cambridge Scholars, 2014.

Sasso, Alfredo. "The Political Dimension of Ante Marković's Reform Project: 'We Must Develop Democracy and a Third Yugoslavia.'" *Contemporary Southeastern Europe* 7, no. 1 (2020): 25–48.

Schenck, Marcia C. "From Luanda and Maputo to Berlin: Uncovering Angolan and Mozambican Migrants' Motives to Move to the German Democratic Republic (1979–1990)." *African Economic History* 44, no. 1 (2016): 202–34.

Schierup, C., S. Bianchini, and G. Schopflin. *From Fraternity to Fratricide: Nationalism, Globalism and the Fall of Yugoslavia*. Longo, 1998.

Schindler, Seth, Tom Gillespie, Nicola Banks, Mustafa Kemal Bayırbağ, J. Miguel Kanai, Himanshu Burte, and Neha Sami. "Deindustrialization in Cities of the Global South." *Area Development and Policy* 5, no. 3 (2020): 283–304.

Scranton, Phil. "Managing Communist Enterprises: Poland, Hungary, and Czechoslovakia, 1945–1970." *Enterprise & Society* 19, no. 3 (2018): 492–537.

Scranton, Phil, and Patrick Fridenson. *Reimaging Business History*. Johns Hopkins University Press, 2013.

Sekulić, Dubravka. "Energoprojekt in Nigeria: Yugoslav Construction Companies in the Developing World." *Southeastern Europe* 41 (2017): 200–229.

Sekulić, Dubravka. "Constructing Non-Alignment: The Case of Construction Enterprise Energoprojekt, 1961–1989, Architecture, Construction Industry and Yugoslavia in the World." PhD diss., ETH Zurich, 2020.

Shafir, Gershon. *Immigrants and Nationalists: Ethnic Conflict and Accommodation in Catalonia, the Basque Country, Latvia, and Estonia*. State University of New York Press, 1995.

Sharma, Devika, and Frederik Tygstrup. *Structures of Feeling: Affectivity and the Study of Culture*. De Gruyter, 2015.

Shields, Stuart. "Historicizing Transition: The Polish Political Economy in a Period of Global Structural Change—Eastern Central Europe's Passive Revolution?" *International Politics*, no. 43 (2006): 474–99.

Shields, Stuart. "The European Bank for Reconstruction and Development and the Lessons from Eastern Central Europe for Middle East/North African Transition." *Spectrum Journal of Global Studies* 7, no. 2 (2015): 45–67.

Sicurella, Federico Giulio. *Speaking for the Nation: Intellectuals and Nation-Building in the Post-Yugoslav Space.* John Benjamins, 2020.

Siefert, Marsha, ed. *Labor in State-Socialist Europe.* CEU Press, 1945.

Sirc, Ljubo. *The Yugoslav Economy under Self-Management.* Macmillan, 1979.

Skoda, Hannah. "Nostalgia and Pre-Modernity." *History and Theory* 62, no. 2 (June 2023): 251–71.

Slobodian, Quinn. *Comrades of Color: East Germany in the Cold War World.* Berghahn Books, 2015.

Spaskovska, Ljubica. "Landscapes of Resistance, Hope and Loss: Yugoslav Supra-Nationalism and Anti-Nationalism." In *Resisting the Evil: [Post-]Yugoslav Anti-War Contention,* edited by Bojan Bilić and Vesna Janković. Southeast European Integration Perspectives. Nomos, 2012.

Spaskovska, Ljubica. "The 'Children of Crisis': Making Sense of (Post)Socialism and the End of Yugoslavia." *East European Politics and Societies and Cultures* 31, no. 3 (2017): 500–517.

Spaskovska, Ljubica. *The Last Yugoslav Generation: The Rethinking of Youth Politics and Cultures in Late Socialism.* Manchester University Press, 2017.

Spaskovska, Ljubica. "Building a Better World? Construction, Labour, and the Pursuit of Collective Self-Reliance in the 'Global South,' 1950–1990." *Labor History* 59, no. 3 (2018): 331–51.

Spaskovska, Ljubica. "Constructing the 'City of International Solidarity': Non-Aligned Internationalism, the United Nations and Visions of Development, Modernism and Solidarity, 1955–1975." *Journal of World History* 31, no. 1 (2020): 137–63.

Spaskovska, Ljubica. "'Crude' Alliance: Economic Decolonization and Oil Power in the Non-Aligned World." *Contemporary European History* 30 (2021): 528–43.

Spaskovska, Ljubica, and Anna Calori. "A Nonaligned Business World: The Global Socialist Enterprise between Self-Management and Transnational Capitalism." *Nationalities Papers* 49, no. 3 (2021): 413–27.

Stanek, Łukasz. *Architecture in Global Socialism: Eastern Europe, West Africa, and the Middle East in the Cold War.* Princeton University Press, 2020.

Stanojević, Miroslav. "Workers' Power in Transition Economies: The Cases of Serbia and Slovenia." *European Journal of Industrial Relations* 9, no. 3 (2003): 283–301.

Stanojević, Miroslav. "Conditions for a Neoliberal Turn: The Cases of Hungary and Slovenia." *European Journal of Industrial Relations* 20, no. 2 (2014): 97–112.

Stark, David, and Laszlo Bruszt. *Postsocialist Pathways: Transforming Politics and Property in East Central Europe.* Cambridge University Press, 1998.

Stiglitz, Joseph. "Quis Custodiet Ipsos Custodes? Corporate Governance Failures in the Transition," Governance, Equity and Global Markets, Proceedings from the Annual Bank Conference on Development Economics in Europe, June 1999, edited by Pierre-Alain Muet and J. E. Stiglitz. Conseil d'Analyse économique, 2000. (Originally presented as keynote address at the Annual Bank Conference on Development Economics in Europe, Paris, June 23, 1999.)

Štiks, Igor. "Nationality and Citizenship in the Former Yugoslavia: From Disintegration to European Integration." *Southeast European and Black Sea Studies* 6, no. 4 (2006): 483–500.

Štiks, Igor. "'Being a Citizen the Bosnian Way': Transformations of Citizenship and Political Identities in Bosnia-Herzegovina." In *From Peace to Shared Political Identities: Exploring Pathways in Contemporary Bosnia-Herzegovina,* edited by Sylvie Ramel and Francis Cheneval. Institut de sociologie de l'Université libre de Bruxelles, 2011.

Stojanov, Dragoljub. *Economics in Peacemaking: Lessons from Bosnia and Herzegovina.* London: Portland Trust, 2009. https://portlandtrust.org/wp-content/uploads/2019/12/epm_bosnia_herzegovina.pdf.

Storey, Andy. "Economics and Ethnic Conflict: Structural Adjustment in Rwanda." *Development Policy Review* 17 (1999): 43–63.

Strangleman, Tim. "Work Identity in Crisis? Rethinking the Problem of Attachment and Loss at Work." *Sociology* 46, no. 3 (2012): 411–25.

Strangleman, Tim. "Exploring an Industrial Structure of Feeling: Creating Industrial Gemeinschaft in a Twentieth-Century Workplace." In *Stretching the Sociological Imagination*, edited by M. Dawson, B. Fowler, D. Miller, and A. Smith. Palgrave Macmillan, 2015.

Strangleman, Tim. "Deindustrialization and the Historical Sociological Imagination: Making Sense of Work and Industrial Change." *Sociology* 51, no. 2 (2017): 471.

Strydom, Hennie. "The Non-Aligned Movement and the Reform of International Relations." *Max Planck UNYB* 11 (2007): 1–46.

Stubbs, Paul, ed. *Socialist Yugoslavia and the Non-Aligned Movement: Social, Cultural, Political, and Economic Imaginaries.* McGill-Queen's, 2023.

Šupek, Rudi. *Omladina na putu bratstva: psiho-sociologija radne akcije.* Mladost, 1963.

Sustersić, Janež. "Political Economy of Slovenia's Transition." In *Slovenia: From Yugoslavia to the European Union*, edited by Mojmir Mrak, Matija Rojec, and Carlos Silva-Jáuregui. World Bank, 2004.

Svejnar, Jan. "Transition Economies: Performance and Challenges." *Journal of Economic Perspectives* 16, no. 1 (2002): 3–28.

Svejnar, Jan, and Milica Uvalić. "Why Development Patterns Differ: The Czech and Serbian Cases Compared." In *Institutions and Patterns of Economic Development*, edited by Masahiko Aoki, Timur Kuran, and Gerard Roland. Palgrave Macmillan, 2012.

Svetličić, Marjan, et al., *Ekonomski odnosi Jugoslavije sa zemljama u razvoju.* Istrazivački projekat privredna, politička, kulturna i naučno-tehnička sarandnja Jugoslavije sa zemljama u razvoju, 1971.

Tagliabue, John. "How a Yugoslav Company Built an International Market." *New York Times*, March 28, 1983.

Taylor, Lisa. "Landscapes of Loss: Responses to Altered Landscape in an Ex-Industrial Textile Community." *Sociological Research Online* 25, no. 1 (2020): 46–65.

Tchalakov, Ivan, and Nikula Jouko. *Innovations and Entrepreneurs in Socialist and Post-Socialist Societies.* Cambridge Scholars, 2013.

Ther, Philipp. *Europe since 1989: A History.* Princeton University Press, 2018.

Thorpe, J., M. Cannon, and S. Emili. *"Empresas Recuperadas": Argentina's Recovered Factory Movement, Case Summary No. 4.* Institute for Development Studies, 2019.

Ticktin, Hillel. "Why the Transition Failed: Towards a Political Economy of the Post-Soviet Period in Russia." *Critique: Journal of Socialist Theory* 30, no. 1 (2002): 13–41.

Toal, Gerard, and Carl T. Dahlman. *Bosnia Remade: Ethnic Cleansing and Its Reversal.* Oxford University Press, 2011.

Todorova, Maria. "The Trap of Backwardness: Modernity, Temporality, and the Study of Eastern European Nationalism." *Slavic Review* 64, no. 1 (2005): 140–64.

Tomasi di Lampedusa, Giuseppe. *Il Gattopardo.* Feltrinelli, 1958.

Tomka, Béla. "Globalization in Socialist Eastern Europe: A Turn in Research and Its Discontents." *European History Quarterly* 53, no. 4 (2023): 685–96.

Tomka, Béla. *Globalization in State Socialist East Central Europe*. Palgrave Macmillan, 2024.

Trecker, Max. "Circle of Debt: How the Crisis of the Global South in the 1980s Affected the Socialist East." *Cold War History* 20, no. 1 (2020): 1–19.

Trecker, Max. *Red Money for the Global South: East-South Economic Relations in the Cold War*. Routledge, 2020.

Trecker, Max. "Entrepreneurs as Saviours of Socialism? The Complicated Relationship between East German State Socialism and Entrepreneurship." *Business History* 65, no. 7 (2023): 1209–25.

Turner, Bryan S. "The Erosion of Citizenship." *British Journal of Sociology* 52, no. 2 (2001): 189–209.

Unger, Corinna R. *International Development: A Postwar History*. Bloomsbury, 2018.

Uvalić, Milica. *Investment and Property Rights in Yugoslavia: The Long Transition to a Market Economy*. Cambridge University Press, 1992.

Uvalić, Milica. "Trade Liberalisation in Southeast Europe: Recent Trends and Some Policy Implications." *European Journal of Comparative Economics* 3, no. 2 (2005): 171–95.

Velikonja, Mitja. "The Past with a Future: The Emancipatory Potential of Yugonostalgia." In *Transcending Fratricide: Political Mythologies, Reconciliations, and the Uncertain Future in the Former Yugoslavia*, edited by Srđa Pavlović and Marko Živković. Nomos, 2013.

Venn, Couze. "Identity, Diasporas and Subjective Change: The Role of Affect, the Relation to the Other, and the Aesthetic." *Subjectivity* 26 (2009): 3–28.

Venugopal, Rajesh. "Privatization, Private-Sector Development and Horizontal Inequalities in Post-Conflict Countries." In *Horizontal Inequalities and Post-Conflict Development: Conflict, Inequality and Ethnicity*, edited by Arnim Langer, Frances Stewart, and Rajesh Venugopal. Palgrave Macmillan, 2012.

Venugopal, Rajesh. "Neoliberalism as Concept." *Economy and Society* 44, no. 2 (2015): 165–87.

Verdery, Katherine. "Fuzzy Property: Rights, Power, and Identity in Transylvania's Decollectivization." In *National Research Council*, edited by Joan M. Nelson, Charles Tilly, and Lee Walker. National Academies Press, 1998.

Verdery, Katherine. "Privatization as Transforming Persons." In *Between Past and Future: The Revolutions of 1989 and Their Aftermath*, edited by Sorin Antohi and Vladimir Tismaneanu. Central European University Press, 2000.

Vladisavljević, Nebojša. "The Breakup of Yugoslavia: The Role of Popular Politics," in *New Perspectives on Yugoslavia: Key Issues and Controversies,* edited by Dejan Djokić and James Ker-Lindsay. Routledge, 2011.

Vodopivec, Nina. "Social Memory of Textile Workers in Slovenia." *Slovene Studies* 30, no. 1 (2008): 63–78.

Vodopivec, Nina. "Yesterday's Heroes: Spinning Webs of Memory in a Postsocialist Textile Factory in Slovenia." In *Negotiating Normality: Everyday Lives in Socialist Institutions*, edited by Daniela Koleva. Transaction, 2012.

Vučetić, Radina, and Paul Betts, eds. *Tito u Africi*. Muzej Jugoslavije, 2017.

Westad, Odd Arne. *The Global Cold War: Third World Interventions and the Making of Our Times*. Cambridge University Press, 2005.

Woodward, Susan L. *Balkan Tragedy: Chaos and Dissolution after the Cold War*. Brookings Institution, 1995.

Woodward, Susan L. *Socialist Unemployment: The Political Economy of Yugoslavia, 1945–1990*. Princeton University Press, 1995.

Woodward, Susan L. "The Political Economy of Ethno-Nationalism in Yugoslavia." *Socialist Register* 39 (2003): 73–92.

Wright, Peter Quinn. "Between the Market and Solidarity: Commercializing Development Aid and International Higher Education in Socialist Yugoslavia." *Nationalities Papers* 49, no. 3 (2021): 462–82.

Wright, Peter Quinn. "'Are There Racists in Yugoslavia?' Debating Racism and Anti-Blackness in Socialist Yugoslavia." *Slavic Review* 81, no. 2 (2022): 418–41.

Yuzhou Sun, Jodie. *Kenya's and Zambia's Relations with China, 1949–2019.* Boydell and Brewer, 2023.

Zapp, Kenneth. "The Economic Consequences of National Independence: The Case of Slovenia." *International Journal of Politics, Culture, and Society* 7, no. 1 (1993): 57–74.

Živković, Andreja. "From the Market . . . to the Market: The Debt Economy after Yugoslavia." In *Welcome to the Desert of Post-Socialism*, edited by Srećko Horvat and Igor Štiks. Verso, 2015.

Životić, Aleksandar, and Jovan Čavoški. "On the Road to Belgrade: Yugoslavia, Third World Neutrals, and the Evolution of Global Non-Alignment, 1954–1961." *Journal of Cold War Studies* 18, no. 4 (2016): 79–97.

Žuk, Piotr. "Employment Structures, Employee Attitudes and Workplace Resistance in Neoliberal Poland." *Economic and Labor Relations Review* 28, no. 1 (2017): 91–112.

Zukin, Sharon. "The Problem of Social Class under Socialism." *Theory and Society* 6, no. 3 (1978): 391–427.

INDEX

ANNA CALORI is Lecturer in Contemporary Economic History at the School of Social and Political Sciences, University of Glasgow.

FOR INDIANA UNIVERSITY PRESS

Lesley Bolton, Project Manager/Editor
Anna Garnai, Production Coordinator
Sophia Hebert, Assistant Acquisitions Editor
Samantha Heffner, Marketing and Publicity Manager
Katie Huggins, Production Manager
Gigi Lamm, Director of Sales and Marketing
Annie L. Martin, Editorial Director
Bethany Mowry, Acquisitions Editor
Dan Pyle, Online Publishing Manager
Jennifer L. Wilder, Senior Artist and Book Designer